Identity, Gender and Teaching English in Japan

NEW PERSPECTIVES ON LANGUAGE AND EDUCATION

Series Editors: Professor Viv Edwards, *University of Reading, Reading, Great Britain*

Two decades of research and development in language and literacy education have yielded a broad, multidisciplinary focus. Yet education systems face constant economic and technological change, with attendant issues of identity and power, community and culture. This series will feature critical and interpretive, disciplinary and multidisciplinary perspectives on teaching and learning, language and literacy in new times.

Full details of all the books in this series and of all our other publications can be found on http://www.multilingual-matters.com, or by writing to Multilingual Matters, St Nicholas House, 31-34 High Street, Bristol BS1 2AW, UK.

NEW PERSPECTIVES ON LANGUAGE AND EDUCATION: 47

Identity, Gender and Teaching English in Japan

Diane Hawley Nagatomo

MULTILINGUAL MATTERS
Bristol • Buffalo • Toronto

Library of Congress Cataloging in Publication Data
A catalog record for this book is available from the Library of Congress.
Nagatomo, Diane Hawley, author.
Identity, Gender and Teaching English in Japan/Diane Hawley Nagatomo.
Bristol; Buffalo, NY: Multilingual Matters, [2016] |
New Perspectives on Language and Education: 47 | Includes bibliographical references and index.
LCCN 2015044280| ISBN 9781783095209 (hbk : alk. paper) | ISBN 9781783095193 (pbk : alk. paper) | ISBN 9781783095216 (ebook)
LCSH: English language–Study and teaching–Japan. | English language–Study and teaching–Japanese speakers. | English teachers–In-service training–Japan. | English teachers–Japan. | Women teachers–Japan. | Japan–Languages.
LCC PE1068.J3 N26 2016 | DDC 428.0071/052–dc23 LC record available at http://lccn.loc.gov/2015044280

British Library Cataloguing in Publication Data
A catalogue entry for this book is available from the British Library.

ISBN-13: 978-1-78309-520-9 (hbk)
ISBN-13: 978-1-78892-584-6 (pbk)

Multilingual Matters
UK: St Nicholas House, 31-34 High Street, Bristol BS1 2AW, UK.
USA: UTP, 2250 Military Road, Tonawanda, NY 14150, USA.
Canada: UTP, 5201 Dufferin Street, North York, Ontario M3H 5T8, Canada.

Website: www.multilingual-matters.com
Twitter: Multi_Ling_Mat
Facebook: https://www.facebook.com/multilingualmatters
Blog: www.channelviewpublications.wordpress.com

Copyright © 2016 Diane Hawley Nagatomo.

All rights reserved. No part of this work may be reproduced in any form or by any means without permission in writing from the publisher.

The policy of Multilingual Matters/Channel View Publications is to use papers that are natural, renewable and recyclable products, made from wood grown in sustainable forests. In the manufacturing process of our books, and to further support our policy, preference is given to printers that have FSC and PEFC Chain of Custody certification. The FSC and/or PEFC logos will appear on those books where full certification has been granted to the printer concerned.

Typeset by Deanta Global Publishing Services Limited.
Printed and bound in Great Britain by the CPI Books Group.

Contents

Conversation	xiii
Acknowledgements	xv
Glossary of Some Key Japanese Terms	xvii
Foreword	xix

1	Introduction	1
	English Language Learning and Teaching in Japan	1
	See the World and Teach English Abroad	3
	Rationale and Motivation for the Study	5
	Overview of the Book	8
2	The Japanese Context	10
	Introduction	10
	Yakudoku as a Teaching and Learning Method	10
	Japan's First Exposure to European Languages	12
	English Gains Importance	14
	English in the Meiji Era (1868–1912)	16
	Missionaries as English language teachers	17
	Japanese go abroad	19
	Foreign experts and foreign language teachers	20
	Replacing the foreign experts	22
	Decline in English Ability	24
	English in the 1900s	25
	Harold Palmer	26
	Before and During WWII	28

	Postwar English	28
	English in the 1970s	30
	Summary of Chapter 2	33
3	1980s until Today	35
	Introduction	35
	Eikaiwa	36
	The business side of *eikaiwa*	37
	Ideologies surrounding *eikaiwa*	38
	Eikaiwa teachers	39
	Secondary Schools	41
	Public education vs. private education	41
	The JET program	42
	Outsourced and direct-hire ALTs	45
	Attitudes toward ALTs	47
	Stand-alone teaching	48
	Higher Education	49
	Standard and nonstandard positions in Japanese universities	51
	Part-time teachers	52
	Contracted full-time teachers	54
	Tenured positions	56
	Japanese and foreign teachers are different	57
	Summary of Chapter 3	58
4	Gender Issues Surrounding English in Japan	60
	Introduction	60
	Interracial Romance Between Japanese and Westerners	60
	Interracial Relationships from the 1880s to the Wartime Years	63
	Japanese war brides	65
	Hollywood-Constructed Relationships	67
	Mismatched Relationships?	68
	Booming economy and Japanese women	69
	International Marriage Today	70
	Summary of Interracial Relationships	74

	Gendered Issues and Language Learning and Language Teaching	75
	Japanese women and English studies	75
	Charisma Man	77
	The fine line between flirting and harassment	79
	Sexually charged university classrooms	80
	It's a Man's World	82
	Male and Female University Teachers	84
	Hostilities against Women	86
	Summary of Gendered Issues in Language Learning and Language Teaching	88
	Conclusion of the Background Chapters	88
5	Methods	91
	Introduction	91
	Teachers' Professional Identity	91
	Narrative as a Research Method	92
	The Participants	93
	Interviews	95
	Transcription Method	96
	Process of Analysis	98
	Participant Confirmations	99
	The Theoretical Frameworks: Gee (2000) and Wenger (1998)	99
	Gee (2000)	100
	Wenger's (1998) Communities of Practice (CoP)	102
	My Position Within the Study	103
	A Word of Caution	104
	Organization of Discussion Chapters 6–9	104
6	Destination Japan	106
	Introduction	106
	Deciding to Come to Japan	106
	The JETS	110

Louisa	110
Margaret	112
Victoria	114
Pat	115
Theresa	116
Carrie	117
The Other Teachers	119
Annie	119
Andrea	120
Lisa	121
Sarah	122
Reactions to their Marriages	124
The women's families	124
The husbands' families	125
Acceptance from the husbands' families	127
Summary of Chapter 6	127
7 Running an *Eikaiwa* Business	**129**
Introduction	129
Getting Up and Running	130
The Students	131
Children versus adults	132
Dwindling enrolment	132
Reasons for fewer students	133
Problem students	133
Fighting Against the Ideologies of *Eikaiwa* and *Eigo*	134
Is *Eikawa* just fun and games?	135
More Than English Lessons	135
Teaching Adults	136
Socializing at *eikaiwa*	136
Friendly with students, but not really friends	137

Money Matters	138
Financial dependence/independence and taxes	138
Collecting tuition	140
Misunderstandings about *eikaiwa* teachers' incomes	141
Louisa and Margaret's Futures	142
Examining Margaret and Louisa's Identities Through Gee's (2000) Theoretical Lens	143
Summary of Chapter 7	144
8 The Jugglers	146
Introduction	146
Victoria: Priest and English Teacher	146
Victoria's schedule	147
School bus driver	148
Identity conflicts as a priest and a teacher	148
Victoria's teaching	150
Being an ALT	151
Private teaching	154
Victoria: In conclusion	155
Lisa: A 30-Lesson-a-Week Teacher	156
Teaching in the aftermath of the earthquake	157
High-school Teaching	159
The daycare centers/kindergartens	160
Private lessons	161
Lisa: In conclusion	161
Louisa: From *Eikaiwa* School Owner to University Lecturer	163
Developing a new professional identity	164
Becoming an proficiency examiner	164
Teaching in tertiary education	165
Understanding the hierarchy of university teaching	166
Finding her own way as a university teacher	167
Differences in running an *eikaiwa* school and being a part of larger organizations	169

You can't go back	169
Louisa: In conclusion	170
Summary of Chapter 8	171
9 The Full Timers	**173**
Introduction	173
Andrea: From Public High School to Private University Lecturer	174
Going to Graduate School	175
Deciding to leave	176
Moving to a university	177
Collaboration and camaraderie	178
University students versus high-school students	179
Andrea and CoP	180
Annie: A Private High School Teacher	183
In the beginning	183
Developing a reputable English program	184
The strengths of team teaching in a global studies program	184
On being a language teacher	185
Improving Japanese skills	186
On being a working mother and raising a bicultural child	186
Retired life	188
On being an insider foreigner living in Japan	188
Comparing Annie and Andrea's degrees of belonging to their schools' CoP	189
Sarah: A Tenured Professor	191
The university's English program	191
Outsourcing teachers	192
Traveling abroad with students	194
The teaching	195
Graduate degree	196
Promotion	197
On being marginalized	197

Sarah's future	198
Sarah's placement in her CoP	199
Summary of Chapter 9	199
10 Concluding Comments	201
Introduction	201
Summing It All Up	203
Time of arrival	204
Location	204
Resourcefulness	205
Being a non-Japanese native English speaking teacher	207
Gender issues	209
Closing Thoughts	211
References	213
Author Index	229
Subject Index	233

Conversation

Conversation between Random Foreign Male (RFM) and Heather

The conversation I always seem to have

H: Hi.
RFM: Hi. What do you do?
H.: I'm an English teacher.
RFM: Ohhhh........(eyes glazing over)
H.: You?
RFM: I'm a university teacher and author. You?
H.: Eikaiwa [English conversation]
RFM: (Slightly patronizing) Ohhhhh..... Adults?
H.: Nope. I mainly teach children in the 1-8 age group with a smattering of adult classes, mostly women and senior citizens.
RFM: Ohhhhhhh, well, nice to meet you...(wanders off)

The conversation I never seem to get to have

H.: Don't judge me by my job. I have a BA/Bed (Hons) in ESL Education and Japanese. I'm a qualified secondary school teacher in Australia. I speak Japanese. I spent a year at Osaka University of Education. I have been teaching in Japan for 14 years. I have taught at pre-schools, kindergartens, elementary and junior high schools, businesses and a university. I know what's out there. I have found my niche in children's English teaching. I enjoy it, my students enjoy my classes and I'm good at it. I'm not waiting for an opening at the university. I'm not studying for my Masters (although I haven't ruled out further study in early childhood education). I'm not hoping for that elusive direct hire ALT position and I'm not writing a book. I'm not here for the money and I'm not looking to get into a career outside of teaching. I hope *to be teaching children English conversation, a bit of culture, and a love of language and learning for many, many years to come.*

Oh. Nice to meet you, too.

(Fukase, 2015)

I wouldn't have the confidence to do what I'm doing now if I didn't come here. My feeling is I have to continue giving back to Japan my whole life because Japan gave me myself. There are so many things that drive me nuts about Japan, but Japan helped me discover me. Before that I was so afraid of just everything. I always know that I can do things, but it is hard to convince other people I can do them. I'm kind of humble and not good at selling myself. My husband is very relaxed for a Japanese man. I'm very shy and quiet for an American. So we meet each other halfway. (Carrie)

Acknowledgements

It is my pleasure to thank the many people who have helped make this book possible. First and foremost, my heartfelt gratitude goes to the ten women who took time out of their busy personal and professional lives to take part in this study: Andrea, Annie, Carrie, Lisa, Louisa, Margaret, Pat, Sarah, Theresa and Victoria. Without the candidness, warmth and friendship they offered before, during and after the multiple interviews, this book could never have been written.

A very special thank you goes to Professor Thomas Farrell of Brock University for providing the foreword to this book.

I am also extremely grateful to Dr Melodie Cook of the University of Niigata Prefecture for being an excellent friend and a wonderful colleague. Even though we live and teach in different prefectures, her personal and academic presence in my life continues to inspire me on a daily basis. In particular, I would like to acknowledge how much I appreciate Melodie's keen editorial eye and her valuable feedback on early drafts of this book.

In addition, I would like to extend my gratitude to Assistant Professor Thomas Lockley of Nihon University for his comments and advice on an early draft of Chapter 2. I am also grateful to Gloria Ishida for sharing with me some historical details on early foreign wives of Japanese men and for her feedback on some parts of Chapter 4. In addition, I would like to say thank you to Jeanette Dennison for allowing me to use her lovely wedding photo for the cover of this book.

A condensed version of Andrea's story from Chapter 9 appeared in the *Asian EFL Journal* [2015, 17 (3), 111–130], and I thank the chief editor for permission to expand on it and include it in this book.

This project could never have evolved into book form without the support and expertise of the staff at Multilingual Matters. I appreciate the series editor, Professor Viv Edwards, and the editorial staff, Kim Eggleton and Sarah Williams, for making the production process so smooth.

As always, I am extremely grateful to my husband Shin for his never-ending support and encouragement.

Finally, I would like to dedicate this book to the members of the Association of Foreign Wives of Japanese (AFWJ). During my 35 years of membership in this wonderful organization, I have witnessed the triumphs and difficulties of these women (many of whom are English teachers) as they navigate the gendered and sociopolitical waters of life in Japan. These women are the reason why I decided to write this book in the first place, and so this book is for them.

Glossary of Some Key Japanese Terms

ALT:	Assistant Language Teacher
Eigo:	English language
Eikaiwa:	English conversation
EIKEN:	test in practical English proficiency
JET:	the Japan Exchange and Teaching Program
Juken:	English for examination purposes
Gaijin:	foreigner
Gaikokujin:	foreigner (more polite than *gaijin*)
MEXT:	Ministry of Education, Culture, Sports, Science & Technology
Yakudoku:	a Japanese version of the grammar translation method

Foreword

In the emerging literature on teacher identity in second-language teaching, it is uncommon to find a book that makes specific links to gender, identity and a particular context. As sociocultural approaches to research seem to be taking center stage in the profession of teaching English as a second language (TESOL), Diane Hawley Nagatomo's book, *Identity, Gender and Teaching English in Japan* fills in this void as she explores the personal and professional identity development of ten foreign women, all with Japanese spouses, who teach English in different contexts in Japan. I know of no other such book that explores such a complex subject, and as such, this work is a blueprint for all educators in Japan and beyond who are interested in teacher identity development.

This book gives a detailed analysis of how second language teaching developed in Japan, from Japan's first exposure to Europeans to when the missionaries first arrived prior to the Meiji era, to World War II and beyond. There is a special emphasis in this discussion that covers the 1980s to today, describing the current teaching realities faced by foreign English teachers in Japan. Nagatomo then initiates a very interesting discussion centered on gender and teaching by focusing first on interracial relationships between Westerners and Japanese and then by exploring various gender-related issues that shape English language learning and English language teaching in the Japanese context. As Nagatomo points out, these two gendered threads not only shape the lives of all women living and working in Japan, but also in particular those of the ten participants that are detailed in her study.

This book – written by a knowledgeable insider, an American woman with a Japanese spouse who has been living and teaching English in Japan for many years – begins to fill the gap in our knowledge about the very real impact of gender on identity in both a professional and personal manner. The background chapters offer a very realistic discussion of how gender and interracial relationships can shape teachers' professional and personal lives. Some may not want to acknowledge the impact such relationships may have on teaching English as a foreign language (EFL), but it nonetheless has important implications for language educators worldwide in terms of language teaching and language-teacher identity development.

The core of the book is the study of ten foreign female EFL teachers married to Japanese men and their identity development as English language teachers in Japan. Through her participants' narratives, Nagatomo discusses how personal and professional identities are discursively constructed. What follows is a fascinating account of how these women adapted to (and even adopted) their new surroundings, both personally by marrying a Japanese man and professionally by developing their identity as teachers: being non-Japanese, being native English speakers and being female. Although this book reports on a sensitive topic, Diane Hawley Nagatomo does so with tact and sensitivity. This book has made a huge contribution to our knowledge of personal and professional English teacher identity development, not only to English teaching in Japan but also to the TESOL profession as a whole. As Nagatomo herself explains, 'My analysis and interpretation of these women cannot apply to all female EFL teachers in Japan with Japanese spouses, but I do believe the stories my participants told might resonate with other foreign teachers in Japan as well, whether or not they are male or female or whether or not they are married to Japanese' (p. 269). I fully agree.

Thomas S.C. Farrell
Brock University, Canada

1 Introduction

English Language Learning and Teaching in Japan

English language teaching (ELT) in Japan and its surrounding industries is a multibillion-yen business. It is taught and studied in formal educational contexts, such as primary, secondary and tertiary institutions, as well as in informal educational contexts, such as *eikaiwa* (English conversation) schools, community centers, and people's homes. Those studying English range in age from toddlers to senior citizens (Ministry of Trade and Industry, 2005, 2015).

In formal educational contexts, at least through secondary schools, English is generally a required subject, and it is accorded great importance because of its gate-keeping role in entrance exams (e.g. LoCastro, 1996). Through English exams (and those of other academic subjects), students gain access to secondary and tertiary institutions that will determine the course of their lives. In other words, the higher the level schools students are able to enter and ultimately graduate from, the brighter their futures are likely to be (e.g. Honda, 2004; Ishida, 1993; Kariya & Rosenbaum, 1987; McCormick, 1988; Okano & Tsuchiya, 1999; Ono, 2001, 2003). Therefore, priority in schools is often given to teaching *eigo* (English language), which focuses on the structure of English for *juken* (English for entrance examination) purposes, and these classes are mainly taught by Japanese English teachers.

Despite recent recommendations by the Ministry of Education, Culture, Sports, Science and Technology (MEXT) for teachers to teach in English and to focus more on communication, attention is mainly on providing grammatical explanations about English in Japanese. Teachers often have students translate English sentences into Japanese because of beliefs that such skills are necessary for passing the exams mentioned above (e.g. Butler & Iino, 2005; Gorsuch, 1999, 2000, 2001; Nishino & Watanabe, 2008; Nishino, 2011; Sato, 2002).

Nowadays, most private and public elementary and secondary schools have some communication-based classes. These classes usually have foreign[1] teachers acting as assistants to Japanese English teachers or, in some cases, teaching alone. However, these classes are often viewed more as a means for students to *touch* English than to actually learn how to speak it. In most cases, teachers, parents and students attach greater importance to classes that are believed to provide greater educational opportunities to the students (e.g. Geluso, 2013; Law, 1995; Sato, 2002).

English is also an important subject in tertiary education, and it is taught by both foreign and Japanese teachers[2]. Foreign teachers usually teach communication-based classes, and Japanese teachers teach English-related subjects such as literature or linguistics (e.g. Fraser, 2011; Whitsed & Wright, 2011). Although at this stage there is no longer any need to conduct English classes as if students would be taking entrance exams, many Japanese teachers who do teach English language in university teach in ways that mirror those that are used in high school (Nagatomo, 2011, 2012a).

English is also studied informally and voluntarily in *eikaiwa* schools. The reasons why students enroll (or students' parents have them enroll) in such institutions vary. Some believe that to master English it is essential to supplement the English that is taught in schools, which is widely acknowledged to be insufficient. Others may study English because of concrete educational and/or career goals. But there are also many who have no clear purpose for studying English other than having a general liking for the language and/or for cultures of the English-speaking world. A key point of *eikaiwa* school attendance, regardless of students' intentions, is the opportunity to learn English as taught by a foreign (especially a *Western*) teacher (e.g. Bailey, 2006, 2007; Kubota, 2011; Mizuta, 2009; Takahashi, 2013).

As with any educational system, whether it is formal or informal, the teachers are its heart. What the students learn is highly dependent upon the teachers, regardless of whether or not they are native speakers or nonnative speakers of English or whether or not they are Japanese or non-Japanese. What individual teachers know, think and believe about teaching has been found to be of great importance in mainstream education (e.g. Clandinin, 1985, 1986; Elbaz, 1983; Shulman, 1986), as well as in foreign language education (e.g. Clark, 2009; Fichtner & Chapman, 2011; Gatbonton, 1999; Golembek, 1998; Nagatomo, 2011, 2012a; Phan Le Ha, 2008; Tsang, 2004; Tsui, 2007; Woods, 1997). It is now understood that English-language teachers are not teaching machines that merely apply an appropriate methodology in a classroom for students to absorb (Nunan, 1988; Nunan & Richards, 1995); they bring to the classroom their own sense of identity, and this shapes both teaching and learning.

In Japan, as mentioned above, both native and nonnative English-speaking teachers teach English to Japanese language learners. However, as we shall see throughout this book, the historical, cultural and legal roles of these teachers, and their pedagogical styles, differ. In fact, attitudes surrounding English in Japan taught by Japanese and non-Japanese teachers have led to parallel modes of English language learning: *eigo* and *eikaiwa*. Because these two types of learning are generally not in sync with each other, a cohesive English-language education system has not yet been successfully established, and English-language education in Japan has been, and continues to be, highly criticized (e.g. Harasawa, 1974; Imamura, 1978; Law, 1995; Mizuta, 2009).

In order to understand more about these two pedagogical systems and the teachers that work in them, it is necessary to examine the teachers. The focus of this book is on those teachers who mainly engage in what could be called the more communicative side of English language teaching in Japan – that is, the foreign teachers.

See the World and Teach English Abroad

Japan is not the only country that has both native English-speaking and nonnative English-speaking teachers. In fact, because English-language proficiency is viewed as an essential skill, it is studied and taught in classrooms over the world.[3] The teaching of English as a second/foreign language generally follows two types of pedagogical practices. The first is that which has evolved from the 'Inner Circle' countries (Canagarajah, 1999; Kachru, 1985, 1992), such as Britain, Australasia and North America, which Holliday (1994) calls BANA countries. There, the focus is mainly on theories and methodologies that have been developed in the West. BANA teachers are generally native English speakers or those who have studied in BANA countries. The second is that which has evolved from countries where English is not spoken but is taught as a foreign language (EFL) by teachers who are natives of those countries in their own tertiary, secondary and primary (TESEP) educational institutions. The methodologies employed by those teaching in TESEP contexts have usually been locally developed and adapted for the purposes of those countries (e.g. Holliday, 1994; Phan Le Ha, 2008).

Many language learners throughout the world wish to study English with native English speakers, and as a result, many native English speakers from BANA countries have found work teaching English in TESEP countries. Some teachers have taken EFL/ESL (English as a foreign language/English as a second language) teaching courses prior to departure for these countries, but others have not (e.g. Caesar & Bueno, 2003; Neilsen, 2009).

People often seek ELT employment abroad because of an interest in foreign cultures and/or a desire to see the world (e.g. Johnston, 1997,

1999; Neilsen, Gitsaki & Honan, 2007; Neilsen, 2009, 2011). Work can be easily found in the Middle East, the Far East and Latin American countries. In general, remuneration for language teaching is related to the supply of and demand for teachers, and it is higher in countries that are considered difficult to live in (such as Saudi Arabia) than those countries that are considered pleasant to live in (such as the south of Spain) (Neilsen, 2009).

Although native English–speaking teachers often enjoy greater prestige and greater opportunities in ESL contexts than nonnative English–speaking teachers do (e.g. Braine, 1999a, 1999b; Kamhi-Stein, 2004; Rampton, 1990; Tang, 1997), this is not always the case in EFL contexts. Neilsen (2009: 46–48) for example, described how precarious expatriate ELT teachers' employment actually is and how they are often marginalized: In Brunei, one Afro-Caribbean British woman was dismissed after four years of employment for 'not being British enough'; in Sweden, foreign EFL teachers were paid substantially less than Swedish teachers for doing the same work; in Italy, foreign teachers were downgraded to 'non-teaching staff' while Italian graduate students were upgraded to tenured positions. As we shall see throughout this book, such issues are also problematic for foreign teachers in Japan.

Few ESL/EFL teachers remain in the field permanently because it is 'an unstable, marginalized, impermanent occupation' (Johnston, 1997: 707). Some who began teaching as a means to support travel or to have overseas experiences move into entirely different professions. Others quit because of the low salaries and the low status associated with the field. In fact, salaries and benefits are usually less for teachers in both ESL and EFL settings than they are for those teaching mainstream subjects. In addition, language schools, which are generally private for-profit commercial businesses, often exploit EFL teachers because of the constant supply of eager new teachers willing to replace them. When working abroad, EFL teachers often have no recourse in the case of discriminatory treatment or shady employment practices, and they often feel marginalized due to unstable employment contracts and unpredictable conditions (Neilsen, 2009, 2011). Those who do remain often travel from country to country as what Neilsen (2009: 49) considers culturally adept global nomads. He says,

> The kind of person who continues to work in ELT must then be flexible, have a high tolerance for change in life circumstances. ELT is largely a market-based field with few or no support structures in place for the teacher working away from home.

It is true that those living abroad need to have flexibility and a capacity to accept the challenges of constant uncertainty. But many teachers, particularly those who have migrated to another country, are not, as Neilsen writes above, necessarily *working away from home*. Many *are at home*, albeit a newly adopted one.

Thus, my general question that guides this book is the following: how do teachers who have chosen to settle down in one country manage the surrounding difficulties of living and teaching English in that country? If personal and professional difficulties arise for temporary sojourners, they can always move to greener teaching pastures, or they can even return to their home countries. Such mobility, however, is not possible for all teachers engaged in language teaching abroad, especially if deep personal and professional roots have been established in their new country.

Rationale and Motivation for the Study

The purpose of this book is to explore the personal and professional identity development of one group of foreign English language teachers (EFL) in Japan who have chosen to live in Japan permanently: Western women with Japanese spouses. Most of the women in this study began their lives in Japan as language teachers who had planned to stay only for a few years. Through marriage to Japanese nationals, however, they have essentially become permanent migrants. As the wives and mothers of Japanese citizens, they now have a stake in Japan and they have established deep roots. And while they are not entirely outsiders to the local communities in which they live, they are not exactly insiders either.

It is true that Western men with Japanese spouses also have deep roots and they are also members of their communities. As we shall see later in this book, both Western men and women share many professional difficulties as foreign English teachers in Japan. However, Western women also need to contend with societal gendered constraints that shape the lives of all women in Japan because, according to Liddle and Nakajima (2000: 317), women's place in society is defined 'primarily by their relationship to domesticity, reproduction and the family'. Attitudes that men are supposed to work for money and women are supposed to support that work from the home front are carried over into attitudes toward Western women teaching and living in Japan. These attitudes are not only seen in Japanese people but in some instances in Western men living in Japan as well (e.g. Appleby, 2014; Kobayashi, 2014; Nagatomo, 2014, 2015).

Statistically speaking, there are more Western men married to Japanese women (89%) than there are Western women married to Japanese men

(11%) (Yamamoto, 2010). One of the reasons for this, as we shall see in Chapter 4, is that Japanese men have not been considered such a good catches for Western women because of negative stereotypes. Nonetheless, such marriages are not all that rare either, and many of those women with Japanese husbands do teach English. In fact, I am also one such woman. I have been teaching English in Japan for 36 years (31 of those years in tertiary education) and I have been married to a Japanese national for 35 years.

Therefore, the motivation for this study stems partly from my personal experiences, but it also comes from witnessing the resilience and struggles of other foreign women teaching English in Japan who are also in the same boat, so to speak. As a member of the Association of Foreign Wives of Japanese (AFWJ), a support group for foreign women with Japanese spouses founded in 1969 with nearly 500 members, I have heard stories (in person and in online discussion groups) describing the members' personal and professional difficulties *and* their large and small triumphs. It is certainly not easy to navigate the gendered waters of being a wife and mother in Japan as a foreigner while at the same time trying to establish and maintain a career as an English teacher.

As a qualitative researcher, I became more and more curious as to how these women manage their personal and professional lives and what impact these women have on the English abilities of the students that they teach. Some of these women live and work in such remote areas that it is hard to imagine their students would ever have the opportunity to use English outside of their classes. Thus, I decided to investigate this group of teachers more systematically.

In 2011, I constructed a survey that asked foreign female teachers in Japan about their personal and professional circumstances and posted it to Survey Monkey. Through snowball sampling, I collected usable data[4] from 191 female respondents (143 with Japanese spouses and 48 without Japanese spouses) from 15 different countries. Participants were asked to respond to issues such as those concerning relationships with colleagues, relationships with family members, income from teaching, and balancing family and professional life. There were also a number of open-ended questions where respondents could write freely.

I found that the women teach English in their homes and neighborhoods, in cultural centers, in kindergartens and nursery schools, in established *eikaiwa* (conversation) schools, in private and public elementary and secondary schools and at two- and four-year universities and technical colleges. Some women taught English for pocket money, while others supported their families entirely through their teaching. In addition to teaching English, some respondents engaged in other types of professional work such as translation, interpretation, proofreading/editing, freelance writing, fiction writing, web-page design and voice narration. Others taught classes unrelated to language learning, such as cooking, baking and/or craft making. Nearly all of the respondents had college degrees, with those teaching in higher education generally holding at minimum an MA and those with tenure a PhD. In some cases, the degrees (especially the MAs and PhDs) were specifically related to English-language education, but many women had specialized in entirely different fields, such as science or business. The results from the questionnaire survey and the subsequent e-mail correspondence with several of the respondents provided data for my preliminary studies (Nagatomo, 2013, 2014b). While analyzing the data from the questionnaire survey, I came to feel that I was only scratching the surface of the respondents' professional and personal experiences in Japan. To paint a more complete picture of foreign female English-language teachers in Japan, especially those with Japanese spouses, I felt needed to have a more in-depth understanding of their lives. To do that, I conducted a narrative study (Pavlenko, 2002), which meant letting the participants speak for themselves at length in multiple interviews and then analyzing their stories in relation to the sociopolitical and sociocultural context of Japan. The narratives reported on in this study were examined through two theoretical lenses that deal with identity: (1) Gee (2000: 99), who simply defines identity as 'being recognized as a certain kind of person in a given context'; and (2) Wenger (1998) who views identity as that which forms while participating in groups called *communities of practices* (CoPs).

Why examine the lives of foreign women teaching in Japan? As mentioned earlier, I have a vested interest in this particular group of teachers. But importantly, accounts of women living abroad, especially as English teachers, are historically rare. According to Appleby (2014: 43):

> Both the official and unofficial histories of English abroad have been populated, until quite recently, almost exclusively by men: from sailors, castaways and naval commanders, to interpreters, applied linguists and teachers. In earlier centuries, the possibilities open to Western men to travel and work abroad inevitably meant that the language activities that occurred as a consequence of international trade and diplomacy were primarily the province of men.

While it is understandable that women's voices might not have been heard in earlier times because they were not adventuring throughout the world, this is no longer the case. As we shall see, all of the women in my study met their husbands in Japan while they were on their own adventures. Although the stories that will be told in this book are uniquely the participants' own stories and cannot be generalized to others, I believe that the themes that will be brought up will resonate with many other foreign teachers in Japan, regardless of their marital backgrounds. I also believe that these women's stories will dispel some stereotypical images of foreign EFL teachers in Japan, of foreign women married to Japanese men and of Japanese men married to foreign women.

The research questions that have guided this study are the following:

(1) How do foreign women with Japanese spouses develop and sustain careers in Japan as English language teachers?
(2) What factors shape the personal and professional identity development of these women?

Overview of the Book

To conclude this introductory chapter, I give an overview of the rest of the book, which is comprised of ten chapters, of which the first four provide background information for the study.

Following this introduction is Chapter 2 ('The Japanese Context'). This chapter locates the study within a historical and sociopolitical context starting in the 1600s and closes with a discussion of issues surrounding English education in the 1970s. Chapter 3 ('1980s to Today') covers the modern era of English education in Japan and focuses particularly on the areas of English that are taught mainly taught by foreigners. Chapter 4 ('Gender Issues Surrounding English in Japan') focuses on two perspectives of gender. First, it describes the historical background of interracial relationships between Japanese and Westerners, and then it discusses gendered issues that shape English-language learning and English-language teaching in Japan.

Chapter 5 ('Methods') briefly introduces the ten participants of this study, the means of data collection and how that data was analyzed, and the theoretical frameworks that guided the analysis. In this chapter, I also discuss my insider position within the study.

The analytical portion of this book begins from Chapter 6 ('Destination Japan'), where the participants are introduced in detail, and their stories are examined through the theoretical frameworks of Gee (2000) and Wenger (1998). The chapter explains the participants' motivations for coming to Japan, their early days of living in Japan, how they met their spouses and their families' reactions to their wanting to marry Japanese men. Three of the participants' current employment situations are also discussed in this chapter.

Chapter 7 ('Running an *Eikaiwa* Business') focuses on two of the participants who run successful *eikaiwa* schools from their homes. Chapter 8 ('The Jugglers') discusses three of the women who piece together numerous part-time jobs to make a living, and Chapter 9 ('The Full Timers'), the final discussion chapter in this book, covers the three women who are employed full time by academic institutions.

Chapter 10 concludes the book by reexamining the themes explored in Chapters 6–9 and offers some thoughts toward the future exploration of English-language teaching in the Japanese context.

Notes

(1) I purposely choose to use the word 'foreigner' when I refer to non-Japanese in this book, but I will also use 'Westerner' where I wish to emphasize the Caucasian race. I believe that the English term 'foreigner' best describes non-Japanese in Japan, especially from the perspective of Japanese. The more polite and formal term is '*gaikokujin*' (an outsider from a foreign country), but it is usually shortened to '*gaijin*' (outsider). These two words are among the very first that foreigners hear upon arrival, and they soon begin to shape their identities. Other terms that have been used to describe foreign language teachers, such as 'expatriate' or 'transnational' teachers, seem to me to imply a sense of temporariness.

(2) Throughout this book, I mainly use the term 'teacher' to refer to all those who teach, regardless of the type of educational institution they work for or their academic titles.

(3) It is beyond the scope of this book to discuss the important issues surrounding power and language in the field of English-language education. See Phillipson's (1992) book *Linguistic Imperialism* for a full account, but also Canagarajah (1999) Kubota (1998), Pennycook (1994), Liu, D. (1998), Liu, J. (1999), Phan Le Ha (2008). For a discussion concerning the differences between native-speaking and non-native-speaking teachers, see Davies (1991), Edge (1996) or Rapton (1990).

(4) Initially more than 200 people responded to the questionnaire, but some did not fit the research perimeters and were eliminated (i.e. they were male teachers, or they were female teachers not residing in Japan). Other questionnaires were discarded because only a few questions had been answered. Apparently, there were also attempts to sabotage my study by supplying outlandish answers, such as having 25 children, working as prostitutes and/or in the porn industry, and having a monthly income running into millions of yen. Such responses appeared immediately after I had solicited participants via an online social network group in Japan called 'Gaijin Pot'. As soon as I had posted my request for female participants, the discussion thread, led by several foreign men, sunk into such smutty talk that the forum's moderator needed to delete my legitimate request and its ensuing discussion. Although my survey respondents had complained about such behavior, I had unwittingly fallen into my first and only real experience of gender harassment by foreign men in Japan.

2 The Japanese Context

Introduction

In the previous chapter, I briefly described two prevalent modes of English language education in Japan: *eigo*, which is generally taught by Japanese teachers; and *eikaiwa*, which is generally taught by foreign teachers. *Eigo* is considered essential to pass entrance exams, and *eikaiwa* is considered essential to gain communicative skills. The purpose of this chapter is to introduce the sociopolitical context that has shaped these two pedagogies, and as we shall see, English education in Japan has historically wavered back and forth between English for communicative purposes and English for examination purposes (Butler & Iino, 2005). An examination of English language teaching and learning from a historical perspective can provide some insight into how and why it is carried out the way it is in Japan today.

I begin the chapter with a brief overview of Japan's most enduring language instructional method, which is followed by descriptions of Japan's first contact with Europeans and their languages in the 1500s, through the period beginning in 1639 and ending in 1854, in which Japan isolated itself from the West. Next, I describe the Meiji era (1868–1912), when Japan began its rapid modernization. During this era, hundreds of foreign experts, advisors and instructors came to Japan and imparted Western knowledge in their own languages, which were quickly learned by Japanese. Once knowledge came to be disseminated *in* Japanese *by* Japanese, however, there was no need for foreign-language proficiency, and the communicative skills of Japanese immediately declined. However, as we shall see, foreign language study, particularly English, came to be used as a selection tool to gain admission into higher education. The chapter concludes with a discussion concerning English language education in the 1970s.

Yakudoku as a Teaching and Learning Method

Before embarking on a historical tour of English language education in Japan, it is first necessary to examine the most prominent and enduring means of teaching foreign languages in Japan: *yakudoku*. *Yakudoku* shares some similarities with the grammar-translation method, but its purpose is to extract information from a foreign language by retaining Japanese word order in the other language translation so as to better understand the content in *Japanese* (e.g. Henrichson, 1987; Hino, 1988; Tajima, 1978). Hino (1988: 46) provides an example of how the *yakudoku* method is used to study a foreign language:

[Target language sentence] She has a nice table in her room.

Stage 1 [The reader mentally makes word-by-word translation.]
She has a nice table in her room
kanojo motteiru hitotsu-nosutekina teburu naka kanojo-noheya

Stage 2 [Translation reordered to match Japanese syntax.]
kanojo kanojo-no heya naka hitotsu-no sutekina teburu motteiru

Stage 3 [Recoding in Japanese syntax.]
Kanojo-wa kanojo-no heya-no naka-ni hitotsu-no sutekina teburu-wo motteiru.

For centuries, *yakudoku* was the means by which Chinese literature, art, law, architecture and thought were imported into Japan. It was also the means of importing Western knowledge and technology during the centuries Japan had closed its doors to the world. However, as a system for studying language, it has been widely criticized. In the case of Chinese language study, Confucianist Sorai Ogyu (1666–1728) complained in the following terms: '[T]he traditional method of reading Chinese is a misleading one, which should be avoided. You cannot truly understand Chinese in this way. Chinese should be read as Chinese' (Kawasumi, 1975 in Hino, 1988: 50). Later, in 1788, Gentaku Otsuki criticized *yakudoku* as an instructional method for learning Dutch by saying,

In reading Dutch, beginners may use the method for reading Chinese, but it is desirable for advanced readers to read directly in the original word order. You can understand the contents more clearly this way. Dutch often loses its meaning if rendered into Japanese. (Kawasumi, 1975, 1978 in Hino, 1988: 50).

Yakudoku as an instructional method was clearly ineffective in teaching foreign language communication as also demonstrated in the 15 June 1857 diary of Townsend Harris, the first American counsel in Japan. In an excerpt describing the signing of the treaty, he makes an incidental remark on not only the archaic choice of language used by the Japanese but also their peculiar request relating to word order. He writes:

> Today we signed the Convention, having been some nine days in setting the wording of the Articles, which by the way is a work of much difficulty, as the Dutch of the Japanese interpreters is that of the ship captains and traders used some two hundred and fifty years ago. They have not been taught a single new word in the interim, so they are quite ignorant of all the terms used in treaties, conventions, etc., etc. This, joined to their excessive jealousy and fear of being cheated makes it exceedingly difficult to manage such a matter as the present one. They even wanted the words of the Dutch version to stand in the exact order they stood in the Japanese! Owing to the difference of grammatical structure this would have rendered it perfect gibberish. (Minakawa, 1955: 48–49)

Much later, in 1911, Yoshizaburo Okakura criticized *yakudoku* in his book *Eigo Kyoiku* (English Education), saying that it should not be employed in studying English despite its popularity. He argued:

> In reading Chinese, it is best if you understand the meaning of a text in the original word order. The contents are understood well enough in this way. As a matter of fact, this is the best way to achieve understanding. Likewise, direct reading is the best way of reading English in terms of time, energy, and efficiency. (Kawasumi, 1978, in Hino, 1988: 50)

Yakudoku persists today in Japanese English education because it is believed that such skills are necessary for students to pass entrance exams (e.g. Gorsuch, 2000, 2001; Guest, 2000; Nishino, 2008; Butler & Iino, 2005). Harasawa's (1978: 77) comment, even though it was made in the 1970s, reflects attitudes toward English language study today and sums up Japan's strong adherence to the *yakudoku* method in the following terms: 'In Japan English is not English at all, in the people's subconscious, unless and until it is rendered into Japanese.'

Japan's First Exposure to European Languages

Despite the prevalence of *yakudoku* as an instructional method of teaching languages in Japan, there have been periods when practical knowledge of foreign languages was necessary, and some Japanese people managed to develop excellent communication skills. The following sections, which cover a 400-year period, show how communicative and practical language learning in Japan involved interaction with foreign people.

Japanese people's first exposure to European languages occurred after the Portuguese traders and missionaries arrived in Kyushu in 1543. The Jesuit priest Francis Xavier (1506–1552), who came to Japan in 1549 bearing gifts in exchange for permission to preach Christianity, developed enough proficiency in Japanese to convert more than 500 people (e.g. Keene, 1969; Minakawa, 1955). Another Christian, Italian priest Allesandro Valignano (1537–1606), established a system to train Jesuit priests to be able to deliver sermons *in Japanese* with the same aim. Some of these priests developed sufficient proficiency to act as interpreters between the powerful feudal lords and the visiting Europeans. Valignano also established a college for Japanese, and, according to Minakawa (1955: 26),

> The students made progress in any subject of studies more rapidly than the foreign teachers had expected. Even in the study of European languages which greatly differed in grammatical structure from their mother tongue, they were proficient enough to read and write well in the course of several months. They also studied Latin, the language which was regarded as a difficult one by Europeans themselves.

Valignano sent four Japanese Catholics to Europe to meet the Pope. Their return eight years later led to a craze in Japan for European clothing, for Christian items (such as rosaries and crucifixes) to be worn for fashion, and for Catholic prayers and songs to be learned by heart. By the 1600s, there were more than 300,000 Catholic converts, and concern developed that Christianity (and by default, Western ideas) was damaging the political and ethical structure of Japan. In 1587, Toyotomi Hideyoshi[1] expelled the Jesuit missionaries from Nagasaki, crucified numerous Christians, and banned Christianity entirely in 1597 (e.g. Brown, 1994; Keene, 1969; Minakawa, 1955).

The strict ban on Christianity eased when Tokugawa Ieyasu came into power after Toyotomi's death. Tokugawa was keen to learn more about the Western world, and a printing press, which was brought to Japan, published books in Latin and Portuguese, exposing Japanese to the Roman alphabet for the first time.

In 1600, an Englishman named William Adams (1564–1620) (fictionalized as the character John Blackthorne in the popular 1975 novel *Shogun* by James Clavell) was shipwrecked off Kyushu. Tokugawa first communicated with Adams through a Jesuit interpreter and a Japanese Catholic, but Adams, an English Protestant, quickly learned Japanese because of his mistrust of the

Portuguese Catholics. Adams taught Tokugawa '"jeometry," "navigacion," "mathematickes" and any other subjects of science that he had known of' (Minakawa, 1955: 69) and built the first Western-style ships in Japan. During this period, there were attempts to establish trade agreements between England and Japan, but after Tokugawa's death in 1616, the business did not do well and the English left in 1623 (Ike, 1995).

By 1639, Japan had closed its doors to most of the outside world. Christianity was banned again, Japanese Christians were persecuted, the Japanese were prohibited from having contact with Europeans and traveling abroad – or attempting to travel abroad – was a capital offense. The Portuguese were expelled from Japan, but the Dutch remained trade partners with strict restrictions. Few ships were permitted to land, and Dutch were allowed only on Dejima Island in Nagasaki, except during yearly tribute missions to Edo (e.g. Keene, 1969; Minakawa, 1955; Ike, 1995; Henrichson, 1987, 1989).

Language learning through direct contact with speakers of foreign languages ceased for ordinary people, and information about and from the Western world was filtered into Japan via translated Dutch and Chinese documents. This translation work fell to the *Nagasaki Tsuji* (Nagasaki interpreters), which became an official government bureau in 1604. This was a jealously guarded (Keene, 1969) hereditary profession among a group of about twenty families, with son succeeding father (Torikai, 2009), and it included 'hierarchical ranking, training and testing, as well as a detailed "code of conduct" with *Oh-tsuji,* chief interpreter, overseeing the entire profession' (Hayashi, 2000, in Torikai, 2009: 29). The main interpreters for Western materials were the *Oranda-tsuji* (Dutch language officers), who not only translated documents but also dealt with the Dutch crew on the arrivals of the ships, accompanied the Dutch on required gift-giving trips, and interrogated shipwrecked sailors (Keene, 1969; Torikai, 2009).

English Gains Importance

The need for knowledge of English became clear after the British warship HMS *Phaeton* sailed into Nagasaki Harbor in 1808 under a Dutch flag. Miscommunication caused the English to riot, and the Nagasaki governor committed suicide by way of taking responsibility for the resulting chaos (Ito, 1978; Jansen, 2000; Keene, 1969; Tanabe, 1978; Pomatti, 2007). Thus, in 1811, the Shogunate ordered the Nagasaki interpreters to study English (as well as some other European languages) to avoid future problems with Western ships. There were neither native English speakers nor English language materials to learn from. The first English grammar book to appear in Japan was the error-ridden Dutch translation of *Murray's English Grammar,* written by Lindley Murray in 1795. The first 'English teacher' was probably Jan Cook Blomhoff of the Dutch factory, who developed, with the help of the interpreters, two textbooks that shaped English language learning for the next 70 years: *Angeria kokugowage* (English Lessons for Beginners) and *Angeria gorintaise* (English Vocabulary, about 6000 words). *Katakana* (a Japanese pronunciation key for foreign words) was also developed to assist learners in reading foreign words. Unfortunately, Blomhoff's English ability was limited, and the pronunciations ascribed to the English words in those books were often incorrect (Omura, 1978; Henrichsen, 1987).

The Nagasaki interpreters' spoken English improved greatly in 1848 with the appearance of Ranald MacDonald, a 24-year-old Scots-Irish Indian from the North American territory of the Hudson Bay Company, who purposely shipwrecked himself off the coast of Hokkaido in northern Japan because he wanted to visit the country. He was promptly transported to Nagasaki, the designated point of expulsion for white foreigners. Unlike previous shipwrecked sailors who had been in Nagasaki, MacDonald seemed refined and educated and had brought many English books with him. During the 10 months he was held prisoner, he taught English to the interpreters while he learned Japanese (Schodt, 2003). MacDonald describes a typical English lesson as follows:

> Their [the students] habit was to read English to me: one at a time. My duty was to correct their pronunciation, and as best I could in Japanese explain meaning, construction, etc.... [The students were] all very quick and receptive. They improved in English wonderfully for their heart was...in the work, and their receptiveness...was, to me, extraordinary; in some of them phenomenal. (In Schodt, 2003: 283–284)

The Nagasaki interpreters were thus able to publish a two-part dictionary called *Egeresu-Jisho-Wakai* (Japanese Translation of a Dutch-English Dictionary) in 1850 (Omura, 1978; Henrichson, 1987). Later, MacDonald's star pupil, Moriyama Einosuke, interpreted for Commodore Perry when he arrived in Japan in 1853 with an American naval fleet and demanded that Japan open its doors for trade. Schodt (2003: 281) goes so far as to argue that MacDonald's role was crucial in the forthcoming Japanese–American negotiations:

> Without the skills of these interpreters it would have been difficult for Japan to preserve her independence in the mid nineteenth century. Instead of experiencing a successful political, social, and technological revolution and eventually becoming a ranking world power, Japan

might have been colonized or carved up by Europeans or Americans, as happened to the rest of Asia.

The translation profession expanded beyond Nagasaki because of the increasing importance of disseminating Western knowledge in Japan. The *Bansho-shirabedokoro* (also called *Bansho-shirabesho*) (An Office for the Translation or Examination of Barbarian Books) was established in Edo (Omura, 1978). Dutch studies (*rangaku*) in classrooms, called *shijuku* (which also taught mathematics and literacy skills), became popular as a means for career advancement among low-ranking samurai (Pomatti, 2007). Widespread interest in English and in the West continued during the latter part of the Tokugawa period, and the *shijuku* began adding English classes. By 1850, there were around 10,000 *shijuku* nationwide.

The doors to Japan officially opened in 1854 after the Treaty of Friendship was signed, and America established a consulate office there (Henrichson, 1987). Those Japanese who had left Japan illegally, either by design or by accident, could now return without fear of execution. They brought Western knowledge with them, and they played an important role in modernizing the country (Henrichson, 1987; Jansen, 2000). One of these, Nakahama Manjiro, a shipwrecked Japanese sailor who spent 10 years studying in the United States, returned to Japan in 1859 and wrote *Ei-Bei Taiwa Shokei* (A Shortcut to Anglo-American Conversation). This book, which used *katakana* as a pronunciation key and the *yakudoku* style of teaching Chinese classics, influenced later English books published in the Meiji era (1868–1912) (Ike, 1994). Another exile, Niijima Jo, who had swum out to an American whaling ship off the shore of Hokkaido and asked to be taken to America, returned to Japan as an ordained minister and later established Doshisha University, the oldest Christian college in Japan, in 1866 (Minakawa, 1955; Jansen, 2000).

Dutch was quickly recognized as an impractical language for negotiating with Westerners, and many, including Fukuzawa Yukichi (1835–1901), who later became the founder of Keio University, switched from Dutch to English (Henrichson, 1987, 1989; Jansen, 2000). The *Bansho Torishirabe-dokoro* (Institute for the Investigation of Barbarian Writings) was established in 1856 with a focus on English, German and French rather than Dutch (Numata 1957, in Henrichson, 1987).

English in the Meiji Era (1868–1912)

This section will discuss the various developments that mark English language learning and teaching during the Meiji era. Many foreign experts, none of whom could speak Japanese, came to Japan in numerous capacities to assist in its modernization. Therefore, it became necessary for Japanese people to develop proficiency in various languages in order to acquire the knowledge that the foreign experts had brought with them. Over time, as we shall see, reliance on the foreign workers to modernize the country decreased, and as a result, communicative proficiency was no longer essential, and the purpose of foreign language study changed.

Missionaries as English language teachers

One of the most influential groups of people during the early part of the Meiji era were missionaries, who began arriving in Japan in 1864. Although preaching Christianity was prohibited and Japanese were forbidden to become Christians, the hard work ethic of American Protestant missionaries, which was admired by the Japanese, allowed them to gain a foothold in Japan, mainly through teaching (Minekura, 1956; Jansen, 2000). Although they came to Japan with the primary goal of propagating Christianity, their main contribution was to modernize and Westernize Japan through education. Japan had a relatively high literacy rate during the Tokugawa Period because of the *terakoya* (temple schools) and *shijuku*. A centralized, compulsory and coeducational system became established in 1871 with two mandates: (1) to educate the masses to be obedient citizens and (2) to educate an elite class to lead the country. Elementary school became compulsory from 1872 for everyone for six years from the age of six; imperial universities were established to produce elite bureaucrats and government officials, and normal schools were established to train teachers for lower-order institutions throughout Japan. Missionaries taught in various schools but particularly those attended by elite students. These students then became key leaders during the first few decades of the Meiji government (e.g. Ion, 2009; Jansen, 2000; Koike & Tanaka, 1995; Ota, 1994; Poole, 2010; Pomatti, 2007).

One of the most notable missionaries during the Meiji era was Guido Fridolen Verbeck (1830–1897), who came to Nagasaki in 1859 and remained in Japan until he died in 1897. His influence was so great that his biographer William Elliot Griffis (1900: 219) said, 'I felt convinced before I left him, that this quiet, forceful man, was then, as I know now, from 1859 until 1898, not the least among the living leaders and actual makers of new Japan.'

Verbeck began his career in Japan by teaching English and German in his home. His reputation spread, and he was asked to open other schools throughout Kyushu. In 1866, two of his students went to the United States and, through his letters of introduction, gained admission to the US Naval Academy and Rutgers University respectively. Approximately one hundred more of his students would eventually follow to study in the United States. They were the sons of the elite, who later became political leaders and provided Verbeck with inside access to government power (Earns, 1997). This is evident in a letter Verbeck wrote in 1867:

> More than a year ago I had two very promising pupils, Soyeshima and Okuma, who studied through with me a large part of the New Testament and the whole of our national constitution. The former of these is now a member of the new parliament, lately formed at Miyako, to revise the ancient constitution of the empire. The latter is a member of the privy council of the Governor-General of Kiushiu [sic], and is to start in a few days for the capital, Miyako, in connection with the revision of the constitution. On Saturday last, I was invited to a special meeting of some leading members of the said privy council to be consulted on matters in regard to the revision of the national constitution, and to-morrow a similar meeting is to take place. (In Griffis, 1900: 174)

Verbeck was called to the new capital, Tokyo, where he helped establish what was to become the University of Tokyo. He also proposed a diplomatic mission to his former student from Nagasaki, Okuma Shigenobu, (who was then the Deputy Minister for Finance). This mission became known as the 'Iwakura Mission', and although its unofficial goal was to reexamine the humiliating unequal treaties Japan had been subjected to, the stated goals were to (1) study the law and government of Western countries; (2) study aspects of trade, including banking, taxation and transportation; (3) study aspects of education; and (4) investigate military equipment and military training procedures (Jansen, 2000; Ruxton, 1998).

Other missionaries (among hundreds) who helped shape English language education include James Curtis Hepburn, a medical physician and Presbyterian missionary who practiced medicine and founded the Hepburn School, which later became Meiji Gakuin University. He published Japanese and English phrase books and developed the Hepburn romanization of Japanese characters commonly used in Japan. His colleague, Samuel Rollins Brown, who arrived in Yokohama in 1863, was concerned with women's education and education for the blind and deaf. He helped translate the New Testament and also published Japanese language textbooks. He opened a language school in 1862 with the assistance of one of the official interpreters (Henrichson, 1989). According to Griffis (1902: 202),

One hundred young men of the higher class were to be taught in English, and [these] missionaries were to have charge of the work. Dr. Hepburn's Japanese–English dictionary was nearly ready for the press. Groups of from two to three, or six or seven young men came to the missionaries' house to read the English Bible, preferring this to the study of schoolbooks.

Ando, the Japanese consul in Hawaii and a former student, later said this about his lessons with his teachers:

> It was about the year 1865 that I met Dr. S.R. Brown in a school at Yokohama belonging to the Customhouse, and though very poorly provided, it was then the only English school in Japan in which instruction was received directly from foreign teachers. These were all Americans, consisting of Drs. Brown and Hepburn, and the Rev. J. H. Ballagh and David Thompson. All the teachers were kind and diligent, but Dr. Brown was particularly noted for his strict and skillful methods of teaching pronunciation and grammar. (Griffis, 1902: 208)

Missionary English teachers like those described above, who viewed themselves as 'creators of the New Japan', felt that Japan could only become modernized and civilized through the spread of Christianity (Schwantes, 1950, cited in Pomatti: 137). In fact, the Iwakura Mission was called 'The Great Embassy to Christendom' by Griffis (1900), and Verbeck's conviction that he was doing God's work is reflected in his statement, 'Whatever happens, I am not called here by a mere chance, and that I have a work to do, in the doing which, being quite aware of my insufficiency, I look to the Master for counsel and guidance' (Griffis, 1900: 185–186).

Japanese go abroad

Although some members of the elite class had already studied abroad with the assistance of their missionary teachers (Griffis, 1900, 1902) and through the financial backing of their local feudal lords (Jansen, 2000), Tokugawa first gave official permission for Japanese to travel abroad in 1866 for business and academic studies but prohibited them from adopting Western ways, for example by changing their hair styles or wearing Western clothing (Hara, 1977). The new Meiji government began to financially sponsor students to study abroad from 1868, and that program became officially regulated in 1871. Students from all over Japan applied, and they were selected on the basis of ability, character and proposed field of study. Applicants were instructed that 'going abroad should not be for the sake of the individual but for the sake of the country, and that no student would be permitted to become a Christian' (Hara, 1977: 450). The maximum period abroad was to be 10 years, and students were to specialize in areas such as politics, medicine, law, science, agriculture and mining. Hara (1977: 451) writes:

> Students were required before their departure to pay a visit to the Shinto shrine of their native places, where they would pray that they might repay their debt to their country; they were, furthermore, to drink a cup of sacred *sake* and vow that they would not disgrace their country while abroad.

However, controlling students once they were overseas proved difficult. Some switched areas of academic specialization, and others returned to Japan with no academic degree. The program was halted in 1873 because of its financial drain, which, according to Hara (1977), consumed 18% of the total expenditures (1,380,000 yen) of the Ministry of Education in 1873.

The program resumed in 1875 but with stricter conditions. Candidates, mainly from the prestigious Tokyo Kaisei Gakko, were rigorously screened for academic ability and linguistic proficiency. The period abroad was limited to five years, and students who returned with no degree were subjected to further examinations. Furthermore, the 'scholarship' was considered a loan, which the students were expected to repay over a 20-year period. Finally, to ensure proper behavior, 'foreign student advisors' were sent to each country (mainly America and England) to supervise the Japanese students. Also, for the first time, a few Japanese women were sent abroad to study, including Tsuda Umeko (the youngest member of the Iwakura Mission), who later founded Tsuda Juku, the first women's university in Japan (Hara, 1977).

Foreign experts and foreign language teachers

According to Umetani (1965, cited in Hara, 1977), the Japanese government employed more than 500 foreigners between 1872 and 1885 as specialists in areas relating to government, education, business, diplomacy and banking, as well as technicians in areas such as transportation and construction. Ogata (1961, cited in Hara) states that during the Meiji era from 1867 to 1912, government agencies and universities employed a total of 348 high-level experts, with the greatest number (78) between the years 1873 and 1877.

However, there was still a shortage of qualified English teachers to fit the demand of people who wanted to learn English. Keenleyside and Thomas (1937, cited in Pomatti, 2008) identified four prevalent types of English teachers at that time: (1) Japanese who had returned from abroad, (2) foreign experts who taught their area of expertise *in English*, (3) foreigners with no knowledge of language or pedagogy who somehow ended up in Japan, and (4) missionaries who used language teaching as a means of converting people to Christianity.

Schwantes (1950, cited in Pomatti, 2008: 129) says that the desire to have a foreign teacher – *any* foreign teacher – was so strong that foreigners could often go straight from a waterfront bar to establish themselves as language teaching professionals, He says, 'In time better professional standards and procedures of recommendation were evolved, but as late as 1890 the impulse to economize sometimes led a Japanese school to engage a beached sailor as an English teacher.'

These teachers had few pedagogical methods at their disposal, and language learning was based on direct communication with the students in English. In addition, the texts they studied from were also in English. Thus, in spite of their dubious credentials, Schwantes (1950, cited in Pomatti, 2008) believes that these students often developed a better grasp of English than those who studied English as an academic subject under Japanese teachers who still taught through *yakudoku*.

Those with access to private English instruction or who had the means to attend private language academies studied under native English-speaking teachers, often missionaries like those discussed above, who seemed to teach language effectively (Pomatti, 2007; Ota, 1994). For example, they prepared students to be able to understand, without difficulty, the foreign professors in tertiary institutions lecturing in their fields of expertise in their own languages. William Smith Clark, the president of Massachusetts Agricultural College, who came to Japan to be the president of Sapporo Agricultural College, claimed that his Japanese students were more proficient at reading and writing in English than the Americans back home. Edward S. Morse, a professor of zoology at the University of Tokyo, found no language barrier between him and his students (Ota, 1994). In fact, Nitobe Inazo, one of Japan's intellectuals at that time, whose portrait is currently on the 5000-yen note, wrote that he was more comfortable in English than in Japanese. All of his school subjects were taught in English, which was also the means of communication and correspondence between himself and his friends. As a result, educated people in that period were comfortable code switching between Japanese and English (Ota, 1994).

Some supporters of Westernization had wholeheartedly embraced Western ideas, and the Minister of Education in 1883, Mori Arinori, who had studied abroad himself, went so far as to propose abolishing Japanese and adopting English as the official language in Japan. He said:

> [O]ur meager language, which can never be of any use outside of our islands, is doomed to yield to the domination of the English tongue, especially when the power of steam and electricity shall have pervaded the land...The laws of state can never be preserved in the language of Japan. All reasons suggest its disuse. (Okubo, 1972, cited in Ota, 1994: 202)

However, not everyone agreed. In 1877, Kato Hiroyuki, the Head of the Faculties of Law, Science and Arts of the University of Tokyo, expressed concern to the Ministry of Education over the decline in Japanese language ability, saying, 'Those who boast themselves to be graduates of the University of Japan may be proficient only in English and incompetent in Japanese' (Miyake, 1946, cited in Ota 1994: 202). According to Ota (1994: 205), some of the intellectuals during that period later came to feel that the English immersion education that they had received came at a price. The internationally famous botanist, Miyabe Kingo, called this situation 'abnormal' and wrote that he 'suffered serious inconveniences because of that'. Later, even Nitobe agreed that such an education might 'overtax the brain linguistically and was not conducive to good intellectual development' (Nitobe, 1969, cited in Ota, 1994: 205).

Replacing the foreign experts

The Japanese government began to reduce the number of foreign experts and to rely more on native talent who had returned from abroad or who had received training in Japan. In the 1870s, the government employed more than 500 foreign specialists, but the numbers decreased to 132 in 1883 and to fewer than 100 in the 1890s. In 1877, 27 of 36 professors at the University of Tokyo were foreigners, but by 1883, only 13 foreigners remained, and in 1878, Japanese became the official language of the University of Tokyo, with nearly all instruction taking place in Japanese (Ota, 1994).

The foreign teachers' salaries varied, ranging from 600 yen for the Ministry of Education's top advisor, David Murray, to 50 yen for an English instructor in Kochi prefecture. In some cases, foreign teachers received 250 yen or more per month, nearly 2.5 times the salary of school principals. In fact, foreign instructors at the University of Tokyo were paid equal to, if not more, than the 400-yen salary of the university president (Ota, 1994).

According to Ogata (1961, cited in Hara 1977), the salaries of the foreign instructors at the University of Tokyo during the fiscal year from July 1877 to June 1978 represented more than one third of the university's total annual budget. The president considered that either more funds were needed or that foreign staff would have to be replaced by Japanese. Likewise, the Ministry of Public Works wanted to replace the expensive foreign technicians – whose salaries consumed nearly half of its annual budget – with new graduates from the College of Technology. Replacing the foreigners with Japanese instructors and workers was an essential cost-effective measure (Pomatti, 2007).

There was also a shift in the public sentiment from the adoration of 'all things Western' in the early Meiji era to an 'all things Japanese' movement. For example, Shiga Shigetaka visited the Pacific Rim Islands and witnessed firsthand the negative impact of colonialism, describing its dangers and calling for a sense of Japanese identity in his 1881 book *Nihon Jin* (The Japanese) (Ike, 1995: 5). Others who had returned from abroad may have had unsatisfactory experiences, in particular related to racism. Still others reported that their eyes had been opened to the contradictions of Western ideals and realities (Pomatti, 2004). Upon returning to Japan, these people wanted to create a unique Japan in which further modernization would be carried out under the supervision of Japanese experts in various fields rather than by outside Western experts. These Japanese who had returned from abroad came to view their own function in helping the Meiji system catch up with the West in terms of *specialized academic research* rather than that of being merely *educated by* the West (Hara, 1977).

Thus, the Japanese returnees ultimately replaced foreign specialists. According to Hara (1977), this generation not only brought Western knowledge and technology to Japan, they also 'Japanized' Japan at the same time. This helped develop a new ideology wherein Japan could adopt Westernization and yet retain its own sense of Japaneseness. One way that this was achieved was to dispense Western knowledge through the Japanese language. In other words, Westernization was no longer being driven directly by foreigners but indirectly by Japanese (Hara, 1977; Pomatti, 2004)

Hatoyama Kazuo, for example, was the first returnee to lecture in Japanese at the University of Tokyo in 1881. By 1883, Japanese had become the official language of the university, and by 1885, lecturing in Japanese was standard. The importance attached to Japanese as the medium for transmitting information is evident in a speech delivered by an assistant at Tokyo Specialty School (which later became Waseda University):

> I have hopes for this school – hopes by ten years from now this specialty school will be improved and will advance and be upgraded to a university in which instruction will be given to the students in Japanese. I want it to aid in the independence of Japanese learning. A country's independence is based on the independence of its people, and the independence of a people is rooted in the independence of its spirit. And the independence of a people's spirit indeed depends very much on independence of learning. (Hishiuki, 1972, cited in Hara, 1977)

Another example of how sentiments were changing was the renaming and refocus of the *Igirisu Hoka Gakko* (England Law School), which was established in 1879 with the goal of teaching English law in English, to *Tokyo Hogakuin* (Tokyo Law School) in 1889, with the goal of teaching Japanese law in Japanese (Hara, 1977). In other words, as the Japanese acquired knowledge of the Western world on their own, their dependency on foreign experts decreased. As a result, there was less need for native English-speaking teachers. With English no longer a priority, Japanese people's communicative ability in English immediately declined.

Decline in English Ability

Now that instruction in universities was *in* Japanese *by* Japanese professors, students no longer needed oral proficiency in English. By 1881, the majority of teachers in elite preparatory schools were Japanese, even the English teachers. This caused an immediate decline in the English abilities of incoming students at the University of Tokyo, as noted by law professor Hendry T. Terry in 1880. By 1883, it was recognized as an ongoing problem. Soseki Natsume, for example, considered one of Japan's greatest novelists, wrote that he felt unprepared for study in England because of his poor listening and speaking ability. Lafacio Hearn, a popular writer of books about Japan in the early 1900s, considered his students' English comprehension in 1896 to be so poor that half of his students could not understand what he said (Ota, 1994).

Despite the fact that students no longer needed aural and oral skills, educational materials continued to be written in English, thus requiring students to have good reading proficiency. As soon as the Ministry of

Education replaced foreign textbooks with Japanese ones in 1911, however, the reading level among well-educated Japanese declined.

Although many hours were still devoted to the study of English (Ota, 1994), some Japanese teachers did not have proficient English skills. Two styles of teaching and learning English were popular at the end of the 19th century. In 1896, Hidesaburo Saito founded an English school called *Seisoku Eigo Gakko*, teaching his new *seisoku* method (similar to the method employed by the foreign missionaries, which involved studying the correct pronunciation as well as the meaning). This approach was in contrast to the more commonly employed *hensoku* method (developed from *yakudoku*), which involved translating the meaning without regard to the correct pronunciation or to the rules of syntax. Tanabe (1978: 55) calls Saito the 'official initiator of learning English as a workable foreign language'.

Hensoku methodology, however, prevailed in spite of criticism by those who were proficient in English. Nitobe Inazo, for example, commented, 'Its sole object is to get the sense of a sentence and therefore it gives no heed whatever [to] how a word sounds. If it is necessary to pronounce an English word...as little respect is paid to the pronunciation of the original as in the case of Kango' (Nitobe, 1929, cited by Omura, 1978: 94). However, Nitobe, perhaps under pressure due to increasing nationalism, later qualified his criticism, and admitted,

> It must be said to its praise that students who are trained this way have usually much more accurate and precise comprehension of what they read than those who are taught to read parrot-like one sentence after another without thinking fully of the meaning. (Nitobe, 1929, cited by Omura, 1978: 94–95)

One reason for the success of *hensoku* was because of its use by Fukuzawa Yukichi at his private school, Keio Gijuku, which later became the prestigious Keio University (Omura, 1978). Thus, studying English through translation – *yakudoku* or *hensoku* – became the norm as practical (communicative) English knowledge became unnecessary.

English in the 1900s

Politicians and scholars debated the value of English in the Japanese educational curriculum during the first years of the 20th century. Some looked for practical means to solve the decline in students' English abilities, but others questioned the importance of English in Japan in the first place. Japan had become more aware of the West's discriminatory attitudes toward Asians, in particular the Japanese, which was a blow to its pride and a reason for this debate (Henrichson, 1988).

In 1911, the Japanese government removed foreign textbooks from the curriculum and replaced them with Japanese ones, leading to a decline in English reading ability. Ironically, when English shifted from being a practical necessity to an academic subject, students needed to study harder in order to keep abreast of developments in the West. For example, students entering the elite Number One Higher School *learned about* English as a subject for nine hours per week, in stark contrast to previous generations, who studied various subjects *in* English (Ota, 1994).

What influenced English education in Japan more than anything else, however, was the increased competition to enter universities. The development and expansion of compulsory education meant that more students were graduating from middle schools, and there were more applicants for higher education than there were spaces. By the first decades of the 1900s, only one out of 20 applicants was accepted. English became used as a selection tool, and thus, its importance in entrance exams was greater than the need to learn English for practical purposes (Ike, 1995; Kitao & Kitao, 1995; Ota, 1994).

According to Kinmouth (1981, cited in Pomatti, 2007), extracts from a series of popular self-help books written by an American named Orison Swett Marden were used as English entrance-exam questions. Kinmouth describes Marden's work as inadequate for testing purposes: It was filled with run-on sentences and obscure words. By using such materials, examinations became a means to eliminate applicants rather than to test their actual ability, and as a result, language learning came to focus on minute details rather than on developing a global understanding of it. At the same time, English came to be seen as a means to cultivate students' minds and deepen their understanding of themselves as Japanese (Ishikawa Rinshiro, cited in Ota, 1994). According to Sasaki (2008), such a philosophy led to a greater focus on the translation of literary works than on more practical applications.

Harold Palmer

By the 1920s, the Japanese had trouble making themselves understood while overseas. Nonetheless, several prominent Japanese who had traveled and lived abroad believed that a working knowledge of English was essential for Japan to advance economically. Dr Masataro Sawayanagi, president of the Imperial Education Association, was impressed by a lecture given by the prominent linguist and language teacher Harold Palmer, and steps were taken to invite him to Japan in 1921 as a 'linguistic advisor' to the Department of Education. Interestingly, Palmer's position was not funded by the government but by private business leaders (Nakao, 1978; Henrichson, 1987, 1989). Palmer established the semiofficial Institute for Research in English Teaching (IRET) in 1923 and began editing the *IRET Bulletin* (which would much later evolve into the *ELT Journal*) (Smith, 2007). At first, he saw his role in Japan as follows:

> I will mainly observe the practical side of the English teaching methodology at the high schools in various places, and...I intend to make the most of the good points and make up for the defects of the current teaching methods. My basic plan is to teach pronunciation first instead of teaching letters which have been taught first up to now. (Yamamoto, 1978: 152)

By 1926, Palmer realized that reading and writing were considered more important in Japan than he had originally thought, and so he tried, together with Japanese educators, to develop methods and materials that could be used effectively within the constraints of the Japanese educational system (Smith, 2007). The reforms he attempted to implement included 'reduced class sizes, increased freedom for teachers in textbook selection, improved in-service teacher education and more effective involvement of native speaker teachers' (Smith & Imura, 2004: 32). He also called for university entrance examinations to include listening and speaking components and to reduce emphasis on obscure literary terms.

Unfortunately, Palmer's suggestions for reform were not widely adopted. By the time he arrived in Japan, discriminatory immigration laws concerning Japanese nationals in the United States had led to a deterioration of relations with the United States. This unleashed a wave of anti-American sentiment, including demands to cease teaching the language of a hostile country in the schools. Such a sentiment was reflected in a series of articles in the Tokyo Asahi Press in 1924 entitled *Beigo o Ooiharae* (Drive Away American English) and *Eigo Tsuiho Ron* (The Ousting of English from the Middle School Curriculum) (Ike, 1995). These articles led to harsh criticism of Palmer's work, which had come to be considered as too non-Japanese. For example, Palmer's book *Thinking in English* was misinterpreted as a means for the Western nations to colonize Japan (Nakao, 1978).

In 1936, Palmer retired as Director of IRET and, because of the political turmoil in Japan, returned to England, where he lived until his death in 1944.

Before and During WWII

English education in Japan deteriorated further during the years leading up to World War II. Fewer students studied in English-speaking countries during the 1920s and 1930s. In 1932, 127 students went to Germany, but fewer than 20 went to the United States (Bryant, 1956, cited in Henrichson, 1989). By 1937, under the influence of the military government, the Ministry of Education reduced foreign language requirements from five years to three years in secondary schools, and 'English teachers had the hardest time ever experienced. Finally English was regarded as the language of the enemy and the study of the enemy's language was considered to be undesirable' (Imura, 1978: 135). During the war, English education in the girls' middle-school curriculum was eliminated, and the number of English classes for boys was reduced further (Koike & Tanaka, 1995). In addition, all schools were required to use only officially approved educational materials (Ike, 1994). It is interesting, however, that the Japanese Naval Academy continued teaching English for communication, perhaps, as Koike and Tanaka (1995: 17) suggest, to ultimately 'prepare them [naval academy students] for reconstruction of a new Japan [as leaders of the world in the event that Japan should win the war]'.

After war broke out between the United States and Japan, enemy foreigners were deported or placed in detention, and English effectively disappeared from the curriculum (Henrichson, 1987); in 1944, Doshisha University, Kansai University and Rikkyo University closed down their English literature departments entirely (Ike, 1995).

Postwar English

Japanese education was completely overhauled after World War II. Compulsory education became coeducational and was extended for three years to include middle school. With the increasing number of students attending middle school, there was an immediate need for more teachers and for more educational facilities (Henrichson, 1987). English also returned to the curriculum. An American linguist who helped developed the *Course of Study* (a national curricular document that prescribes educational goals in all public schools in all subjects) for English after the war, *recommended* that English in Japan should be taught using Harold Palmer's methods, but the wording in the *Course of Study* was flexible so that it could be adapted to local contexts. As a result of such flexibility, however, no real changes were ever made, and the subsequent course of studies developed by the Ministry of Education became 'precise, rigid, and inflexible' (Imura, 1978: 137). The earlier emphasis on speaking and listening disappeared, and instructional methods for English language education using *yakudoku* methodology once again became widespread.

One reason for the lack of postwar change in English language education was teachers' poor English abilities. Torii (1978: 60) recalls that the new educational curriculum was hastily established toward the end of 1946, and Japanese students would be required to study English. This resulted in a severe shortage of qualified teachers:

> Prewar middle school English teachers began teaching at the newly established high schools, but the majority of the English teachers at junior high schools at the start were those who had until then nothing to do with education. A number of these teachers were repatriates from the front who upon return found their places of employment had burned down during the war, and having nothing else to do became English teachers. A few of them were very proficient in the use of English and turned out to be excellent teachers, but most of them lacked proficiency not to mention an acquaintanceship with teaching languages. But not withstanding these drawbacks, it was these people who planned various kinds of organizations for the improvement of English teaching as a part of compulsory education, and somehow made it work.

Bryant (1955, cited in Henrichson: 228) supports Torii's description of how English education was established during the postwar years, writing that students '[were] taught by some 85,000 teachers, few of whom have ever heard the language spoken by a native – except, perhaps, over the radio.... It is a serious fact that only about one-third of the lower secondary school English teachers hold regular teaching licenses.'

Despite the low number of proficient English speakers in Japan, interest in learning English increased during the American occupation. Furthermore, an attempt to develop oral educational methods was made with the financial backing of the Rockefeller Foundation and the establishment of the English Language Exploratory Committee (ELEC) in 1956 (which later changed its name to the English Language Education Council in 1963). This program introduced the modern method (the Oral Approach) developed at the University of Michigan by Charles C. Fries. The details of this plan and how it was implemented have been thoroughly discussed by Henrichson (1987, 1989) but will be described briefly below.

A conference for English specialists was held in Japan in 1956 with funding from J.D. Rockefeller III. Rockefeller stated that the 'ultimate goal' of ELEC was 'the transformation of English language teaching methods in schools and universities throughout Japan' (Henrichsen 1989: 194). The conference invited linguists such as Americans Charles C. Fries and W. Freeman Twaddle and Englishman A.S. Hornby to discuss modern principles of language learning. The Americans impressed the Japanese with the scientific approach that they believed could revolutionize language learning in Japan. Thus, recommendations were made to develop teaching materials aimed at developing students' oral proficiency through contrastive principles. Until 1959, under the guidance of Fries and Twaddle, textbooks were developed with a communicative focus and teachers trained to teach them.

After 1959, Japanese staff at ELEC and foreign teachers hired by ELEC carried out the work, but unfortunately ELEC was unable to institute major and lasting reforms in English language education in Japan (Henrichson, 1987, 1989). However, with the advancement of technology, some schools such as Tsuda Juku (the university founded by Tsuda Ume, the first woman sent abroad to study during the Iwakura Mission) opened language laboratories so students could practice aural/oral English (Ike, 1995). In spite of various problems at this time, the roots for practical communication may have been established directly or indirectly because of the ELEC project. By 1960, when Japan was preparing to host the 1964 Tokyo Olympics, the Ministry of Education established the Council for Improvement of English Teaching, and emphasis was placed on teaching the four skills (reading, writing, listening and speaking) to develop students' English comprehension and expression (Koike & Tanaka, 1995; Yoshida, 2002).

English in the 1970s

By the 1970s, the importance of English for Japanese was once again discussed in what was called the *Eigo Dai Ronso* (A Great Debate on the Teaching of English in Japan) between Hiraizumi Wataru, a member of the House of Councilors; and Watanabe Shoichi, a Professor at Jochi University (Matsuyama, 1978). Hiraizumi argued for the abolition of compulsory English education. He felt that current teaching methods were inefficient and ineffective, and that 95% of students studying English had no need for it. He strongly felt that investing so much time and energy into passing the English component of university entrance exams was a waste of time and money. Hiraizumi, a fluent English speaker (but not an English teacher), may have been unaware of the difficult conditions faced by Japanese English teachers, but he was able to garner a certain amount of support for his ideas (Matsuyama, 1978). Professor Watanabe, in contrast, argued that English is an excellent medium for Japanese students to broaden their knowledge of the world and their knowledge of Japan and Japanese culture and to cultivate their minds (Ike, 1995).

Following that debate, an ambitious 917-page book entitled *The Teaching of English in Japan*, which was edited by Koike et al. (1978) and featured more than 80 chapters, was published in 1978. The contributors (mainly Japanese) identified problems and issues associated with English language education in Japan. Articles include the history of language education in Japan, English language teaching in various Japanese educational contexts, teaching methodologies and materials, language testing and technology. Although some articles, particularly those related to technology and methodology, may now be outdated, many of the issues raised remain relevant.

Harasawa (1974, 1978), a professor at Keio University, for instance, identified surface-structure and deep-structure reasons as to why Japanese have been unsuccessful at acquiring English. Deep-structure reasons, he maintained, stem from the self-perceived uniqueness of Japanese people in terms of the country's language and history, which he believed prevents them from having the necessary psychological ability to learn English. He considered that, because the Japanese are insular and have fought off linguistic influence in their language for centuries, successful foreign language learning can never take hold. He asserts, 'The Japanese are unduly addicted to or intoxicated by their own language – so much so that neither English nor any other foreign language can ever succeed in invading their linguistic subconsciousness' (p. 76), adding that this is why nearly all books concerning English are written in Japanese. In his view, *'In Japan English is not English at all, in the people's subconscious, unless and until it is rendered into Japanese'* (italics in original) (p. 77).

Harasawa was not optimistic that deep-structure problems could be addressed. However, he saw a 'ray of hope' (p. 78) that the following surface-level problems – which have hindered language learning – could be changed if the following recommendations were taken on board: (1) Entrance exams must test actual language, (2) obtaining an English teaching license must be more difficult, (3) training of secondary and tertiary teachers should be improved, (4) university professors should not place too much priority on academic English at the expense of practical English, (5) more attention needs to be paid to current scientific methods of language acquisition, and (6) teachers should eliminate their 'excessive fondness for hair-splitting discussion of grammatical details' (p. 75).

According to Harasawa, other problems with English language education include the shortage of native English-speaking teachers, oversized classes, too much use of Japanese in the classroom, too much focus on translation and too few opportunities for English teachers to actually use English. The single greatest deterrent for students learning English, he argues, is the 'defective entrance examination… because…it flagrantly distorts not only six years of English teaching at school but subsequently higher education as well' (p. 76). He suggests that if universities voluntarily eliminated English from their entrance examinations, teaching would become more effective, and students' abilities and motivation would improve. In other words, he believes that not all Japanese students should be required to learn English. In conclusion, Harasawa makes a rather pessimistic observation:

> There is hardly any immediate hope for innovation, much less for drastic change, but in respect for the surface structure there is, theoretically at least, some hope for the future: that the university entrance examination will some day be made to attach 50 percent weight to the oral-aural skills, thereby ceasing to distort the teaching of English at junior- and senior-high-school level. (p. 78)

Harasawa (1974: 78), then, called for more attention to be given to teaching rather than to research and for university professors to cease thinking of teaching as a 'necessary evil'.

Imamura (1978: 16), a professor and director of the English Language Center in Michigan, on the other hand, blames teachers for teaching English in the same ways as in the 1950s and earlier and not necessarily the entrance exams. He points out that if the teachers were teaching language properly, the students would automatically do well on entrance examinations. Instead, he criticizes university teachers, in particular literature professors, who cannot separate literature study and language teaching; and linguistics professors, who are more interested in examining disconnected pieces of language rather than encouraging students to understand it as a whole. He dispels the commonly stated notion that Japanese are proficient at the passive skills of reading and writing even though they cannot speak English with the comment: 'My conviction, after many years of teaching and testing Japanese students in the United States, is that the Japanese can read and write English no better than they can understand and speak it' (p. 19).

Likewise, Matsuyama (1978: 40) accuses university teachers of failing to implement language innovations in their classrooms and, for the most part, of being uninterested in language education. He notes that only a few joined the organization to improve university English education in Japan, the Japan Association of College English Teachers (JACET), established in 1962.

Summary of Chapter 2

This chapter has provided a general overview of how foreign languages were taught and learned from the time the first Europeans arrived in Japan during the 1500s up until the 1970s. As we saw, in general, language learning for Japanese has been rooted in the desire to obtain knowledge of the outside world that would be of benefit to Japan. At first, such knowledge entered Japan via China, shaping many areas of Japanese culture, including religion, architecture, philosophy and language. The means by which this knowledge was transferred into Japan was through a translation method called *yakudoku,* which was a system of converting the information from Chinese into Japanese (Hino, 1988). When the first Europeans arrived in Japan in the 1500s, it is likely that conversational fluency was achieved through face-to-face interactions in areas where the Europeans stayed and, according to Minakawa (1955), some Japanese studied European languages diligently, including Latin, and even became literate in them. Whereas the Japanese were keenly interested in the Western technology the Europeans had brought with them (for example, gunpowder and shipbuilding knowledge), the Europeans, particularly the Catholic priests, were interested in propagating Christianity. The Japanese became increasingly wary of the Europeans' intentions and expelled most Europeans in 1639. After that, Japan's exposure to Western knowledge was via the Dutch, who remained trade partners with Japan but only under strict conditions and limitations. A hereditary profession of interpreters in Nagasaki was responsible for bringing in this knowledge, which they did through *yakudoku* translations.

When Japan reopened its doors at the end of the Edo era and began to modernize, it was clear that there was a lot of catching up to do. Many foreign experts in numerous fields acted as advisors and instructors, and Japanese needed to learn their languages in order to acquire their knowledge. To do that, students became competent in all four language skills. After several decades, however, such information could be disseminated by Japanese *in Japanese,* and as a result, reliance on the foreign experts lessened and proficiency in foreign languages was no longer necessary. This caused an immediate decrease in students' speaking skills, followed by a decrease in reading ability once textbooks came to be published in Japanese (e.g. Hara, 1977; Ike, 1995; Ota, 1994).

English then became an academic subject that was utilized as a measurement tool to select candidates entering higher education, even during the periods of nationalism leading up to and during World War II. When the educational curriculum was entirely overhauled after the war, English became a required subject for all students for the last three years of compulsory education and then for a further three years as more students advanced to senior high school. Despite the fact that students had six years of English language study, English language teaching came under much criticism because of its seeming failure, which was tied to ineffective teaching and the entrance examination system. The chapter closed with a discussion of these key issues, which were brought together in a 1978 volume entitled *The Teaching of English in Japan*.

The next chapter covers the next four decades, beginning with curricular reforms of the 1980s, which were shaped by Japan's growing economic power. These reforms resulted in many foreigners coming to Japan as English language teachers. During that period, as we shall see, the focus is once again on language proficiency, but in a very Japanese kind of way.

Notes

(1) The names of historical figures in Japanese will generally be presented in the Japanese way; that is, family name will precede given name.

3 1980s until Today

Introduction

The previous chapter described how the purposes of teaching and learning foreign languages in Japan shifted over several hundred years and showed how language learning and language teaching were related to ongoing sociopolitical events. In this chapter, I focus on the language teaching that has been mainly carried out by foreign teachers from the 1980s onward. During the past 30 years, the number of foreign English teachers has increased substantially, and these teachers now live in urban and rural areas and teach in formal and informal educational institutions throughout Japan.

One reason behind this increase is the economic boom of the 1960s and 1970s. By the 1970s, Japan's industrial economy had recovered from World War II, and it attained the third largest gross national product (GNP) in the world. This was partly possible due to postwar educational reforms that resulted in a highly educated workforce, so that by the 1970s, nearly all Japanese graduated from high school, and nearly 50% attended university. Despite the educational and economic achievements, however, there was great dissatisfaction concerning English language education as discussed toward the end of the previous chapter (Koike *et al.*, 1978). It was not until industry began demanding graduates with better English proficiency (as well as other academic skills) that sweeping reforms influencing secondary and tertiary education took place (e.g. Kempner, 1996; Aspinal, 2005; Butler & Iino, 2005; Nakata & Mosk, 1986). These reforms included various measures, many of which focused on improving language education at the secondary-school level through several revisions of the course of study. These revisions encouraged teachers to move away from test-oriented English to focus on more communicative-oriented English (e.g. Butler & Iino, 2005). As a result, more and more foreign English language teachers came to be employed in Japan.

One area where foreign teachers have traditionally worked is in the *eikaiwa* industry. For many years, it was understood that because there were two parallel types of English language education: *eigo* (English language, which mainly focused on exam-oriented English) and *eikaiwa* (English conversation, which took place out of school). Those wanting to learn English needed to supplement *eigo* with *eikaiwa*. The *eikaiwa* industry, as we shall see, developed into a multibillion dollar industry by the 2000s, and in the past several decades it has employed tens of thousands of foreign teachers.

Foreigners also came to be employed in most secondary schools after the Japan Exchange Teaching (JET) program was established in 1986, hiring native English speakers as assistant language teachers (ALTs). Today, more than 60,000 participants from 63 countries to date (JET Programme, n.d.) have participated in JET, but there are also many foreign ALTs who are hired to work at schools directly or through dispatch companies. In addition, there are some public and private schools that hire foreigners as regular classroom teachers; these staff do not assist Japanese teachers but are in charge of their own classrooms.

In tertiary education, the number of foreign English teachers has also increased. Prior to the 1980s, English education in universities was mainly related to English literature and/or English linguistics, and Japanese professors mainly taught these content-based classes in Japanese. Some universities might have had several foreign teachers on staff, but those in regional areas (where few foreigners lived) generally did not. With the booming economy and with more students entering higher education, many universities expanded their language programs to include communicative courses and hired foreign teachers to teach them. Currently, nearly half of all universities in Japan employ native English speakers, at least as part-time teachers (Yoshida, 2002). Foreign teachers are also employed in full-time positions as well. The majority fill limited-term contracted positions, but many hold tenured positions as well.

This chapter discusses the sociopolitical and ideological issues that surround these three English language teaching contexts. My discussion opens with the *eikaiwa* industry, which provides informal and supplementary English education and where attendance by students is voluntary. Then I describe how the JET program began and some of its glitches in the early years to set the stage for the current context of secondary-school English teaching. Finally, I discuss English language teaching in tertiary education. University teaching is considered to be the pinnacle of teaching English as a foreign language (EFL) in Japan, but as we shall see, a three-tiered employment system means that not all university employment is equal in terms of status and security.

Eikaiwa

I begin my discussion in this chapter with *eikaiwa* teaching, which generally occurs in informal educational contexts and is considered supplementary to the *eigo* taught in schools. *Eikaiwa* teaching is often considered to be at the bottom of the EFL teaching hierarchy in Japan. The teachers are often (but not always) relatively inexperienced transient sojourners to Japan. Many are fresh out of college, and they want to have an overseas experience before embarking on other careers (Caesar & Bueno, 2003).

The business side of *eikaiwa*

As mentioned in Chapter 2, foreign language proficiency, particularly in English, was essential for educational and career advancement in Japan in the early to late 1800s, but as Western knowledge became available in Japanese, proficiency was no longer necessary. After World War II, English became a required subject for all students, but as it was used as a measurement tool to select secondary and tertiary students, the focus was mainly on *yakudoku*. At that time, the parallel industry of *eikaiwa* began. It first consisted of mainly radio (and later, television) programs and conversational books, which led to numerous English clubs being established throughout Japan (e.g. Mizuta, 2009; Sugiyama, 2010). *Eikaiwa* came to represent an American world – unattainable, affluent and exotic. According to Sugiyama (2010: 44), it provided a 'feeling of liberation from the depressing and miserable atmosphere of the previous war'.

Nowadays, *eikaiwa* and the professions surrounding it comprise a huge part of the leisure-industry business sector. *Eikaiwa* schools, as registered businesses, fall under the jurisdiction of the Ministry of Economy, Trade and Industry (METI) and they are grouped together with other for-profit businesses such as wedding service companies, culture centers, and fitness clubs. The *eikaiwa* industry in the 1990s was worth approximately 1 trillion yen[1] (Tsuda, 1995, cited in Takahashi, 2013), which included not only language teaching itself but also the production of audiovisual materials, TV and radio broadcasts, proficiency tests, and advertising (Takahashi, 2013). By the 2000s, the English teaching industry had expanded to have more than 30,000 full- and part-time teachers (15,000 of whom were foreign) (METI, 2005).

At the industry's peak in 2005 and 2006, more than 9 million Japanese attended commercial language schools, with 92.9% of the lessons focusing on English. Annual sales were 192 billion yen, which included 19 billion yen for educational materials and 7 billion yen for schools' entrance fees. Students paid an average annual fee of 176,000 yen, with larger schools charging more than smaller ones. The majority of learners were under 20 years old, although there was an increase in learners over 60 years old. In addition, 60% of *eikaiwa* students are female (METI, 2005), and the implication of this will be discussed in more detail in Chapter 4.

By 2015, the number of *eikaiwa* students had dropped to less than five million. This was because of a downturn in the foreign language market and the bankruptcy of the major *eikaiwa* chain Nova (METI, 2015; Sugiyama, 2010). The number of registered *eikaiwa* businesses decreased from 4303 in 2005 to 3741 in 2009. During the same period, sales related to tuition and educational materials dropped from 136 million yen in 2006 to 81 million, and the number of teachers (including full- and part-time teachers) fell from 13,580 to 9602. The employment status of *eikaiwa* teachers also changed: In 2006, there were 8120 full-time teachers and 5460 part-time teachers, but in 2015, the number of part-time teachers (6461) was nearly double that of full-time teachers (3141) (METI, 2015).

The majority of language-school businesses operate in the greater Kanto area (Tokyo and the surrounding prefectures), but there are established language schools in the main cities of every prefecture (METI, 2005). In addition to large language-school businesses, there are also numerous *eikaiwa* schools operating as independent businesses and *eikaiwa* lessons taught by individuals as cottage industry businesses that operate under the tax radar (Nagatomo, 2013).

Ideologies surrounding *eikaiwa*

In postwar Japan, few Japanese actually *needed* English except for *juken eigo* (English for examination purposes). Despite being far removed from people's lives, *eikaiwa* gained popularity, at first via radio and then via television. Affluent people living in urban areas (where foreigners tended to live) could attend *eikaiwa* schools if they so desired. At the heart of *eikaiwa* was the native English speaker, who represented a whole package of language, culture and lifestyle for Japanese to aspire to (Sugiyama, 2010; Takahashi, 2013). Lummis (1976) criticized this by describing his personal experiences as a student in Japan in the 1960s. He was asked to teach English even though he had no linguistic or pedagogical knowledge, and he was shocked to learn that his income was to be higher than his more qualified and more experienced Japanese colleagues. Furthermore, Lummis argued that the trivial conversational topics focusing on an imaginary American lifestyle (such as ordering a milkshake at a soda fountain) during those *eikaiwa* lessons actually created barriers between the foreign teachers and the Japanese students rather than promoting language and cultural understanding (see also Derivry-Plard, 2013; Kubota, 1998; Mizuta, 2009; Rivers & Ross, 2013; Seargeant, 2009, 2013; Sugiyama, 2010; Toh, 2013; Tsuneyoshi, 2013; Yoshino, 2002).

In recent years, the discourse surrounding *eikaiwa* has changed and, rather than aspiring to a more luxurious Western lifestyle, students are lured by images of globalization and internationalization (e.g. Takahashi, 2013). Even though teachers and learners may feel that they are participating in activities that broaden minds and promote shared experiences between Japanese and non-Japanese people, Yoshino (2002: 139) agrees with Lummis (1976) that *eikaiwa* actually promotes distance:

> Many language teachers thus become reproducers and transmitters of discourses of cultural difference and national identity...in fact, it is increasingly in the realm of the English-conversation industry that discourses on Japanese cultural and behavioral distinctiveness, namely *Nihonjinron* [theories and discussions about the Japanese by the Japanese] are reproduced and transmitted.

Such a discourse has contributed to a flourishing industry where many participate but lack clear goals or purposes. Sugiyama (2010: 45) criticizes such language study because it is 'no more a survival tool in reality, but often rather a hobby for complacency'. Kubota (2011: 485), on the other hand, takes a more pragmatic stance toward *eikaiwa* and argues that the personal enjoyment obtained from such classes is a sufficient end in itself. Membership in *eikaiwa* classes enables attendees to be 'part of the social imaginary of *eikaiwa* world – an imagined community of English speakers, which the learners enjoy visiting once every week'. This, she argues, is one of the main attractions of *eikaiwa*, and for the students, a sense of belonging may be of more importance than the possibility of obtaining English language proficiency.

Eikaiwa teachers

Although some *eikaiwa* schools have begun hiring teachers of different racial and cultural origins (see, for example http://www.aeonet.com/application-requirements/), *eikaiwa* schools generally hire teachers for their physical appearance and for personality characteristics that they believe their students want their teachers to have (Kubota, 2011). This has been criticized as being racially and culturally biased (e.g. Heimlich, 2013; Houghton & Rivers, 2013; Kubota & Fujimoto, 2013; Kubota & McKay, 2009; Lummis, 1976; Seargeant 2009, 2013) and in fact, as recently as 2007, a language school specifically advertised for teachers with 'blond hair, and blue or green eyes' (*The Japan Times*, 13 February 2007, cited in Seargeant, 2009: 56). *Eikaiwa* teachers are not only supposed to look the part; they are also supposed to be *'genki'* (energetic) and have a 'good attitude, to feel positive, [and be] eager and outgoing' (Bailey 2007: 596). They are also relatively young (Bueno, 2003) and they act as cultural representatives of the West (usually America) by providing cultural experiences (often in the form of holiday activities) for students (e.g. Duff & Uchida, 1997). There are few requirements (other than holding a BA, which is necessary for visa sponsorship) for obtaining employment in *eikaiwa* schools, indicating that the characteristics described above may be more desirous in the teachers than pedagogical knowledge and experience.

To date, relatively little empirical research has been conducted on *eikaiwa* teachers and/or *eikaiwa* schools (e.g. Bailey, 2007; MacNaughton, 2008; Nagatomo, 2013; Kubota, 2011, Caesar & Bueno, 2003), despite their significant financial impact on Japan. One reason why *eikaiwa* teachers might have been so under researched to date is because, according to Caesar and Bueno (2003: 15), these teachers tend not to examine their own work critically:

> Those who teach below college level for the most part cannot write…. They are younger, their training is poor, their time in Japan is usually brief, and their motivations have more to do with adventure and travel than commitment to the classroom.

While it may be true that there is little empirical research in this area, there is an abundance of autobiographical accounts by the *eikaiwa* teachers. These accounts range from offering practical and/or humorous advice to current and future *eikaiwa* workers (e.g. Brotherstone, 2015) to blogs and/or self-published works bragging about sexual and drunken exploits while teaching in Japan (e.g. Chesney, 2008).

Eikaiwa teaching is generally considered to be at the bottom of the EFL hierarchy in Japan in terms of salary, prestige and benefits. Most *eikaiwa* teachers do move on to other careers, particularly those who are employed by corporate organizations. There are those, however, who wish to remain in Japan and/or who wish to make English language teaching their career. Some then, like Blackstone (2015) and several of the women in my study, establish and operate their own language schools. Others, wishing to obtain more stable employment in formal educational institutions (often with better working hours and more holidays), obtain graduate degrees in order to move up the language-teaching ladder. Many university professors in Japan, myself included, began their teaching careers with *eikaiwa*. Furthermore, even those currently teaching in other areas may continue with some *eikaiwa* classes, especially long-running ones where mutual feelings of friendship have developed between the teachers and the students (Nagatomo, 2013).

Secondary Schools

Now I would like to turn our attention toward English in formal educational settings. Although English has been a compulsory subject in elementary schools since 2011, I mainly focus on the situation in secondary schools. First, I describe the differences between private and public schools and how these schools impact not only the students who attend them but also the teachers who work for them. Then, I describe the conception and implementation of the JET program, which has brought tens of thousands of young foreigners into Japanese secondary schools and changed the language-learning experiences of Japanese students throughout Japan. Although the number of JET teachers has recently dropped due to changes in hiring practices, the number of ALTs in the classroom has been increasing. Despite the impact that the JET program has had on English language education in Japan, the symbolic and legal positioning of the foreign teachers and the Japanese teachers (e.g. Hashimoto, 2013) has contributed to two separate and not equal positions of foreign and Japanese teachers, resulting in two separate approaches toward learning English: *eigo* (English language), which is generally for test purposes; and *eikaiwa,* which is generally for fun (e.g. Law, 1995; Nagatomo, 2014).

Public education vs. private education

As mentioned in the previous chapter, the length of time to be spent in compulsory education in Japan expanded after World War II to nine years. Secondary-school attendance increased so that today nearly all students attend high school, and nearly 50% attend university. Most children attend neighborhood public elementary schools (98%) and public junior high schools (92%), which are free and follow the standardized curriculum prescribed in the official course of study by the Ministry of Education, Culture, Sports, Science and Technology MEXT (MEXT, n.d.). Students do not automatically advance to high schools, which are academically ranked; instead, they must take entrance exams. The decision as to which school to aim for is often guided by junior-high-school teachers, who consider which schools they believe their students have the greatest chance of getting into (Fukuzawa, 1994, 2001). There are also private schools, some of which matriculate children from elementary school and see them through all the way through university without further entrance exams (e.g. Ishikida, 2005). These schools are also academically ranked, with those attached to prestigious universities being the most difficult to gain admission to. Parents who can afford to pay hefty entrance and tuition fees may choose to send their children to these escalator schools from elementary school to spare their children from examination hell. However, many students enter private schools from high school, especially if they were unable to gain entrance into a high-level public school.

The high schools that students attend are of extreme importance because they are considered to be 'an official verdict about one's capabilities and future opportunities' (Kariya & Rosenbaum, 1987: 172). Students graduating from elite academic secondary schools are more likely to attend elite universities leading to employment in large corporations or in government; those graduating from medium-level academic schools are likely to attend less prestigious universities leading to employment in smaller companies; and those graduating from vocational schools will constitute the lower mass strata of the workforce (Okano, 2000). Because educational credentialism is closely calibrated with cultural capital (Bourdieu, 1991; Bourdieu & Wacquant, 1992), which influences lifetime income and social prestige (e.g. Beauchamp, 1987; Ishida, 1993; Ono, 2001, 2004), many parents invest time and money to ensure that their children can attend the highest level schools possible (Ishikida, 2005a, 2005b).

Japanese full-time teachers in both public and private schools have standard employment with social welfare benefits. They have at minimum a bachelor's degree and a teaching license from a Japanese university, and they have passed rigorous teachers' examinations for public and/or private-school employment. Public-school teachers are considered civil servants, and they are regularly transferred between schools within their school districts. Those in private schools also must have the same academic credentials and must pass an examination to teach at a private school, but they can remain at the same school until retirement. Foreign teachers, as we shall see in this chapter and throughout this book, are hired under and are employed under different criteria in both private and public schools.

The JET program

Now, let us turn our attention to the JET program, which is currently one of the largest exchange programs in the world. It began in 1986 with an announcement from the Japanese government that it was to expand two existing small-scale programs: BET (British English Teaching) and MEF (Mombusho English Fellow). From 1977 to 1986, these two programs had dispatched several hundred teachers annually throughout Japan. In 1987, with the launch of the JET program, 847 ALTs (who generally refer to themselves as 'JETs') arrived, and the number of annual participants increased to over 6273 at its peak in 2002. As of 2014, more than 60,000 people from 63 countries (mostly from the United States) have participated in the program. The stated goals of the JET program presented on its homepage are as follows:

> The Japan Exchange and Teaching (JET) Programme aims to promote grass roots internationalisation at the local level by inviting young overseas graduates to assist in international exchange and foreign language education in local governments, boards of education and elementary, junior and senior high schools throughout Japan. It seeks to foster ties between Japanese citizens (mainly youth) and JET participants at the person-to-person level. (JET Programme, n.d.)

Despite these stated goals, McConnell (2000: 35) writes that the JET program was, in reality, a diplomatic exchange strategy devised by the Ministry of Foreign Affairs to address the $50 billion trade deficit. Nose (pronounced No-say), a career official in the Ministry of Home Affairs, explained to McConnell how the program came to be:

> During the year of the trade conflict between Japan and the United States...I was thinking about how to deal with the demands that we buy more things such as computers and cars. I realized that trade friction was not going to be solved by manipulating material things, and besides, I wanted to demonstrate the fact that not all Japanese are economic animals who gobble up real estate.... In order to do all this, I decided local governments must open their doors and let people come and see the truth directly – not just any people, but those with a college degree and under the age of thirty-five, since people start to lose flexibility after that age. I thought this would be a much better way of solving the trade conflict than using money or manipulating goods.

Initial resistance by the Ministry of Education (MoE) (the forerunner of MEXT) to bringing foreigners into the Japanese English classrooms was due to fears that the Japanese teachers' jobs could be threatened by native English speakers. Support for the JET program was given only under the condition that the foreigners would be hired as *assistants* and not as teachers (McConnell, 2000; Hashimoto, 2013). Wada, the representative of the Ministry of Education at that time, explains the rationale behind this decision:

> I myself thought a lot about that [the issue of Japanese teachers worrying about losing their jobs]. I didn't want Japanese teachers of English to think that I didn't pay attention to that aspect. The idea of team teaching has something to do with that issue. When you look at the situation in private schools, they don't do team teaching because the owners of private schools don't want to spend money on both a native speaker and a Japanese teacher.[2] They think they don't need two teachers (Bracketed items are McConnell's). (In McConnell, 2000: 45)

Not surprisingly, numerous problems, both trivial and serious, occurred during JET's early years, most of which were related to miscommunication due to language and cultural differences between the JETs, the Japanese teachers and the boards of education. One common complaint from the JET teachers was that they were underutilized in the classroom and were treated like a human tape-recorder. Others complained of verbal abuse (from students and faculty) while others experienced direct and indirect gender discrimination. Such complaints were handled by CLAIR (Council of Local Authorities for International Relations), but according to one official interviewed by McConnell (2000: 96–97), they were rarely taken seriously. He explained, 'Whenever a call comes into the counseling section of CLAIR from an ALT, the first thing you should know is that we never believe his story outright. We always contact his superior to find out the real circumstances.' As an example, he described how he handled the 'barbaric' complaint of one British woman[3], who said she was being forced to serve tea to the male members of the board of education:

> I listened politely, but then she asked me to tell them to stop. So I told her I would call her superiors, and I called them all right, but rather than asking them to stop, I simply told them that she had called me. I don't think ALTs have the right to make such barbaric demands.

There were also some highly publicized incidents, which included drug possession, drunk driving and even suicide. They led to more careful scrutiny of prospective JET teachers, with applicants being asked to provide personal data such as mental health and criminal records as well as college transcripts. By 1991, the interviewers were instructed: 'Overly sensitive/emotionally fragile, not sociable, cheerful or polite, or does not appear to like children, DO NOT RECOMMEND their acceptance into the program' (McConnell, 2000: 99–100).

Other issues concerned the duration of JET teachers' sojourn in Japan. Fear that the 'wrong' type of teacher would want to renew their JET contract for the 'wrong' type of reasons was behind the three-year limitation on the contract. The official explanation for this was the aim to provide as many young people as possible with the opportunity to be a JET, but according to McConnell (2000: 102–103), 'by setting the three-year limit, Japanese officials were explicitly acknowledging that the ALT and CIR [Coordinator of International Relations] slots would forever be positions for temporary outsiders.' In short, the JETs were supposed to return to their home countries with positive memories of Japan after their contracts were successfully completed. Unfortunately, some were unable to adjust to living in Japan and returned home without completing their contracts, and others broke their contracts after obtaining more lucrative work at *eikaiwa* schools. Those who wanted to remain in Japan made CLAIR worried that the JET program was being used as a stepping-stone to remain in Japan. This motivated CLAIR to ask the MoE to withhold the promised return airfare if the former JETS obtained jobs in Japan, even *after* completing their contracts. To discourage job-hunting, JETs' visas, which had previously been valid for 90 days after completing their contracts, were shortened to 30 days (McConnell, 2000).

Despite the initial difficulties in the establishment and running of the JET program, (McConnell, 2000: 272–273) nonetheless believes that it brought about 'extraordinary change' in individual and localized contexts. Because of JET, no matter how remote the area, every student has had at least one opportunity to 'see, hear, and talk to a foreigner'. This, he feels, is an accomplishment that was previously unimaginable.

Outsourced and direct-hire ALTs

In 1999, a change in the Japan's Worker's Dispatch Law enabled schools to obtain ALTs from outside the JET program. Since each JET teacher cost school boards 6 million yen per year, this was a welcome change for many school districts, and many began hiring local foreign residents directly or through dispatch companies (Takahara, 2008). In fact, by 2009, nearly 50% of the approximately 10,000 ALTs had come from dispatch companies (Flynn, 2009). Boards of education trust these companies to provide reliable and trustworthy teachers and, if problems do arise, the dispatch companies will take care of them and send replacement teachers.

This means schools are provided with a steady flow of foreign teachers that they no longer need to handle (Tope, 2003; Flynn, 2009).

Although schools benefited financially from utilizing dispatch agencies, labor-law violations have occurred. Dispatched teachers are commonly contracted to teach less than 30 hours per week, which gives them part-time status and thus makes them ineligible for medical insurance and other benefits. However, ALTs often work more than that because they take part in non-teaching-related activities, such as eating lunch and/or cleaning the classroom with students. Failing to pay for this overtime work, which essentially gives ALTs a full-time schedule but without the attached benefits, clearly violates the labor law.

Another violation occurs when classroom teachers instruct dispatched ALTs on what to do in the classroom. According to the Worker Dispatch Law, dispatched workers are to receive direct instructions *only* from the companies that employ them and not from on-site employees. This contradicts the foundation on which team teaching is based, because *only* Japanese teachers can be in charge of classes – not ALTs nor the companies that employ them. This concern motivated MEXT to seek advice from the Ministry of Health, Labor, and Welfare (MHLW) in 2009. Notices were then sent to the BOEs throughout Japan that 'outlin[ed] the MHLW's view that team teaching could not be conducted with the outsourced ALTs and urg[ed] them to review the employment conditions of ALTs' (Hashimoto, 2013: 162).

Confusion over how dispatched ALTs should be handled by schools is demonstrated in an article entitled 'A less-than-desirable ALTernative', which originally appeared in the *Daily Yomiuri* in 2010 and was discussed on the *Education in Japan Community Blog* (Kawagoe, 2010). The article provides an extreme example of how misinterpretation of the labor law can occur and can cause problems. It described an elementary-school class in which the Japanese teacher sat silently in the back while the dispatched ALT taught in the front. According to the article, the two teachers did not communicate with each other, and it concludes that fears of violating the labor law made the school 'opt for the safest approach: banning all conversation between teachers and ALTs during class'.

Relying on dispatch companies may also negatively impact the quality of the English lessons. Some dispatch companies provide adequate training for their employees, but others do not (Aoki, 2014), resulting in some schools having better qualified ALTs than others. Furthermore, low salaries contribute to a rapid turnover of dispatched ALTs. Dispatched ALTs only receive 60% of the fees BOEs pay to the dispatch companies, and they earn approximately 20–30% less than JETs (Flynn, 2009). Not surprisingly, many quit without notice if offered better employment. Schools, however, are seldom without ALTs because there are others eager to take their place.

Because of problems surrounding the outsourcing of ALTs, some school boards have eliminated this process entirely (Takahara, 2008). For example, one Tokyo school district hires ALTs directly through interviews and presentations of sample lessons. However, Aoki (2014) fears that a governmental directive to increase the number of ALTs in schools by 2020 will may have BOEs selecting the more economical, but not necessarily better, hiring path.

Attitudes toward ALTs

As discussed earlier, one condition for the establishment of the JET program was that the ALTs would be positioned below Japanese teachers. In fact, ALTs without linguistic and/or pedagogical knowledge were preferred because they would be less likely to be a threat to the Japanese English teachers' careers. Furthermore, the terminology employed in describing the JET program and the JET teachers differs in English and in Japanese, and this difference also contributes to a hierarchal positioning of the teachers. First, there is a discrepancy between the English terms 'JET' and 'ALT' and their Japanese translations. JET stands for 'Japan Education Exchange' in English, but in Japanese, it is *'Gogaku shido nado o okonau gaikoku sei nen sho chi jigyou'*, which means 'project to invite foreign youth who conduct language teaching, etc.'. According to Hashimoto (2013: 161), the latter part of the phrase – 'to conduct language teaching, etc.' – is often omitted and thus contributes to the image the JET program is merely an exchange program and not a teaching one. Furthermore, 'ALT', which stands for 'Assistant Language Teacher' in English, is stated in Japanese as *'gaikoku go shido joshu'*, which directly translated means 'foreign language teaching assistant'. The removal of the word teacher, Hashimoto argues, is another way to position the ALT below the Japanese teacher. And yet another example of the hierarchy is found in the Japanese version of the 2010 Course of Study guidelines. There, team-teaching is described as classes taught by *Japanese teachers* and *native English speakers* (emphasis mine). These examples, Hashimoto argues, emphasize an unequal relationship in the classroom where one group is considered to be real teachers, but the other is not.

Many ALTs who take their jobs seriously wish to be respected for the work they do, and they resent being treated as mere role models whose main function is to provide fun for students (e.g. Geluso, 2013).

Such attitudes toward native English speaking teachers may affect students' attitudes toward learning communicative English, because after becoming aware of their native English speaking teachers' lower status in their schools, they might develop attitudes that communicative English is unimportant. Those students studying English for investment purposes (Norton, 1995), for example, may sense their ALTs' lower position and come to prefer Japanese teachers, who may be perceived as more qualified to help them achieve their academic goals, particularly those related to entrance examinations (Suemori, 2014).

Stand-alone teaching

In addition to ALTs, there are also foreign teachers in both private and public secondary schools that are in charge of their own classrooms. As mentioned earlier, private schools have more leeway in hiring foreign teachers, but foreigners can also teach on their own in public schools, if budgets allow, by receiving special limited-term teaching licenses from local school boards.[4]

Private schools can hire whom they like under whatever conditions they like as long as minimum requirements are met and as long as the school can afford to do so. Some private schools may utilize dispatch companies for convenience, but some hire part-time and full-time foreign teachers directly. Some teachers may have limited-term contracts, but others may be employed under the same conditions as Japanese teachers until retirement. Private-school teachers may engage in team teaching with Japanese teachers, but many are in charge of their own classes as well. One Japanese teacher at an elite academic private secondary school with several branches in the Kanto area said that some foreign teachers at her school are employed as full-timers with full benefits. They are in charge of their own classes, and they have the freedom to choose their own textbooks and develop their own syllabi. To become full time, however, these teachers must have sufficient Japanese to carry out the duties of a homeroom teacher, and they must be willing to take part in extracurricular activities with the students (private e-mail correspondence).

Some private schools, even academically low-level ones, hire native English speaking teachers to attract prospective students as illustrated below in the following comment by a former high school teacher:

> I used to teach at a private high school in Osaka. A very 'bottom of the barrel private high school.' I was hired directly through an introduction by a contact I had. I was able to more or less name my salary, and I

was told I could buy any furniture or electric appliances I wanted and if I wanted to move the school would be my guarantor and pay all the security deposit and key money. Initially I was *hijokin* [part time] with no responsibilities outside teaching my regular classes and English club, but from the second year I was made *jokin* [full time] and a sub homeroom teacher. I only stayed 3 years, but it was my choice to leave. The school wanted to keep me. I was always featured very prominently in their pamphlet as a selling point (private e-mail correspondence).

Higher Education

Now let us examine the type of English teaching that is carried out in tertiary education. By the time Japanese students enter university, they will have studied English for at least six years, and it is likely they will continue to study English, to some extent, at university as well. The majority of English teachers in university are Japanese, many of whom have specialized in English-related areas such as literature or linguistics and whose pedagogical methods often mirror those of secondary-school teachers (Nagatomo, 2011, 2012a).

As mentioned in the introduction to this chapter, demands from industry are one of the motivating factors behind English education reforms, which have led to a greater focus on communicative English. There is, however, another motivating factor for this increase in communication classes, particularly at the university level. Because of a decline in the 18-year-old population, fewer students enroll in universities nowadays and competition to attract fee-paying students is fierce. English education programs populated with foreign teachers are one way to attract students.

Nearly half of all high-school graduates in Japan attend university but, as discussed earlier, not all universities are equal in terms of prestige, academic quality and opportunities for graduates. National universities and the older universities established during the Meiji era are at the top of the hierarchy. Top universities have more professors with advanced degrees, graduate programs and research facilities. Newer liberal arts universities (often called *ekiben daigaku,* or 'Mickey Mouse' universities) are at the bottom (e.g. Daizen & Yamanoi, 2008; Benjamin & James, 1989; Eades, 2005), and they are often operated as for-profit family businesses (Kemper & Makino, 1998; Kenmouth, 2005).

Research universities obtain funds through grants and other sources as well as from students' tuition. Lower-ranking universities, on the other hand, operate mainly on the basis of fees obtained from entrance exam applications, students' tuition payments and government subsidies. Because there are fewer students due to a birthrate decline, many lower-ranking universities are in financial danger because of their reliance upon tuition (which accounts for 60% of private universities' budgets). If student quota drops below 50%, the universities stand to lose government subsidies, (approximately 166,000 yen per student) (Ishikida, 2005a). Fear of bankruptcy has resulted in a 'buyer's' market where universities do whatever it takes to attract and keep fee-paying students.

According to Kinmouth (2005), to survive, universities are taking measures to reduce costs (particularly those that are related to personnel), to attract more nontraditional students (such as foreign students, mature students, disabled students, and minorities) and to recruit students through alternative examination processes. Highly ranked universities remain selective, but those at the bottom, particularly 'F'-ranking schools, admit all those who apply. One way that 'F'-ranking schools (a classification that, he reminds us, only coincidentally corresponds with the English term 'F' for failing) hope to attract more students to sell 'trendy' courses that are 'international' and/or related to 'information technology' (see also Goodman, 2007). Kinmouth explains that in many cases, such courses are falsely labeled:

> That 'trendy' subjects should be associated with enrolment shortfalls is largely to be explained by the lack of content behind these names. Looking at the prospectus of a private college that touts itself as 'international' typically reveals nothing more than the teaching of 'business English' and possibly the presence of several peripatetic foreign teachers of English conversation. (2005: 119)

Thus, English became a selling point for universities, and more native English speaking teachers were hired to teach it.

For many foreign English teachers in Japan, obtaining university employment is much like reaching the 'holy grail' of EFL employment (e.g. Fraser, 2005; Whitsed, 2011; Whitsed & Wright, 2011). University teaching is desirable because the salaries are generally higher than those in other areas of English language teaching. Paid holidays are abundant, and teachers generally receive greater respect. To gain access to employment in higher education, many of those engaged in *eikaiwa* or secondary-school teaching returned to school to obtain MAs and, in some instances, even PhDs.

However, not all university positions are equal in terms of prestige and security. As we shall see in the subsequent sections, foreign university teachers are often positioned quite differently from their Japanese counterparts. This positioning, as many have argued, has resulted in a kind of 'academic apartheid' (e.g. Caesar & Bueno, 2003; Hall, 1998; Hayes, 2013; McVeigh, 2001, 2002; Rivers, 2010, 2011, 2013; Rivers & Ross, 2013).

In the sections that follow, I will discuss the differences between standard and nonstandard employment in tertiary education, followed by a description of part-time, contracted full-time (non-standard employment) and tenured (standard employment) positions that are filled by foreigners.

Standard and nonstandard positions in Japanese universities

In Japanese universities (as well as in other work areas), there are two types of employment: standard and nonstandard. Nonstandard employment includes part-time teaching and contracted full-time teaching. Standard employment is similar to the Japanese corporate tradition of lifetime employment, which includes social welfare benefits and job security, and it usually means tenure (see Shimbori, 1981). Full-time contracted teachers may be eligible for certain social welfare benefits under the terms of their contracts, but part-time teachers must make arrangements for their own insurance and pensions. Tenured teachers, however, enjoy long-term job security, but part-time and limited-term contracted teachers, whose positions are precarious, do not (e.g. Hayes, 2012, 2013; Rivers, 2013).

The minimum requirement for teaching in Japanese universities is a BA, although most universities require an MA (Nagasawa, 2004). Although in the past it was not entirely unusual for foreign teachers (myself included, in 1988) to obtain tenure without graduate degrees on the basis of their native-speaker status, nowadays most universities require both Japanese and non-Japanese applicants to have PhDs in English-related areas and a proven research record. However, the hiring criteria for nonstandard positions (particularly for foreigners) are often much more relaxed (Hayes, 2012, 2013).

Contracted full-time foreign teachers are usually required to have an MA in *any subject* and, depending upon individual universities' hiring policies, they may be fresh out of graduate school without having engaged in much previous research or they may be experienced teachers with a solid research background. The hiring criteria for part-time teachers are often related to supply and demand. Universities in regional areas where few foreigners reside may only require a BA, but in urban areas with many foreigners, requirements are likely to be more stringent. In general, the higher the academic level of the university, the higher the requirements are, even for part-time teachers, and some schools prefer hiring those with tenure and/or who have a certain number of research publications.

In the past, tenured teachers (Japanese and non-Japanese) were often hired because of personal connections at the university (e.g. Shimbori, 1981). Nowadays, tenured positions are announced on official websites like J-Rec (see: https://jrecin.jst.go.jp/seek/SeekTop?ln=1). Applicants' academic specialties must match the requirements of the university (such as TESOL, literature, linguistics or education), and an appointed hiring committee scrutinizes résumés and research papers before conducting interviews. Because tenured teachers have administrative duties in addition to teaching, Japanese language proficiency is usually required.

For nonstandard positions held by foreigners, however, there is more leeway. For part-time positions, universities generally hire locals with personal connections with someone at the university (Hicks, 2013), but there also seems to be a recent trend for universities to rely on dispatch companies to provide part-time teachers. Full-time contracted positions are also usually announced on J-Rec, with those successfully passing the first round of screening being called to the university for interviews. Some universities interview and hire teachers from abroad, especially those with freshly minted MA degrees. Now let us examine these positions in more detail.

Part-time teachers

There are approximately 160,000 part-time teachers, called *hijokin koshi,* in Japan, (MEXT, 2005). These teachers help reduce universities' personnel expenditures and they provide specialist lectures in academic subjects for students in areas not covered by tenured staff (Kinmouth, 2005; Poole, 2010). Some part-time teachers hold tenured positions at other universities as well, but many make their living by teaching in multiple universities.

Many foreigners gain entry into university teaching through part-time work, and since nearly half of all Japanese universities employ part-time foreign teachers (Yoshida, 2002), there are plenty of opportunities available. Compared to other types of EFL teaching in Japan, part-time university work offers various perks, including good salaries, paid holidays and teaching autonomy (Whitsed & Volet, 2013). Most schools pay a fixed amount per class over a 12-month period, but classes are generally in session only 30 weeks per year (15 weeks per semester). Because part-time teachers have no responsibility outside of teaching, they are usually free for those 22 weeks per year during which classes are not in session.

Many schools also give part-time teachers the autonomy to teach their classes as they like.

Despite the benefits of part-time university teaching described above, obtaining and maintaining enough classes to earn a decent salary can be tough, and teachers sometimes supplement university classes with *eikaiwa* or business English classes. Part-time teachers may also spend a great amount of time traveling to different universities, sometimes to two or more campuses in one day. Furthermore, it is not unusual for the total number of English classes taught by part-timers to exceed those taught by tenured and/or contracted full-time teachers.

A survey distributed by a part-time teachers' union to non-Japanese teachers in the Kansai and Kanto area (www.hijokin.org/en2007) revealed numerous concerns held by these teachers, with the main one related to employment stability. Teachers are hired on year-to-year contracts, which are generally renewable. However, changes in a university's curriculum and/or a decision to downsize due to budgetary cutbacks could result in a teacher's classes being reduced, and therefore, teachers are unsure of their schedules from one academic year to the next. Last-minute class reductions could make it difficult for teachers to find replacement classes, and this could result in a substantial loss of income.

The survey respondents also complained that despite having years of experience, seniority went unrecognized and their salaries never increased. They also felt excluded from the behind-the-scenes decision making that influenced their classes and excluded from the professional opportunities made available for full-time teachers (i.e. being able to publish in the university's journal and/or having access to research funds. (See also Fraser, 2011; and Whitsed & Violet, 2013).

Many teachers, particularly young ones, hope that part-time teaching will lead to full-time work. Once a good teaching schedule is established, however, some part-timers may hesitate giving up classes for a full-time limited-term contracted position. Although there are numerous advantages to working full time (which will be discussed in the next section), there is no guarantee of obtaining another position once that contract is completed. It might be difficult to regain enough part-time classes to reassemble a good schedule.

There is also some recent concern as to whether or not part-time teachers' contracts can be automatically renewed after the implementation of a new Labor Contract Law in 2013. The law was designed to protect all part-time workers by requiring companies who have employed them for five years to continue to employ them indefinitely. However, many fear that employers will simply fire part-timers before they reach the five-year limit. Whether or not this law is applicable to those teaching in universities is as yet unclear (General Union, 2013), but it seems that some universities are already taking action by establishing time limits on contracts and/or by implementing a six-month cooling-off period during which part-time teachers will be asked not to work (e.g. Brooks, 2015). If such practices become widespread, then part-time teachers' livelihoods can become even more precarious.

Contracted full-time teachers

The second area of nonstandard university employment for foreign teachers is contracted full time, which is called *ninkisei* in Japanese. Contracted positions usually include perks such as a good monthly salary, generous paid vacation time, insurance benefits, research funds, and an office or designated work space. Teachers are often given autonomy in teaching but, unlike part-time teachers, they usually have on-campus duties in addition to teaching.

When there were relatively few foreign teachers in Japan, one-year, indefinitely renewable contracts were common. Some private universities had a few tenured positions for foreigners, but these positions were rare (Evanoff, 1993). At national universities, foreigners were hired as *gaikokujin kyoushi* (foreign instructors). They could not be given tenure (because tenured professors at national universities were considered national civil servants) until a special law was passed in 1982. For decades, the *gaikokujin kyoushi* were given full teaching loads, but they had no administrative duties and no chance of promotion. However, the salaries were high, housing was often provided and visits to the teachers' home countries were generally paid for. Although some national universities began hiring foreigners (such as myself, in 1995) for tenured positions, most continued employing them as *gaikokujin kyoushi*. However, the MoE advised national universities to eliminate this position in 1992 as a way to economize, and instead of moving the *gaikokujin kyoushi* into tenured positions (like my university actually did for our *gaikokujin kyoushi*), many interpreted the MoE's directive as instructions to fire foreign teachers who had been employed for many years (even those who had had verbal guarantees of permanency) and to rehire younger ones on limited-term contracts (e.g. Masden, 2013; Houghton, 2013). Private universities followed suit and began limiting the term for which foreigners could teach full time at their institutions.

By having a constant flow of teachers at entry-level positions that will never advance in terms of seniority and salary, universities are able to significantly cut personnel costs. If student enrolment drops, the number of teachers hired by the university can be adjusted, which is of utmost importance for schools that are struggling financially. However, such measures, which are mainly (but not always) directed at foreign teachers, have been criticized as being discriminatory and prejudicial. Treating teachers as interchangeable commodities and processing them in and out of the universities because of a 'conveyer belt mentality' (Rivers, 2013: 77) ensures a constant supply of fresh foreign teachers. Apparently, this freshness is a key to Japanese students' language learning success, at least according to Kitakyushu University's Professor Noriguchi (2008, cited in Rivers, 2013: 77). In his article for the *Asahi News*, he claimed (apparently without empirical evidence) that foreign teachers residing in Japan for more than a decade are undesirable because they 'have adapted to the system and have become ineffective as teachers…their English has become Japanized and is spoken to suit the ears of the Japanese students'. Although this attitude may seem unbelievably far-fetched, such an ideology was also behind the dismissal of teachers, some of which resulted in several highly publicized lawsuits (e.g. Houghton, 2013; Masden, 2013; Worthington, 1999).

Unfortunately, term limitations means that these teachers must constantly search for future jobs, and such employment instability can ultimately lead to teacher burnout. Murray (2013) writes about this burnout and describes the life of a full-time contract teacher, 'James', by drawing a composite of his acquaintances' experiences in such situations. James came to Japan on the JET program in the 1990s and decided to remain. After obtaining an MA, he found a contracted position at a private university in Tokyo. Now in his 40s, he has already completed several sets of contracts with universities in his area. A married man with two children, he hesitates to uproot his family once again after his current contract expires. He has published articles and presented at conferences but has been unable to obtain a permanent position. Furthermore, it is becoming more and more difficult to engage in professional development because the conditions of his contract require him to spend nearly 40 hours per week on campus, where he has ten 90-minute required English classes for first- and second-year students. He has little teaching autonomy because the textbooks, the syllabus and the evaluation methods have been determined by administrators and tenured staff. James is also expected to engage in nonteaching duties while on campus as well, such as proofreading English documents written by his Japanese (tenured) colleagues. Such a life, according to Murray, can lead to teacher burnout, which not only affects the teachers' own professional identities but also their students' learning experiences.

Contracted teachers' disillusionment has been noted by other researchers as well. Although many wish to view themselves as professional educators, some have come to feel that they are little more than commodities that are sold to students, who are, in reality, the universities' customers. As customers, they are to be kept happy at all costs. This has resulted in universities siding with students in disputes concerning grading and/or cheating, and this makes the teachers feel even more deprofessionalized (e.g. Burrows, 2007; Fraser, 2011; Whitsed & Volet, 2013; Stewart, 2006).

Tenured positions

Now let us turn our attention to tenure, which is considered the peak of the EFL teaching hierarchy. Many foreign teachers understandably desire tenure, but openings are rare and competition is fierce. In fact, non-Japanese teachers hold only 3% of all tenured positions in Japan[5] (MEXT, 2006) and, as discussed earlier in this chapter, the hiring criteria for both Japanese and non-Japanese are very stringent.

Different universities have different expectations for their tenured teachers, which, according to Poole (2010), are related to two prevailing ideological discourses: *uchimuki* (inward-looking perspective) and *sotomuki* (outward-looking perspective). These two ideologies operate on a continuum, with professors often straddling both perspectives. Schools leaning toward an *uchimuki* perspective place priority on activities that occur within the school. Teachers build social and professional capital through working hard on behalf of the university and by building relationships with students, teachers and administrators. For those working for *sotomuki* schools, social and professional capital is established by gaining recognition from external activities, such as publishing in international journals and presenting at international conferences. In general, tenured teachers in all universities are expected to engage in work on behalf of their schools *and* to produce results related to their research. However, research-focused universities may require their professors to build more outside capital than those smaller, private (and often family-run) universities.

There are also different degrees of belonging within universities, which can affect teachers' experiences in them and their rate of advancement.

According to Wenger (1998), some members in a community of practice (such as a university) are on trajectories that enable them to attain insider status and gain access to positions of power, while others permanently remain on peripheral trajectories. Factors shaping tenured teachers' degrees of belonging within their schools include issues such as race (non-Japaneseness) (e.g. Wordell, 1992) and/or gender (e.g. Kobayashi, 2014; Nagatomo, 2012a, 2012b, 2014b, 2015).

Although obtaining tenure may be difficult, it is not impossible, according to McCrostie (2010), who analyzed 133 job advertisements for tenured positions at 99 universities between 2008 and 2010. Among those advertisements, he found that 56 explicitly stated there were no nationality restrictions, 33 called for native English speakers and 17 required 'native speaker Japanese language ability' (p. 32). Only 65% of the advertisements required applicants to have a doctorate, suggesting that there is some leeway if applicants have proved themselves through their research and experience. However, he notes that successful applicants for the tenured positions had more than the minimum publication and presentation requirements, and they had high levels of spoken Japanese (with some discrepancy between schools' requirements concerning reading and writing ability). Importantly, he adds, applicants must be flexible and willing to relocate to other areas of Japan.

Tenure guarantees employment until retirement, and there is no longer any need to worry about uprooting families while chasing the next contract. Once permanent employment is established, obtaining housing loans and/or permanent residency becomes much easier for foreigners. As a result, permanent roots can be established in Japan, which is another reason why these positions are highly prized.

Japanese and foreign teachers are different

In each of the three employment positions discussed in this section, foreign teachers are perceived differently from Japanese teachers by students, by Japanese teachers and by administrators. Foreign teachers are generally evaluated by different standards. Whereas Japanese teachers' academic knowledge and their ability to transmit that knowledge is considered important, foreign teachers, on the other hand, are evaluated by having positive personality traits such as kindness, friendliness and cheerfulness (Hadley & Yoshioka Hadley, 1996) or by being entertaining and easy for students to approach (Shimizu, 1999). These attitudes are reflected in the types of classes that foreign teachers are often assigned to teach. While it is true that tenured teachers teach some specialized courses, foreign teachers, especially those in contracted and part-time positions, usually teach required language courses (Murray, 2013). This has made some university teachers feel as if they are still engaged in *eikaiwa* teaching, and one of Rivers' (2013: 82) participants complained that his university was like a 'glorified conversation school' that utilized the foreign staff as advertising models to say, 'look how many happy foreigners we have here.' Beliefs that foreign teachers should be outgoing, friendly and helpful shape not only student expectations of classes taught by foreigners (e.g. Hadley & Yoshioka Hadley, 1996; Shimizu, 1999) but also the expectations of those who hire them (e.g. Hayes, 2012, 2013; Yphantides, 2013).

Summary of Chapter 3

In this chapter, I have described the three main areas of EFL employment in Japan that foreigners have engaged in over the past 30 years, and I have discussed the various pros and cons of working within these contexts. It is important to note that teachers may work in any or all three simultaneously, because there is a great amount of professional border crossing. Part-time university teachers, as mentioned earlier, need to piece together a sufficient number of classes to make ends meet, and so they might engage in all three types of teaching. But it is also possible that tenured teachers engage in a little part-time *eikaiwa* teaching as well, especially for classes that have been continuing for years.

It is also important to state that each individual employment context is unique and provides a myriad of experiences for the teachers and students involved. Nonetheless, this chapter has attempted to describe the type of professional world surrounding foreign English teachers in Japan in order to show the context in which the participants in my study work. In the next chapter, I shall provide further background for my study by introducing issues pertaining to gender.

Notes

(1) In this section, and in the following chapters, money will be discussed. Therefore, it might be useful for the reader to have a brief explanation concerning the yen–dollar exchange rate. However, the yen rate has fluctuated quite a bit during the past 30 years, ranging from approximately 250 yen to the dollar in the 1970s and 1980s to as low as 80 yen to the dollar during several periods in the 1990s and 2010s. At the time of writing this book, the exchange rate was 123 yen to the dollar.
(2) Wada's assumptions of team teaching may not be entirely accurate. As we shall see in Chapter 9, one private school in Tokyo made good use of team teaching with Japanese and non-Japanese teachers.

(3) Although there is no proof, it is possible that this official is referring to Victoria, one of my participants, who will be featured in Chapter 8.
(4) Theoretically, foreigners can also be in charge of their own classes if they have a Japanese teaching license obtained at a Japanese university and if they have passed the teachers' exam. In this case, they will be hired in exactly the same manner as Japanese. However, to my knowledge, I do not know of any such instance, except for those who have received Japanese undergraduate education. An example of this would be my former student from Taiwan who was educated entirely in Japan.
(5) This number includes *all* foreign teachers, who may be teaching courses other than English.

4 Gender Issues Surrounding English in Japan

Introduction

In the previous two chapters, I described English language education from a historical perspective and from the standpoint of its current status. This chapter focuses on two gendered threads that shape the lives of women living and working in Japan and those of my study's participants in particular. The first thread is concerned with interracial relationships between Westerners and Japanese. As we shall see, until the Meiji era, all such relationships were, to my knowledge, exclusively between Western men and Japanese women; and after the Meiji era, until fairly recently, relationships between Western women and Japanese men have been quite rare. One reason for this imbalance in interracial relationships is, of course, proximity; historically there were far more Western men in Japan than there were Western women. However, another reason for this imbalance lies in the racially constructed attitudes toward Western and Japanese men and women. Japanese women have been portrayed as ideal partners for Western men, but not vice versa. Such attitudes can and do shape the experiences of foreign teachers in Japan today, especially if they have Japanese spouses.

The second thread examines gender issues surrounding the learning and teaching of English. Although English is important for *all* students because of its role in entrance examinations (LoCastro, 1996), Japanese women may have different motivations for studying English than their male counterparts, and these motivations are often connected to images of interracial relationships (e.g. Kelsky, 2001; Takahashi, 2013). Such student attitudes can shape the experiences of both foreign male and female teachers of English as a foreign language (EFL) in Japan.

Interracial Romance Between Japanese and Westerners

As in this book I examine the professional identities of foreign women who are married to Japanese men, I wish to show in this chapter the background of interracial relationships. As we shall see, the majority of such relationships have occurred between Western men and Japanese women. Western men have been fascinated by Japanese women since the 1500s when the first Europeans arrived in Japan through the postwar years of the American occupation and up till today. In this section, I first describe such relationships from a historical perspective and then I discuss the current state of interracial and international marriages in Japan.

Leupp (2003), in his book titled *Interracial Intimacy in Japan: Western Men and Japanese Women 1543-1900*, provides a chronological account of interracial relationships, which will be discussed over the next few paragraphs. Japanese and Europeans began to intermarry and/or establish domestic relationships from the 1500s with the arrival of the Portuguese. These relationships were exclusively between Western men and Japanese women, because it is unlikely that Western women visited Japan at that time. In some instances, the early interracial marriages were with converted Christians, but many men purchased temporary wives, as they were already married in their home countries. Japanese women were not stigmatized by these relationships, and they were often able to save a dowry for marriage with a Japanese man later.

From the first contact with Japanese, European men wrote favorably of Japanese women, whom they considered as racially white and as representing the best of Japan – diligent, assertive and confident. These women helped their 'husbands' gain access to Japanese culture. One notable marriage at that time, for example, was that between William Adams (who was fictionalized as John Blackthorne in Clavell's novel *Shogun*) and Oyuki, a Christian aristocrat.

In 1624, however, marriages between Japanese and Westerners became illegal, and most Westerners were expelled from Japan. From 1639 to 1859, foreign women were prohibited from entering Japan entirely, and the Dutch, who were confined to Dejima during their stay, were provided with temporary 'wives'. Such relationships were objects of curiosity for Japanese, and their imagined sexual exploits were often depicted in popular pornographic woodblock prints in the 1700s and 1800s.

The social position of Japanese women had shifted by the time Japan opened its doors to the West at the end of the Edo era. In contrast to the more equal relationships between men and women in the 16th century, Japanese women had become more subdued, because their societal roles had become strictly defined through the teachings of *Onna Daigaku*, a Confucian text translated into Japanese by Ekiken. This text had prescribed women's roles in a stratified hierarchical society, which required their total obedience and submission. Women were strictly positioned under the control of their fathers when girls, under the control of their husbands when wives and ultimately under the control of their oldest sons when widows (Ekiken, 1914).

Western men, many of whom had come to Japan during the Meiji era to train Japanese people in areas such as construction, transportation and modern military tactics, entered into sexual relationships with Japanese women, which, according to Leupp (2003: 214), were a 'part of the exotic residential experience'. The philosophy of *Onna Daigaku* that shaped Japanese women's lives made them into idealized fantasy partners:

> The western male in late-nineteenth-century Japan encountered, therefore, a culture that promoted his patronage of Japanese women as prostitutes, temporary consorts, or wives in marriages differing from western marriages in the wife's greater submission and docility. For many western men, this was a delightful prospect. (Leupp, 2003: 166)

Books published about Japan between 1888 and 1904 presented romantic relationships between Western men and Japanese women as unequally balanced, with the Japanese female being totally submissive to her Western partner. Lafcadio Hearn, one of the most famous writers on Japanese culture, also 'idealized the selfless affection of the Japanese woman for her mate' (in Leupp, 2003: 179). *Madame Chrysanthème,* a semiautobiographical novel written by Pierre Loti in 1887, is considered to have influenced Western images of Japanese women as tragic creatures, and John Long's wildly successful short story *Madame Butterfly* (based on Loti's novel) solidified this image and inspired subsequent renditions of this story for decades, which included Puccini's opera of the same name, numerous novels and even Hollywood movies. Japanese women were portrayed as feminine, sensual and mysterious on the one hand; and yet as innocent, childlike, passive and subservient on the other hand. Specifically, they were portrayed as more desirable partners for Western men than Western women were (Leupp, 2003).

Edward Said (1978: 186-8), in his book *Orientalism,* criticized such portrayals of Asian women, who seem to have unlimited sensuality but at the same time are also depicted as rather stupid. He argues that these images are the result of a power fantasy wherein the masculine West dominates over the feminine East. This theme will be taken up again in a later section of this chapter.

Interracial Relationships from the 1880s to the Wartime Years

Koyama (1995, republished in Wetherall, 2008, 2002) published a comprehensive study of marriages between Japanese and foreigners that took place between 1873 and 1899. He wrote that the Japanese government first became aware that some foreign men in Japan wished to return to their home countries with their Japanese spouses after an inquiry was made in 1867 to the magistrate of Kanagawa concerning the legality of marriages between Japanese and foreigners. This led to the 1873 Great Council of State Proclamation No. 103, which enabled foreign men and women to become legal spouses of Japanese. At that time, such marriages were called *naigai kekkon* (inside–outside marriage) and *zakkon* (mixed marriage).

All of such marriages, whether in Japan or abroad, required the permission of the Japanese government. Japanese women who legally married foreigners lost their Japanese standing (at that time there was no concept of 'citizenship') unless their husbands were officially adopted into their families and thus the husbands gained Japanese standing instead. A foreign woman who legally married a Japanese man came to be considered Japanese, although losing her citizenship was dependent upon the laws of her own country (Wetherall, 2008).[1]

The first such legal marriage is believed to have been between Minami Teisuke (1847–1915) and a British woman named Eliza Pittman (1849–1902). In 1865, Minami had been secretly sent to England to study with two others by the Choshu clan, which advocated the overthrow of the Tokugawa government. Minami and Pittman married in London in 1872 after receiving approval from Japanese officials belonging to the Iwakura Mission, which was the de facto government. The marriage became legally recognized in Japan in 1873 after Minami and Pittman submitted translated documents of their marriage to officials in Yamaguchi, who then notified the Ministry of Foreign Affairs. Allegedly, Minami wanted to marry a Caucasian to produce 'mixedblood children' because he believed in 'race improvement through intermarriage',[2] but in the end the couple had no children. Their marriage ended after ten years, because Pittman could not adjust to life in Japan and because she was violent toward Minami and his family – she even cut him with a sword.

The first legally registered marriage between a Japanese woman and a foreign man was that of Kitagawa Sei and William Henry Freame, an unrefined instructor with an unsavory reputation at a common school in Shiga Prefecture. Kitagawa lost her Japanese nationality upon marriage, but she never acquired British nationality because Freame, already married to a woman in Australia, had never registered their marriage at the British Consulate. After their divorce in Japan, however, she regained her Japanese standing (Koyama, 1995; cited in Wetherall, 2008).

There were 230 legally recognized marriages between Japanese and non-Japanese between 1873 and 1897. Among these marriages, 50 Japanese men married women from Great Britain (12), Belgium (1), France (5), Germany (18), Spain (2) and the United States (12); and 180 Japanese women married foreign men mainly from Great Britain (61), China (56), France (10), Germany (14) and the United States (13) (Koyama 1995, cited in Wetherall 2006). Among these marriages are several noteworthy examples, such as that of writer and scholar Nitobe Inazo (1862–1933), prominent educator and the author of *Bushido: The Soul of Japan*, who married Mary Patterson Elkington in 1880; and that of author Patrick Lafcadio Hearn (1850–1904), mentioned earlier, who married Koizumi Setsu in 1896.

Although it was more common for Japanese women to marry foreign men during the Meiji and Taisho eras, there were a number of foreign wives with Japanese husbands, some of who became well known. For example, Scotswoman Jessie Roberta Cowan (Rita) married Taketsuru Masataka in 1920 and became known as the 'Mother of Whiskey' for the effort she and her husband made to establish the whiskey market in Japan. Their story was depicted by the public television station NHK in their 2014 popular morning drama series entitled *Massan*. Another famous relationship was that between the poet Noguchi Yone and the American Léonie Gilmour. Although their marriage in 1903 was not legally recognized, their son Noguchi Isamu grew up to become a well-known sculptor. Léonie's struggles were dramatized in the film *Leonie* in 2013 (Marx, 2013).

In 1928, Shinichi Suzuki (1898–1998), famous for devising the Suzuki Method of violin teaching, married Waltraud Prange. Waltraud translated his book *Nurtured by Love* (Suzuki: 1969) into English, giving him a wider audience for his work; and her autobiography, *My Life with Suzuki* (Suzuki, 1987), provides a glimpse into their courtship, early marriage and life in Japan during the war. Gwendolyn Harrold, who married Japanese diplomat Terasaki Hidenari in 1931, also wrote a poignant memoir about her life, including her own difficult wartime experiences in Japan in her book *Bridge to the Sun* (Terasaki, 1956, 1985), which was made into a film in 1961 and later, in the 1980s, was dramatized for Japanese television as *Mariko*. Waltraud and Gwen both experienced physical and emotional hardships in Japan as foreign wives of Japanese living in Japan during World War II, but they also write positively about their husbands and about the many kindnesses they received from friends, relatives and strangers during those difficult years.

Japanese war brides

After World War II, more than 350,000 American GIs were stationed in Japan, a country in ruins. Although brothels were established by the Japanese government to protect Japanese women's virtue from the rapes they anticipated (Molasky, 1999; Kelsky, 2001; Dower, 1999), the occupation headquarters closed them within months because of a large outbreak of venereal diseases. Troops were then prohibited from fraternizing with Japanese women in bars, cafés or restaurants. Nonetheless, there were many Japanese women working on or near bases as waitresses, clerks, nurses or maids, and many of the young people of the two nations living and working in close proximity with each other formed romantic relationships. Some of these relationships were temporary flirtations, and abandoned women came to be known as 'butterflies' after the main character in *Madame Butterfly*. Others became more permanent. In the Japanese women's eyes, the GIs had wealth, were undamaged from the war, and above all, were gentlemen. American men brought romance and affluence into these women's lives, and they often shared military supplies with them, which provided much-needed food and other essentials for them and their families.

Like the Western men who visited Japan in earlier times, the GIs were also enamored with Japanese women's femininity and compared them positively to American women, who had made great strides toward independence and gender equality during the war. Journalists Frank Kelly and Cornelius Ryan (cited in Shibusawa, 2006: 39) reported that men were 'swept off their feet by the deference and obedience of servile Japanese women', which made them feel that a Japanese woman's heart was 'twice as big as those of her American sisters' (p. 42). John La Cerda (another journalist cited by Shibusawa, 2010: 42) wrote that GIs 'praised the Japanese women for their kindly qualities, their submissiveness, and their eagerness to make the men comfortable' and quoted one GI as saying, 'The American girls could take a lesson in respect from these people over here.'

In addition to seeing Japanese women as being hyperfeminized, the GIs considered themselves to be good catches. Romance between young Japanese people was unheard of in prewar Japan, and so with their 'ladies first' attitudes, they felt superior to the Japanese men that they had classified as domineering and chauvinistic. Aware that a little romance toward Japanese girls went a long way, the GIs accepted their devoted attention. (e.g. Ishigaki, 1940/2004; Shibusawa, 2006; Crawford *et al.*, 2010; Kelskey, 2001).

As Simpson (1994, cited in Kelsky, 2001: 70) wrote, 'The Japanese-female-American male romance almost instantly emerged as the symbol of the relationship between a grateful gracious, and feminized Japan in thrall to the American military men who had liberated her.' With thousands of young men of a marriageable age meeting thousands of young women also of a marriageable age, it is no wonder that many wanted to marry. Furthermore, since Japanese women outnumbered Japanese men because of the casualties of war, marriage with an American man might have been their only chance to have a family (e.g. Kelskey, 2001; Shibusawa, 2006, e.g. Crawford *et al.*, 2010).

However, there were significant legal and social barriers created by racial bias on both sides concerning these interracial marriages. First, Japanese brides could not obtain spousal visas until 1952 due to immigration laws that prevented Orientals from becoming US citizens. Furthermore, antimiscegenation laws in some states made interracial marriages a crime. Obtaining permission to marry involved jumping through incredible bureaucratic hoops (Shibusawa, 2006). Extensive paperwork needed to be perfectly completed, and GIs were advised by the commanding officers and chaplains to reconsider their decision to marry a Japanese woman (Herbison & Shultz, 1990). The Japanese fiancées were subjected to humiliating personal and familial background checks by the Americans to ensure they were not criminals or prostitutes, and they were often ostracized by own their families and friends as well, for it was widely assumed that only prostitutes associated with GIs. In some tragic instances, GIs who had requested permission to marry were transferred out of the country and forced to leave their fiancées, who might have been pregnant, behind (Herbison & Shultz, 1990; Shibusawa, 2006).

Despite such difficulties in obtaining permission to marry, more than 40,000 Japanese women immigrated to the United States between 1947 and 1962 as war brides, and the term *kokusai kekkon* (international marriage) came to be used from the 1950s. The marital experiences of these women varied greatly, as they do in all marriages, and so did their experiences of induction into American society. In some cases they were warmly welcomed and in others they were not (particularly by the Japanese-American community). The term 'war bride', later researchers found, caused pain among these women because of the negative connotations it often had in the United States. Many erroneously believed that all war brides had been prostitutes (Crawford *et al.*, 2010).

Hollywood-Constructed Relationships

Despite difficulties relating to interracial relationships, positive attitudes toward couples consisting of Japanese women and American men gained acceptance, namely through the media, which portrayed such relationships in a positive manner. Dozens of Japan-based Hollywood movies appeared from 1949 to 1967 – some are well known, such as the acclaimed *Sayonara*, but most have long since been forgotten. Shibusawa (2006: 275) says these films were instrumental in shifting American wartime attitudes toward Japan as a vicious enemy to, instead, Cold War attitudes toward it as an important nonwhite ally. Through interracial love stories, often set as a story inside a travelogue to present Japan as a 'charmingly exotic locale', white American men often learned how to be 'more open-minded, understanding, and wise – in short, mature men – through their relations with the Japanese'. These movies generally had 'plots featuring a white American male protagonist who learns to become more competent in his patriarchal responsibilities'.

Despite the popularity of such movies, Hollywood hesitated to cast Asians in romantic roles because they felt they would not be attractive enough for their white American audience. For example, Joshua Logan, the producer of *Sayonara*, first asked Audrey Hepburn to play the film's lead role of Hana-Ogi. She refused, saying, 'I can't possibly play an Oriental. No one would believe me. They'd laugh' (cited in Shibusawa, 2010: 270–271). Logan eventually found Japanese-American Miiko Taka to play the role and then marketed her as particularly attractive for *all* men because of her 'dignified beauty'. Logan had wanted a Japanese male character that went beyond Hollywood's previous stereotypes of Japanese men as 'buck-toothed' and speaking only in 'guttural sounds'. Ironically, he selected a Caucasian – Latino Ricardo Montalban – to do that. He explains that it was necessary to hire a Caucasian to play the part of the Japanese romantic interest of the Western girl because 'he had failed to find in Japan a "virile man who would look romantic to an American girl" and who was also fluent in English. No Japanese man was either "mature" or manly enough for the role' (cited in Shibusawa, 2010: 270–271).

Shibusawa suggests that because of American attitudes at that time, people might have more easily accepted a white man paired romantically with an Asian woman than they would have if the roles were reversed. In fact, she writes that of the three Hollywood movies made that showed white women in romantic relationships with Japanese (one of which had a Western actor playing the hero), all had unhappy endings. In other words, society accepted relationships between Western women and Japanese men, but not vice versa.

Mismatched Relationships?

Although there *were* Western women who married Japanese men, as discussed earlier in this chapter, prevailing beliefs existed that Western women would find Japanese men undesirable, and there were beliefs that Japanese men would dislike Western women as well. Margery Brown, a colonel's wife living in Japan during the occupation, wrote, 'Seldom do we have the restraint, the elegant submissiveness or the subtle charm of their own women. We talk a great deal. We tower over Japanese men in the street and our noses are pointed heavenward' (in Shibusawa, 2006: 43). Japanese men also wrote disparagingly of Western women. During the Meiji era, they thought them to be noisy, unattractive and indecent with superior airs despite being 'frail-bodied and frailer-headed' (Miyoshi, 1979, cited in Kelsky, 2001: 44), and such negative attitudes continued into the 20th century. For example, a 1953 memoir written by journalist Kurata Yasuo, titled *Husband-Wife Study Abroad* (described in Kelsky, 2001: 66), discusses his adjustment to American life during the year he had spent at the University of Oregon with his wife. Although Kurata never mentions his wife by name, Kelsky argues that her presence in the book offers a stark contrast between her (a proper woman) and what he perceived to be loud and abrasive American women with henpecked husbands. He warned, 'Under no circumstances should Japan imitate the United States, least of all in regard to the relations of men and women.'

Other Japanese men in the United States at that time had similar feelings. One study of Japanese researchers abroad (Bennett, Passin & McKnight, 1958, cited in Kelsky, 2001: 66–67), found that the male researchers believed American women were 'frightening' and that a 'traditional passive and obedient Japanese woman was much better'. Although they approved of American 'equality' in principle, such approval did not extend to 'equality between men and women'. They felt that 'American women are so awful, so unfeminine....They show no affection, no grace.'

Not surprisingly, the Japanese female researchers in the same study held opposite views and expressed hesitation about returning to Japan after experiencing the freedom they had had in the United States. It was true that Japanese women had been accorded constitutional rights concerning marriage and the family just a few years earlier in 1947 (see Gordon, 1997). Although women's lives had improved substantially, women still suffered under societal constraints that elevated the status of Japanese men while lowering that of Japanese women.

Booming economy and Japanese women

As discussed in the previous chapters, Japan rapidly expanded its economy after the war and developed its educational system. By the 1980s and 1990s, the hardships of the postwar years were a distant memory, and Japanese women no longer needed to turn to Western (in particular, American) men as a means of improving their economic status. Yet, the image of Western men as gentlemen with 'ladies first' attitudes prevailed in Japan through American movies and television and was capitalized on through the ideologies of English conversation. This *akogare* (desire for) toward the West gives what Piller (2002: 6) calls 'sex appeal' to a language. In particular, this is seen to be a driving force behind English language study and a driving force for women seeking international partners for temporary and/or permanent relationships.

For example, Kelly (2014: 362), now a professor in an American university, wrote of his experiences as a 19-year-old in Japan during the 1970s. He admits:

> For Western men, the availability of Japanese women has been a big attraction. Especially when I first lived in Japan, the romantic image of the Western male was very strong. There was never a shortage of Japanese women in Tokyo who could be met at discos, parties, English classes, or through friends. Some Japanese women accepted the image that Western men were more kind and less sexist as well as more romantic than Japanese men. Western men, including myself often took Japanese women lightly and enjoyed the psychologically secure relationship that we had with them.

Books perpetuating such images were also published, notably those by prolific writer and journalist Boye de Mente. In addition to his books explaining Japanese culture and business, he authored volumes such as *Mistress Keeping in Japan* (1969/2001), *Japan at Night* (1988), and *Sex and the Japanese: The Sensual Side of Japan* (2006)—all of which were aimed at 'the man who has one thing on his mind' (review on back cover of the 2000 edition of *Bachelor Japan* by Boye de Mente).

Despite the previous discourse describing Japanese women as passive 'butterflies' who needed to be rescued by Western men from their lives of drudgery and hardship in the hundred years after Japan opened its doors to the West, the economic miracle of the 1980s gave Japanese women the power to instead actively seek Western men to enhance their cosmopolitan status (e.g. Kelsky, 2001; Takahashi, 2013). When the economy was booming, Japanese women with a substantial disposable income gained notoriety in the Japanese press by supposedly frequenting Tokyo nightclubs and traveling abroad in search of non-Japanese (especially black) sexual partners. They came to be called 'yellow cabs' as in a yellow woman who is easy to catch a ride on. Although it was originally believed that the term came from the men these women were allegedly copulating with, it was later discovered that a journalist named Ieda Shoko had coined it as a sensational means to sell her books (Kelsky, 2001).

According to Kelsky (2001: 137), a 'hypersexualized hysteria' was thus promoted by the media in the form of newspaper and magazine articles, novels, and even soft-porn comic books.

Such widespread media reports of Japanese women's desire to have sex with Western men is probably why some Western tourists, according to Uzama (2012), come to Japan for that specific purpose. Although the 'yellow-cab' phenomena itself was likely a fabrication, playing on people's curiosity about interracial sexual relationships, it does reflect people's curiosity concerning interracial and/or international romance.

International Marriage Today

These days, international marriage has become quite common in Japan. The number of international marriages registered in Japan in 1965 was relatively low at 5,056 (Nitta, 1988), but the number had risen to 34,393 in 2009 (Ministry of Health, Labor and Welfare, 2010). Previously, the majority of marriages between Japanese and non-Japanese occurred between Western men and Japanese women, but this trend shifted in 1975 with more Japanese men marrying foreign women (mainly Korean and Chinese). Currently, 78% of international marriages are between a Japanese husband and a foreign wife, with the majority coming from the Philippines. However, 89% of marriages with Westerners involved Western men and Japanese women (Yamamoto, 2010).

The increase of interracial marriages between Japanese and foreigners (and indeed between the people of other nations in other countries as well) is due to the increasing movement of people across national and regional borders. More Japanese people are studying and working abroad, and more foreigners are working and studying in Japan. This creates opportunities for people to meet at times in their lives when they ordinarily get married. Nitta (1988) found that nearly 75% of the foreign women he interviewed from the Association of Foreign Wives of Japanese (AFWJ) met their husbands outside Japan (as opposed to only 35% of the Japanese members of a similar group for Japanese women married to foreign men). He suggests that the greatly improved socioeconomic status of Japan, compared to the struggle of the postwar years, elevated the desirability of Japanese men as spouses. He also says that Western women might be more attracted to Japanese men because of the better portrayal of Japanese men in the media (for example, Toshiro Mifune in the movie *Shogun*). Most of the couples in his study shared similar educational and economic backgrounds, and the men were, or as students had the potential to be, economically secure. This, according to Kikumura and Kitano (1973, cited in Niita, 1988: 221), was more important in a spouse selection than 'the color of the skin or the slant of one's eyes'.

The Association of Foreign Wives of Japanese (AFWJ) was established in 1969 as a friendship and support group for such foreign women with Japanese husbands. The idea for this group came from Joan Burk, an American woman with a Japanese husband, who had spotted a Western woman who appeared to also be married to a Japanese man with a biracial child on a bus. After making initial contact with potential members through a newspaper column by Jean Pearce that helped foreigners 'get things done', a gathering was held, and the club rapidly expanded; now, more than 45 years later, it maintains a yearly membership of nearly 500 women (AFWJ, n.d.) with members ranging in age from their early twenties to the oldest at 103.

Not all foreign women who are married to Japanese men are members of AFWJ. Some choose to join more loosely organized social groups without an annual membership fee, such as e-mail discussion groups like Married in Japan (MIJ), or they make friends through Facebook groups such as K-Y Japan or Foreign Wives of Japanese People. Some of the foreign wives in these groups have been living in Japan since the 1950s (or even earlier) but others are newly arrived. Foreign wives who arrived in the 1960s and 1970s, as noted by Nitta (1988), tended to meet their husbands in their own, or a third, country (Nitta, 1988). However, many of the younger couples met in Japan, reflecting the increase in foreigners (both men and women) visiting and/or working in Japan from the 1980s.

As discussed earlier, marriages between Western women and Japanese men have been viewed as an enormous mismatch. Nitta (1988) wrote that while conducting his research, he found people's attitudes toward him and his research to be based on assumptions that intercultural marriage is mainly that between Western men and Japanese women.

Stereotypical images of Japanese women as passive, subservient and domestic and of Japanese men as traditional, domineering and chauvinistic have colored other writers' interpretations of such marriages as well. For example, *Alien Rice* (1973), a novel by Ichiro Kawasaki, former diplomat and ambassador to Argentina, attempts to portray the realities of a mixed marriage between a Japanese businessman and an English woman. The novel is poorly written with stilted and unnatural dialog, and Ishida (1973), a foreign wife herself, criticizes Kawasaki for only writing of superficial issues such as differences in food. Because he had by then established himself as 'the layman's Ruth Benedict...to inform foreigners of the inscrutability of his fellow countryman' (par. 1) through his previous nonfiction books on Japanese culture, Ishida felt that readers might 'overlook the poor writing and accept the author's interpretations as truth'. She feared that they would be 'left with the impression that marriages between Japanese men and foreign women are doomed to failure or unhappy forbearance, and that the children of these marriages are outcasts' (par. 4). Apart from the novel being factually wrong in several places (i.e. a British wife does not automatically acquire Japanese citizenship upon marriage) and its being peppered with unnatural dialogs between the husband and wife, it was not well received by the foreign-wife community when it was originally published. AFWJ members of a current Yahoo group recall their outrage when the book first hit the stands. One member said that she 'hated that book but got a few laughs at the most ridiculous parts' (private e-mail 1, 10 July 2014), and another felt that it was 'contrived, full of stereotypes, weird' (private e-mail 2, 10 July 2014). A third member of AFWJ recalls an event where Kawasaki was invited as a guest speaker. She says he was

> just as arrogant and prejudiced as his book. We tried to make him see things differently, but he just 'knew.' In fact he considered himself a man of insight because he had been in a few other countries. At that time, not so many people could go out of Japan and not so many foreigners lived here. (private e-mail 3, 10 July 2014)

Unfortunately, the blurb on the cover calls the book a 'perceptive novel of interracial marriage'. Considering that Kawasaki was widely read at that time for his nonfiction books, which strongly criticized Japan and Japanese, it is likely that many of the readers of *Alien Rice* formed lasting opinions concerning interracial marriage in Japan based on Kawasaki's own interpretation of such marriages.

Even nonfiction work examining cross-cultural relationships runs the risk of being stereotypical and trivial. Journalist Karen Ma, for example, who wrote *The Modern Madame Butterfly* (1995), analyzed cross-cultural relationships through interviews. The book disturbed many people who were in such relationships because of its flimsy and stereotypical analysis. Two thirds of the book focused on relationships between Western men and Japanese women, and she explains Japanese women's interest in these foreign men as follows:

> Most Japanese men have not kept pace with these changes [a modern world with more gender equality]. Still confined to strict, unwritten corporate and social rules, they have neither the time nor energy to attend to women's needs. In frustration, the women may look to Western men, known for their relatively polished social skills and romantic gestures, in the hope of finding better mates. (p. 260)

Ma (1995: 263) characterizes Japanese men as the polar opposites of idealized Western men, but she goes so far as to say it is precisely *these characteristics* (my emphasis) that enticed the Western wives into marriage. She argues that her participants' reasons for choosing Japanese spouses lie in their desire to have a more traditional lifestyle that would enable them to be stay-at-home housewives, which is now a generally unattainable lifestyle in many Western countries. She seemed somewhat surprised that 'the Western image of an insensitive, boorish Japanese husband who has no consideration for his wife is proving to be more of an outmoded Western interpretation of things Japanese'. Nonetheless, she capitalizes on stereotypical images of Japanese men as economic animals and explains 'this makes the industrious, marriage-minded Japanese man seem like a prize to them [those women married to Japanese]'.

Like Kawasaki's book, Ma's book was not too popular among the members of the foreign-wives community either. Her participants were easily recognizable among the members, and readers felt her analysis of them did not realistically reflect the experiences of the women she had written about. Some participants even expressed anger at having their interviews misinterpreted (private e-mails).

Nancy Brown Diggs provided a more balanced examination of American women married to Japanese in her book *Looking Beyond the Mask: When American Women Marry Japanese Men* (2001). She writes, 'The main things that attracts American women to Japanese men are usually the same things that attract them to men anywhere' (p. 14), and she found that the women were attracted to their husbands because they were nice guys with shared experiences and shared values. The ups and downs of the relationships are categorized and discussed in themes surrounding meeting their spouses, enduring culture shock, family life and challenging situations. Although Diggs does not provide details about how her study was conducted nor about how the data was analyzed, her work is refreshing in that it moves beyond stereotypical images of people in interracial and intercultural relationships. The reason for this may be her decision to let her participants' voices be heard.

A final example of Japanese people's fascination with international marriage is the popularity of a best-selling comic-book series entitled *Daring wa gaikokujin (My Darling is a Foreigner)*, which debuted in 2002 and was made into a movie in 2010. The comic introduces humorous episodes in the lives of cartoonist Saori Oguri and her American husband, Tony Laszlo. The popularity of this story indicates that obtaining a Western boyfriend or husband was, and still is, considered an achievement, something worthy of admiration and of interest. I myself have come across such attitudes many times. For example, back in the 1980s, I judged an all-Japan commercial high-school speech contest in which a finalist's speech was entitled 'My Dream is To Marry a Foreigner.' In 2013, when one of my students announced during a seminar that 'foreign men are so cool' and that girls with Western boyfriends are admired by their friends, the other girls in the class nodded their heads in agreement. This sentiment was expressed again several years later, when in 2015, a first-year student wrote in her self-introduction that her goal was to 'marry a cool foreigner'.

Summary of Interracial Relationships

In this section, I have described the historical background concerning interracial relationships in Japan in order to demonstrate how the experiences of Western men and Western women in such relationships are perceived. While it is true that each person's marriage to a Japanese spouse is, like everywhere else, uniquely their own with the ups and downs that all couples have, the sociopolitical attitudes surrounding the appropriateness or the mismatch of such relationships can and do shape aspects of a couple's lives in ways that go far beyond the privacy of their own home. Such attitudes, as we shall see in the next section, have also infiltrated English language education to quite an extent as well. As mentioned at the end of the previous section, foreign men are perceived to be 'cool', and for many students, the only exposure that they have to Westerners is through their English lessons and through their teachers.

Gendered Issues and Language Learning and Language Teaching

In the previous section, I discussed issues concerning interracial relationships and marriages between Japanese and Westerners. I now turn to gender-related issues surrounding English language learning and English language teaching in Japan. Although English is important for *all* students because of its role in entrance exams (Lo Castro, 1996), we shall see that female students have gendered motives to study English as well, which are related to the ideologies surrounding *eikaiwa* as discussed in Chapter 3. The section closes with a discussion of how the experiences of foreign male teachers and foreign female teachers differ.

Japanese women and English studies

As discussed in Chapters 2 and 3, English is important for female and male students because of its important role in entrance exams (LoCastro, 1996), and students generally aim for the highest level of high school and university they can enter because of the lifetime impact such schools have (e.g. Ishikida, 2005a, 2005b). However, there are two gendered educational paths that male and female students tend to take, which result in different career outcomes. Male students aim for tertiary degrees that will enable them to gain 'entry to professions and jobs with high income and social status', but female students often aim for tertiary degrees to signify 'the social class and culture to which they belong' (Amano, 1997: 217). Therefore, many parents who view educating their sons as an important investment in the future will push them through examination hell to attend the highest-level school possible and, once enrolled, male students tend to major in career-oriented subjects. Daughters, on the other hand, are often not expected to have long-term careers, and as a result, parents spare them from examination hell by sending them to less competitive schools closer to home where they study 'feminine' liberal arts subjects that are not career oriented (e.g. Amano, 1997; Brinton, 1988; Fujimoto, 2004, 2005; Fujimura-Fanselow, 1995; Ono, 2004).

One of the most common subjects that Japanese women have studied in two- and four-year universities during the postwar years is English literature and/or language. English was considered an appropriately ladylike area of study that would most importantly enhance women's social capital (Kobayashi, 2002, 2007a, 2007b). At the same time, the study of English was seen as a means to earn money (usually as a teacher) should the need to earn an income arise. Recently, societal attitudes toward women working in Japan have shifted, and now English study is marketed toward women in both the private sector and in the university sector as a necessary career-enhancing skill (Bailey, 2006; Kelskey, 2001). However, Kobayashi (2007b: 567) argues that many female students will be unable to convert their educational capital into careers because, as mentioned above, their educational backgrounds are often inadequate. Well-meaning parents who do not provide their daughters with the same educational opportunities as their sons, as well as corporations, engage in discriminatory practices that 'attach paramount importance to men with certain backgrounds as the legitimate labor force' at the expense of women. Nonetheless, many women major in English because of beliefs that they can earn a supplementary income while married and raising children (e.g. Burton, 2004; Kan, 2009; Nagatomo, 2012a).

In addition to representing career enhancement, English is seen to provide many intangible benefits for Japanese women as well, which include personal self-development and entry into an actual or a virtual cosmopolitan world. Therefore, prior to settling down to marriage and motherhood, Japanese women often undertake language study at home or abroad. These women have a great amount of disposable income, and language schools and study-abroad programs have specific advertising campaigns targeting them (e.g. Burton, 2004; Habu, 2000; Kobayashi, 2002, 2007a, 2007b; Koike, 2000, 2002; Matsui, 1995; Ono & Piper, 2004; Piller & Takahashi, 2006; Raymo, 2003, 2006; Takahashi, 2013).

A drawing factor for pursuing English in informal educational settings is *akogare* (a desire or yearning) for all things Western. Although this yearning toward the West was an important motivator for English study during the postwar years for both men and women, as discussed in Chapter 3, it is particularly strong for women. According to Kubota (2011: 484), '*Akogare* among Japanese women is a key aspect of the consumption of *eikaiwa* learning as a leisure activity....[Attendees] "experience an atmosphere that's a bit different from everyday life" – or to consume the enjoyment of being included in an English-speaking world.' This English-speaking world, Takahashi (2013: 26–27) argues, is all the better if it includes a foreign male teacher: 'Opportunities to spend time in private with the White man are posed as a major motivation for female clients to learn English and, in doing so, position Japanese women as desirers of English-speaking Western men.'

Thus, language schools create compelling images to sell to prospective students. These images often portray a Japanese woman (presumably the student) with a nice-looking Western man (presumably the teacher) in settings that hint at intimacy. Bailey (2006: 110–111) explains:

> A dominant signifier of eikaiwa advertising is an Occidentalist whiteness and/or masculinity, often embodied in the *gaijin* (foreign) instructor, situated in relationship to the young Japanese female, as embodied by the prototypical *eikaiwa* student.... What is imperative is the coupling of this [type of] image in romantic or sexualized proximity with a Japanese female.

The underlying messages in language-school advertisements are that English can lead women to better jobs and to more fulfilled and internationalized selves; that English will enable women to adopt new personas that are free from the cultural and linguistic constraints of being Japanese; and that English can even make women become more beautiful and perhaps help them find a boyfriend (e.g. Bailey, 2006, 2007; Kelsky, 2001; Kobayashi, 2002; Koike, 2000; Mizuta, 2009; Piller & Takahashi, 2006; Takahashi, 2013).

Language-materials developers are also capitalizing on Japanese women's *akogare* toward English and toward Western men. For example, an enterprising iPhone app developer released English-language study materials that fall under the category of 'edutainment' (Bird, 2005) entitled 'What if your boyfriend was a foreigner?' In the app, students 'study' English through interaction with three virtual boyfriends. Through these boyfriends, who are white, cool, rich and powerful, the 'girlfriend' (the language learner) is transported into a cosmopolitan world. Since none of the boyfriends is familiar with Japanese culture, one of the language functions is to explain Japanese culture and to deal with cultural differences. This, criticizes Kennett and Jackson (2014), perpetuates cultural and gendered stereotypical images of Western men and Japanese women and, rather than promoting communication, it inhibits it through establishing barriers.

Charisma Man

How Japanese women's *akogare* is played out and how it is received by Western men is humorously depicted in Larry Rodney's popular 1990s comic strip *Charisma Man* (2013). The story revolves around a skinny and geeky *eikaiwa* teacher who was a fast-food worker in Canada but transformed into a gorgeous hunk – upon arrival in Japan. The character was a composite of some of the Western men Rodney had worked with at an *eikaiwa* school; these men, who were probably not so special back home, were having the time of their lives with Japanese girls (Kashper, 2003; Lewis, 2010). The term 'Charisma Man' has now come to mean 'geeky Western nerds with beautiful Japanese girls' (Rodney, cited in Lah, 2010), and this phenomenon has been widely discussed in the popular media as well as by scholars researching gendered and racial influences on language education in Japan (e.g. Kelskey, 2001; Bailey, 2007; Appleby, 2012, 2013, 2014; Kobayashi, 2014; Rivers, 2013; Piller & Takahashi, 2006; Takahashi, 2013).

Perhaps many foreign male English teachers, particularly the young and single ones, enjoy their popularity and success with Japanese women. For example, *Senseitional: Confessions of English Teachers in Japan* (Chesney, 2008), an apparently self-published book, has the following blurb on the back cover: 'The vast majority of English teachers in Japan are horny and hedonistic young travelers, desperate to delay their adulthood by drinking as much as is humanly possible and shagging anything with a pulse.' Many Western men in *eikaiwa* are understandably upset to be saddled with such a negative stereotype, and those who take English teaching seriously certainly do not wish to be viewed as a Charisma Man – that is, a loser *eikaiwa* teacher on the prowl for Japanese girls. In fact, the Australian men interviewed by Appleby (2013, 2014, 2015) reported that they themselves had never been Charisma Men in Japan, although they admitted that they had had some EFL colleagues who were. Their own job satisfaction as *eikaiwa* teachers decreased as they increasingly realized that they were mainly viewed as commodities by their *eikaiwa* schools and by their female students. They felt they were treated as 'glorified hostess[es]' (2014: 84) at their schools, which were mainly 'a dating service for middle-aged women to meet foreign males' (Appleby, 2014: 84). In fact, some of their schools even sold social event packages such as parties and/or private lunches with teachers, providing the students with access to teachers outside planned lessons. 'Joel', one of Appleby's participants, recalls,

> I didn't think that many people came there for learning. It was just a very – like a meat market I suppose. You come in [and the student says] 'hello, what's your name? are you married?', obviously that was for the young ones, 'do you have a girlfriend?' … This idea that Charisma Man was a sort of predator on unsuspecting Japanese women, to my mind, is not the way I remember it. I'd say that men in some ways were very sort of sexualized by the women if that makes sense, but it's like 'I want to find a foreign boyfriend'. (Appleby, 2014: 83)

Because it was financially advantageous for the schools to encourage flirtations between the teachers and the students, sexual relationships with students were not explicitly prohibited. Appleby's participants reported that teachers were more likely to be reprimanded by bosses for being late or for being absent than for breaking the rules of fraternizing with students. Heads generally turned the other way *unless students complained.*

Understandably, many foreign men, like Appleby's participants, wish to distance themselves from the Charisma Man discourse, especially as they age, settle into long-term and/or permanent relationships and ascend the EFL ladder. It not only deprofessionalizes English language teaching by fueling negative attitudes toward *eikaiwa* and those who teach it; it also demeans legitimate cross-cultural relationships. This is why, according to Appleby (2013, 2014), many teachers exit *eikaiwa* teaching, either by moving into managerial positions at their *eikaiwa* schools or into secondary or tertiary institutions.

Nonetheless, Appleby's participants acknowledged that attitudes toward Western teachers in general and Western men in particular enabled them, while working as *eikaiwa* teachers, to develop the desired lively and outgoing Western personalities (i.e. being friendly, extraverted and cheerful) that that their female students favored. Thus, in a way, they *did* transform into Charisma Man: They became less socially awkward and they developed more self-confidence. As a result, they experienced greater success with women in Japan than they did with women in their own countries. And, like Charisma Man (and other Western men described earlier in this chapter), they also described Japanese women in positive terms but Western women in negative ones. For them,

> Western women were unappealing, both emotionally and physically, in comparison with Japanese women, who displayed the hallmarks of a more traditional femininity in their petite stature, careful grooming, and polite behavior….Western women were described as overweight, difficult, and more demanding in their expectations of Western men.
> (Appleby, 2014: 136)

Although they never painted foreign women as the *enemy* as the comic-strip character Charisma Man did, as we shall see in what follows, they are not exactly portrayed as allies either.

The fine line between flirting and harassment

As discussed earlier, language schools not only accept but also encourage flirtations between teachers and students as a means to attract prospective students and to maintain student enrollment. The seating arrangements due to the man-to-man policy of the conversation school GABA, for example, not only tacitly encourage intimate relationships with teachers but also seem to promote them (Takahashi, 2013; McCrostie, 2014). When *students* complain about teachers' inappropriate behavior, schools are quick to take action. To keep the students happy, 'someone has to go out with the fire extinguisher and get rid of that problem' (Appleby, 2012: 17). On the other hand, if teachers complain about their students, the schools hesitate to take action. Despite numerous complaints filed at the General Union (2007) concerning the sexual harassment of female teachers by male students, *eikaiwa* schools have failed to establish clear policies concerning sexual harassment. Registered complaints include students sitting too close to teachers, inappropriately touching teachers, asking teachers on dates and making lewd comments such as 'I want to drink your breast milk' or 'I want your blow job' (McCrostie, 2014). *Eikaiwa* school managers are unwilling to ban fee-paying students, even those who are known for sexual harassment, so they generally reassign them to different teachers, and those who rely on the school for working visas may feel they have no choice but to teach such students no matter how distasteful this may be. There have even been reports in the media of female teachers being stalked by male students, with the most notable victim of such behavior being Lindsey Hawker, a teacher for Nova, then the largest *eikaiwa* chain in Japan. She was stalked, raped and murdered in 2007 by someone who pretended to be her student at the school.

Sexually charged university classrooms

The teacher–student relationship differs greatly in formal educational contexts compared to informal educational ones. However, it has been noted that there is still a sexually charged atmosphere fueled by female students' attitudes toward their male teachers. The ideologies of *akogare* toward white men, and how this is internalized by men, is illustrated in an article published by a prominent foreign professor in his online EFL column, *The Uni-Files: A candid look at EFL life and lessons from a university teacher's perspective.*

In 2011, Michael Guest offered advice to foreign male university teachers on how to deal with Japanese female students in an article entitled, 'How to Talk to Japanese Women – EFL Version'. While it is true that male teachers are likely to face different issues in regards to their female counterparts, Guest's attempt to humorously explain Japanese women caused outrage among male and female readers (see Mulvey, 2012a). He describes female students as 'chattering' time-wasters with an 'eraser fetish' who position themselves against each other in terms of appearance in vying for their (presumably male) teachers' attention. He warns his readers that if they do not remember all their students' names, the plain ones will believe 'He doesn't remember my name because he hates me and thinks I'm ugly and stupid and he remembers hers because he thinks she is pretty' (para. 6). Guest advises:

> Remember the names of quiet, simple, plain, unobtrusive Fs [females]. They will very much appreciate this. The ones with big personalities or hairdos know you will remember their names soon anyway. And no one can claim that you are remembering names based on some vavoom or pizzaz factor. (para. 7)

Teachers are cautioned that when students with 'vavoom' do appear, like 'Leggy Keiko', with their distracting 'pair[s] of ostentatiously displayed legs', they should not ogle them even if 'the lady showing lotsa leg may not care too much, she may be used to – and may to some extent relish – men checking her out'. He reminds his readers, in a half-hearted way, to maintain professional standards:

> Keep in mind that Leggy Keiko is not dressing up for your entertainment. Leggy Keiko thinks of you as a teacher first and has certain expectations about how a teacher should act. Ogling her probably diminishes your status in her legs... umm... mind.

However joking the tone of Guest's article may be, he highlights the existence of a sexualized university atmosphere that male teachers are apparently quite aware of. Older teachers may feel disturbed by their female students' 'misplaced erotic desire for Western male teachers' as Appleby (2014: 131) found during her interviews with Western male teachers in Japan. For example, her participant 'Grant' explains: 'I'm like, "go away," you know I feel like a geezer nowadays, an 18 year old girl looking at me with goo-goo eyes. I'm 49, I'm like "God I could be your father"' (131). 'Brad' says he takes care when talking to female students because he does not wish to be seen as the type of teacher who enjoys and encourages students' attention, and he admits,

> When talking with such girls I am also sensitive to the observations of the male students or other male teachers who I fear will see me as a predatory foreign man if I engage in carefree conversations with the female students. (p. 132)

Female students may choose to dress provocatively and they may choose to flirt with their male teachers, who *as university teachers* might be considered safe objects of their *akogare*. Male teachers are generally aware of the need to 'control [their] own instinctive, male responses' (Appleby, 2014: 132) as illustrated by Grant and Brad's comments above. However, some male teachers (particularly young ones) may be inclined to read more into their students' behavior, or, as in some instances, take advantage of them (e.g. Stanley, 2012, 2013). This is likely the motivation behind Guest's (2011) article warning foreign male teachers about the sexy students discussed earlier. Despite the article's condescending attitude toward female students, some foreign male teachers evidently need specific instructions on how to handle themselves. Several female university teachers interviewed by Hicks (2013: 157) complained of their male colleagues flirting openly with students and referring to the sexy ones in staff meetings as 'fuck me types', whom they have sit in the front row in the classroom 'in case they spread their legs and offered a peek'.

Such sexually charged banter commonly occurs among foreign male colleagues in private during after-hours socializing and in the workplace in university staff rooms (Appleby, 2013, 2014; Mulvey, 2012b). When such inappropriate talk occurs in front of female colleagues, it is distressing, but Mulvey (2012b) fears that if she halts their fun, it could backfire and she could easily become labeled as *'that* teacher' – an overly sensitive, politically correct party-pooper who becomes the 'next great topic for the gossip mill' (para 11) when out of the room. That foreign women have been censuring such behavior among Western men might be why Appleby (2013: 6) initially had trouble finding male participants for her study. Suspicion that she was 'just another comfy shoe wearing gaijin [foreign] woman with her nose out of joint' was one reason why some men declined to participate in her research.

It's a Man's World

It is impossible to consider the lives of women in Japan today without examining widespread gendered attitudes toward them. As discussed earlier in this chapter, Japanese women had enjoyed a great amount of gender equality during the 1500s and 1600s, but Confucian ideals firmly positioned them in subordinate positions to men and maintained that their main role was to act as wife and mother (Ekiken, 1905). Such attitudes exist today (e.g. Liddle & Nakajima, 2000), as reflected by the low ranking of Japanese women in the World Economic Forum's *Global Gender Report*. This report, which measures women's equality in terms of economic participation in society, political empowerment, educational attainment, health and survival, ranked Japan 104th out of 142 countries in 2014. Japanese women's educational attainment is high compared to international standards and they have the highest life expectancy worldwide, but it is their lack of participation in the public arena that has placed them so low compared to other industrialized countries.

In the field of education, there are many female teachers, particularly in elementary education, but their number decreases at the higher levels, particularly in universities. In 2006, there were 285,860 university teachers in total, but women comprised only 14% (16,659 out of 131,366) of tenured positions and only 24.6% (40,028 out of 162,393) of part-time positions (MEXT, 2006). As explained earlier, one reason for this low number may be that Japanese women have not been receiving the *type* of education to gain entry to professions (Amano, 1997). For those who do work in research fields or in higher education, their careers lag about five years behind their male counterparts because they have less opportunity to develop their careers due to family constraints and also because of power, academic and sexual harassment (Sodei, 2005). Women have complained of hostile atmospheres in Japanese universities, caused by such things as the withholding of research funds, not having the cooperation of male supervisors and/or colleagues, being denied first authorship on papers they had primarily written and being gossiped about in sexually inappropriate ways (McNeill, 2007; Normile, 2001; Sodei, 2005).[3] The Japanese government has acknowledged this problem and it is attempting to raise awareness about harassment and how to prevent it in workplaces. However, official policies have not yet been established due to fears of being unable to handle what may become a flood of complaints (Creaser, 2012).

There are attempts to increase the number of female researchers through proactive programs, such as fellowships and grants, to help women return to research after taking maternity leave (Japan Society for the Promotion of Science, 2006), and some research universities, such as the University of Tokyo, have improved facilities for female researchers. Such improvements include offering better maternity benefits, providing childcare facilities, ensuring safer research environments for pregnant women and holding meetings during the daytime rather than in the evening (University of Tokyo, n.d.). Measures such as these, MEXT (2006) optimistically writes, will ensure a better working environment and will enable more women to enter and stay in the workforce as researchers and as academics.

Nonetheless, for most women in Japan, balancing family life with work is particularly challenging. Kubo (2006), former director of the Gender

Equality Promotion Division in the prime minister's Cabinet Office, said in a workshop on 'Women in Science Engineering and Technology' given in Ottawa, Canada, that one of the greatest issues restraining Japanese women professionally is the lack of practical support from husbands. She calls them 'lazybones' (p. 3), citing statistics that the hours per day they put into household chores are far less than those of their wives. It is true that in Japan, women are often solely responsible for household chores and childcare. In some instances, this responsibility may be due to gendered beliefs held by husbands concerning the roles of men and women, but the structure of corporate employment also contributes to an imbalance in family life by requiring employees to remain late at work and to socialize in the evening. This is why many Japanese women exit the workforce upon marriage (e.g. Amano, 1997) and why many men cannot take a greater role in household matters; it is simply too difficult to balance both work *and* family for both men and women. For foreign career women married to Japanese salaried workers, this is also a great concern, because they are often left to manage household matters singlehandedly. This becomes especially difficult if they are trying to develop careers and have a family. On the other hand, foreign men married to Japanese women can generally expect their wives to deal with daily household matters, giving them more time to focus on work and/or engage in private and work-related socializing, which is often essential for career building. This will be discussed in greater detail from this point onward.

Male and Female University Teachers

In Japanese universities, there are only 5,652 (4%) full-time foreign teachers, and out of these, only 1,347 (24%) were women (MEXT, 2006), although it is unclear how many of these full-time teachers engage in English-related education. Nonetheless, foreign male teachers outnumber foreign female teachers nearly three to one. Appleby's (2014: 135) participants' explanations offered to her male research assistant as to why this is so was related to the simple notion of numbers. They believed that there are just far fewer foreign women in Japan than there are foreign men. While statistically this may be true, their reasons explaining why this is so are interesting, and they reflect the gendered and racial attitudes toward Western and Japanese men and women discussed earlier in this chapter. The study participants believed that foreign women simply 'don't last very long' in Japan due to the fact that they are unhappy because they 'can't find a boyfriend or a husband' since Western men are mainly 'interested in dating Japanese women', and they believed that

Western women 'aren't interested in dating Japanese guys' because they are 'physically unattractive and sexist' (p. 137). This reflects the attitudes toward interracial couples in Japan described earlier in the chapter. They also 'tended to construct Western women as being both emotionally unstable as a result of having no male partner and disgruntled with the good fortune experienced by Western men', who in contrast, are in luckier positions because they could marry and settle down in Japan as respectable citizens (Appleby, 2014). This sentiment is best expressed by the comment by 'Dan' below:

> I don't know why they would come here. ...The [Western] women I've met, you know they're affronted by this Charisma Man syndrome, the fact that the Japanese women treat the men so well, the foreign man. But the other is – the opposite is not true, ... the foreign women don't get treated well by the Japanese men or don't get treated – the way they want. I think that pisses them off. And ah, the recipients of their uh aah their disappointment and their anger is the white male, I think. (Appleby, 2014: 136) [brackets in the original].

While it is true that marriages between Western men and Japanese women are greater in number than those between Western women and Japanese men, such marriages are not uncommon. However, it seems that foreign men are able to tap into Japanese normative expectations of marriage when they settle down with their Japanese spouses, especially since marriage for men symbolizes maturity and career stability; whereas marriage for women (or even the possibility of marriage) symbolizes career instability (e.g. Appleby, 2014; Simon-Maeda, 2004). A Japanese spouse provides a Western man with an insider path into Japanese culture and society, which is seen to increase his value as a more responsible teacher (e.g. Whitsed, 2011) with a means of full integration into Japanese culture. However, this integration also might mean accepting and adopting Japanese attitudes toward men and women that may not be acceptable in their own countries. This is illustrated in Tim's belief of why men like him, without domestic encumbrances, are usually considered better job candidates than women. He not only seems to *understand* the reason for such a policy (if it actually exists), he *accepts it* as normal:

> If I were to apply for a good position in a Japanese university and I was competing with a woman similar to myself from my own society with identical qualifications, in the Japanese situation I think they'd always give me the nod. The justification is they feel that the male is more

likely to slot in with what they want, which is basically you're going to be [there] 16 hours a day if need be to hang around for meetings and you aren't going to rush off because there are domestic attachments. (Appleby, 2014: 110) [bracket in original]

Tim seems to have adopted Japanese gendered bias as his own – women should be at home tending to household matters, freeing the men to be hard-working income earners. Such attitudes might be also transferred to foreign women, particularly those who are married to Japanese. The following example suggests that there might be some hostility toward such women, especially now that the ELT job market is drying up and university positions are becoming harder to come by. A male part timer lodged a complaint at a university when his classes had been cut back but his foreign female colleague's classes were not. He demanded an explanation from the administration for this, citing his years of experience with the school and his role as a breadwinner. Since she had a Japanese husband to support her, he argued that her classes should have been cut instead. Evidently, the school chose the person they deemed more qualified – the one with the MA and who publishes and presents (although it is entirely possible that the school had other reasons for reducing his classes) (Nagatomo, 2014).

Beliefs exist that women in Japan who do work choose to do so as a hobby or for self-fulfillment, despite the fact that many women in Japan (foreign and Japanese) *are* the main breadwinners in their families. Such attitudes can and do shape many aspects of their professional lives, including career trajectories, social welfare benefits and relationships with colleagues (e.g. Hicks, 2013; Nagatomo, 2014). According to Simon-Maeda, (2004: 418), if 'career-oriented wives [of Japanese] do not proactively maintain their jobs, they not only risk being excluded from the dwindling pool of EFL teaching positions but also might have more difficulty entering Japanese society'.

Hostilities against Women

During the interviews, Appleby's (2014: 137) participants expressed sympathy for the difficulties they believed their foreign female colleagues were experiencing. However, by merely being sympathizers and by placing the blame for such difficulties on cultural issues related to Japanese men's discriminatory behaviors, these Western men, she argues, relieve themselves of responsibility for 'any professional discrimination that might be experienced by Western or Japanese women'. In fact, Kobayashi

(2014: 200) also suggests that 'Western male NSs [native speakers] might be tapping into a vein of masculinity in east Asia, which has long marginalized local women and been denounced in the West as Asian men's oriental, backward sexist culture'.

For example, exclusion from the networking that takes place inside and outside of workplaces can mean lost career opportunities. Many job openings, particularly for part-time work, are not openly advertised but are passed around among friends via word of mouth because, as discussed in Chapter 3, universities often prefer hiring those who have been personally recommended for such positions (e.g. Appleby, 2013, 2014; Hicks, 2013; Whitsed, 2011). In other words, careers are often developed through homosocial activities, in which members of the same sex socialize with each other. Women are often excluded from or unable to take part in such gatherings due to family responsibilities, and this can keep them out of the career loop (e.g. Hicks, 2013; Poole, 2010).

In addition to missing out on important job information, as discussed earlier, women are often witness to inappropriate banter or behavior (such as displaying lewd posters of women in public places and/or making jokes with sexual innuendos), which alienates them and can create a hostile atmosphere (Appleby, 2014; Mulvey, 2012). If female teachers do bring forward public and/or private charges of sexual harassment, they can be ostracized for overreacting to what the men might believe to be merely high jinks or shenanigans. Mulvey (2012) writes that she does not want to be labeled as 'that woman' and an example that such labeling can occur is as follows: One of Appleby's (2014: 144–145) participants considered a formally charged harassment complaint in his workplace by a foreign female teacher to be entirely 'inappropriate and unproductive' and that maintaining 'silence' on the matter would have been a preferable course for her to take.

Obviously what some consider 'fun' is not considered that way by others. In some institutions, harassment seems to be systematic and deep rooted, making it difficult to implement changes, even for concerned authority figures. Harshbarger (2012: 9), a former director of a language institute in a prominent Tokyo private university, for example, writes of his difficulty in managing the misogynic and hostile atmosphere that had run rampant in his institute:

> Female instructors almost universally complained about what they perceived as pervasive sexism by a minority of male instructors toward them [female teachers] as individuals and as a group. They felt that this sexism rose to the level of misogyny; a few reported feeling physically,

emotionally and professionally in danger from one or more negative members of the ELP [English Language Program]. Many women felt (and I think justly so) disappointed by the failure of myself and others to stop the pattern of disrespect and hostility directed toward them.

Harshbarger admitted that the problems in his institution lay with a 'few bad apples' who had contaminated the workplace atmosphere, and it is likely that this is true when harassment occurs in other institutions as well. If foreign women who *do* complain publicly about such treatment are painted as hysterical and quick to overreact by men who do not actively take part in harassment activities, those men are, nonetheless, contributing to a hostile environment based on gender discrimination.

Summary of Gendered Issues in Language Learning and Language Teaching

In this section, I have described the role of gender in the way English language learning is approached by many female students and its impact on teachers. I also described some of the sociopolitical gendered issues surrounding foreign men's and women's lives in Japan. However, it is important to note that while these issues might reflect a trend of gendered attitudes, they do not necessarily represent all female English language learners, nor do they reflect the behavior of the male and female teachers. Many language learners do take their language study seriously and many (if not the majority) of teachers are highly professional. As a personal aside, in all the years I have lived and worked in Japan, I have never worked with anyone I would consider to be a Charisma Man, and I have never experienced negative attitudes from any male colleague (foreign or Japanese). However, this might be due to two things: first, I have never worked for an *eikaiwa* school nor have I worked in a tertiary institution with a large number of foreign teachers; and second, I have held a relative position of authority (i.e. tenure) since 1988. These two points, argues Hicks (2013), may result in a power structure that can create a better workplace atmosphere.

Conclusion of the Background Chapters

This chapter is the last of three that situate the sociopolitical context of foreign English language teachers in Japan. In Chapter 2, I showed how English (and other languages) learning and teaching has shifted several times. Attaining language proficiency was generally not the main goal of language instruction; instead, the goal was to obtain important information via the foreign language and then to disseminate that information in Japanese. When communication with the outside world became necessary, Japanese strived for communicative proficiency in all areas, including spoken and written language. Once the information necessary to modernize the country could be disseminated throughout Japan in Japanese, however, the need for communicative proficiency decreased, and the importance of language learning shifted to that of a measurement tool to stratify students into institutions of higher education. Thus, language teaching began focusing on minute and obscure grammatical details for gate-keeping purposes. This resulted in a system where everyone *studied about* English but few people could use it in any practical sense.

In Chapter 3, our attention was turned to English language education from the 1980s onward, focusing on the type of teaching that foreigners usually do in three educational contexts: private, secondary and tertiary. During the 1980s, numerous educational reforms concerning English language education occurred, and the private English education sector expanded, spurred by Japan's economic ascent; Japan simply needed a more linguistically proficient and better-educated workforce. From that period onward, the dual purposes of English seemed to gain a stronghold on two pedagogies: that which focused on language skills (*eigo*) and that which focused on communication (*eikaiwa*). These pedagogies run parallel to each other and have resulted in a hierarchy that places the Japanese teacher engaging in *eigo* at a symbolically and legally higher position than the teacher who is perceived to be engaging in *eikaiwa*. These issues have shaped, and continue to shape, the work that all foreign teachers in Japan do.

Chapter 4, the current chapter, shifted its focus toward gender. It began with a historical description of interracial relationships in Japan, which originally occurred exclusively between Western men and Japanese women. Japanese men did begin marrying Western women from the Meiji era onward, albeit in fewer numbers until the 1980s, when more Japanese began traveling and studying abroad and more Western women began studying and working in Japan, increasing the opportunities for couples to meet and fall in love. Nonetheless, there is, and always has been, the attitude that such couples are a mismatch because of cultural and institutional gendered attitudes in Japan that elevate men and denigrate women. Western men, who are stereotypically portrayed as gentlemen, are often viewed as prizes for Japanese women; but Japanese men, who are stereotypically portrayed as sexist and demanding, are often viewed as completely unsuitable for Western women (e.g. Kelsky, 2001; Takahashi, 2013). These images have been fueled by literary publications (such as *Madame Butterfly*) and by Hollywood film productions (such as *Sayonara* or *Shogun*). On the other hand, Western men in romantic love stories have created enduring images that have contributed to students' motivation to study English in both informal and formal educational contexts, and these images also shape the experiences of the male and female foreign teachers working in them.

The second area of gender discussed in this chapter concerned gender-related constraints affecting professional life. Societal attitudes toward women – both Japanese and non-Japanese – that view women as wives and mothers and men as breadwinners limit women's professional opportunities while creating more opportunities for men. Furthermore, it seems that some Western men have adopted Japanese gendered attitudes in thinking about the roles of foreign male and female teachers in Japan and they, even unconsciously, might be contributing to foreign female teachers' difficulties in professional settings.

Now that the social and political context surrounding English language education conducted by foreign teachers who reside in Japan permanently as spouses of Japanese has been set, let us move on to the analytical portion of the book. In the next chapter, I will introduce the ten women who have participated in my study, and I will explain the methods of data collection, the analytical procedures used and my theoretical framework.

Notes

(1) The children of such relationships gained the citizenship of the husband in the case of legalized marriages, but when children with Japanese mothers were born out of wedlock, they automatically received Japanese nationality. This was the case until 1986 when the nationality laws changed enabling Japanese women to pass on their nationality to their children while being legally married to someone from another country.
(2) Sentiments about improving the Japanese race were also expressed by Mori Arinori (who was to later become the Minister of Education) when he studied in the United States in the 1880s. He 'admonished Japanese students studying in America to take American wives in order to improve the inferior stature of the Japanese race' (Nagai, 1971: 24).
(3) Such issues for female researchers have also been noted in other countries as well. See, for example, Newby *et al.*, (2009) and O'Leary and Mitchell (1990).

5 Methods

Introduction

In this chapter, I outline the data-collection process that I used for this study, which investigates the personal and professional identity development of ten foreign women teaching English in Japan, all of whom are married to Japanese men. First, I briefly describe areas surrounding the study of teacher identity. After that, I discuss narrative research as the means for obtaining data for this study. Then I introduce the study's participants, the interview protocol, the transcription method and the analysis process. Next, I summarize the two theoretical frameworks that are used to interpret the data, and finally I clarify my position as an insider-researcher on this study. The chapter is concluded with a brief explanation about how the remaining chapters of the book are presented.

Teachers' Professional Identity

Teacher identity has been a prominent area of research since the late 1980s as a result of the increasing understanding that teachers are not mere transmitters of knowledge to students but free agents with their own histories and knowledge (Fang, 1996). It is seen as an integration of personal and professional experiences (Elbaz, 1983; Clandinin, 1985, 1986) and an 'ongoing process of integration of the "personal" and "professional" sides of becoming and being a teacher' (Beijaard *et al.*, 2004: 113). This identity is related to three areas – teachers' subject-matter knowledge, teachers' relationships with students and teachers' sense of selves as teachers (Beijaard, 1995) – and it constantly shifts when teachers' knowledge of the content matter, of pedagogy and of didactics changes (Beijaard *et al.*, 2004).

Research into language-teacher identity followed previous research in general education, and language teachers were recognized to hold beliefs, knowledge and attitudes toward language learning and language teaching that shaped all aspects of their teaching. Teachers were no longer seen as transmitters of prescribed methods that would ensure language acquisition (e.g. Freeman & Richards, 1996; Gatbonton, 1999; Golombek, 1998; Woods, 1996), and numerous studies focusing on the integration of the personal and professional aspects of teaching were conducted (e.g. Duff & Uchida, 1997; Kiernan, 2008; Nagatomo, 2011, 2012a, 2014, 2015; Pavlenko, 2003; Simon-Maeda, 2004; Stewart, 2005, 2006; Tsui, 2007). One means of investigating how teachers' personal and professional identity develops is through narrative research, which will be described in more detail in the next section.

Narrative as a Research Method

In this study, I use narrative research to examine the identity development of my participants. This approach is grounded in the tradition of qualitative research (Lincoln & Denzin, 1994), wherein the words that people use to describe their life experiences, usually in the form of autobiographies, biographies, life histories and/or oral histories, are scrutinized (e.g. Casey, 1995–1996; Chase, 2002, 2005; Creswell, 2007; Riessman, 1993, 2002, 2008). These words 'tell the story of individuals unfolding in a chronology of their experiences, set within their personal, social and historical context, and including the important themes in those lived experiences' (Creswell, 2007: 57).

Narrative research enables researchers to explore the complexity of human behavior, and it provides a lens to facilitate deep examination of those under study (e.g. Lyons & LaBoskey, 2002; Webster & Mertova, 2007). Hinchman and Hinchman (2001: xiv) suggest that identity is 'that which emerges in and through narrative', and, if this is true, the stories told by teachers are ideal for analyzing their beliefs, practices and identities. Narrative research has been employed in investigating the identity of teachers in general education (e.g. Clandinin & Connelly, 1987, 1996, 2000; Connelly & Clandinin, 1985, 1990, 1995, 1999; Elbaz, 1983; Shulman, 1987; Watson, 2006) as well as that of teachers in second and foreign language education (e.g. Bell, 2002; Kiernan, 2010; Nagatomo, 2011, 2012a, 2014, 2015; Pavlenko, 2002; Stewart, 2005, 2006; Tsui, 2007).

Narrative research in TESOL (teaching English as a second and/or other language) and SLA (second language acquisition) has generally followed two interrelated paths: *narrative inquiry* and *narrative study*. Narrative inquiry examines the meanings under a person's story (Bell, 2002) and narrative study considers the underlying sociocultural, sociohistorical and social influences during analysis as well (Pavlenko, 2002). Pavlenko (2002: 213) distinguishes the two as follows: 'Narrative inquiry is usually understood to be an ethnographic approach to eliciting understandings, whereas narrative study has a greater focus on narrative construction from a variety of perspectives.' Although these two approaches are quite similar, their differences will be clarified below.

Bell (2002: 209) says that the goal of narrative inquiry is to comprehend the meaning of a speaker's beliefs and their experiences, which is done through examining the story structures that lie underneath a speaker's utterances. Narrative inquiry 'allows researchers to understand experience.... get at information that people do not consciously know themselves.... [and] illuminates the temporal notion of experience, recognizing that one's understanding of people and events change'. She cautions, however, that such an analysis may result in a certain amount of researcher subjectivity. As a result, some researchers may consider that this type of research methodology is not legitimate or, in other words, is not *scientific*.

Pavlenko (2002: 216) also agrees that narrative inquiry has some limitations because it mainly follows an ethnographic approach. It generally views people's stories as factual statements, but it often ignores the sociocultural, sociohistorical and social backgrounds that shape people's lives (and their stories). Pavlenko argues that instead, narratives must be examined for 'whose stories are being heard and why, and whose stories are still missing, being misunderstood, or being misinterpreted'. Narrative study thus investigates the issues that underlie a person's utterances.

In this book, I adopt a narrative study approach to examine the participants' personal and professional identities. I rely upon their verbatim accounts from oral interviews and from written correspondence. From these accounts, I examine the intersection of their personal and working lives in relation to the sociohistorical and sociopolitical contexts of Japan, which were discussed previously in Chapters 2–4.

The Participants

My original research plan was to have 15 participants, five each in three separate educational categories: private (*eikaiwa*), secondary and tertiary. When I started interviewing the participants, however, I found a substantial amount of border crossing between these categories. In some cases, participants were engaged in working in *all three* areas, and in others, participants shifted between employment categories between our interviews. I discovered the difficulty in categorizing the participants strictly according to these employment categories, and so I decided to reduce the number of participants to ten and to examine each in more detail.

Although the women will be introduced again from Chapter 6, Table 5.1 provides brief biographical data in descending order of age. All the names, except where noted, are pseudonyms selected by the participants. These women teach in various contexts in seven different prefectures throughout

Table 5.1 Participants' biographical data

Name	DoB	Nationality	Yrs in Jpn	Education	Prefecture	Teaching history
Sarah	1949	United Kingdom	1974–present	BA, MA	Chiba	Public/private schools, conversation school owner, university
Annie	1949	Scotland	1975–present	BA, RSA	Tokyo	Conversation schools, private teaching, high school
Louisa	1960	United States	1981–82, 1983–present	BA, CELTA	Saitama	MEF, high school, private lessons, conversation school owner, university
Margaret	1966	United Kingdom	1991–present	BA	Hokkaido	JET, private lessons, conversation school owner
Lisa	1967	United States	1989–present	BA	Fukushima	Missionary English conversation school, private, high school, technical colleges, kindergarten
Pat	1967	United States	1988, 1992–present	BA	Iwate	JET, conversation school, university, high school, private lessons
Victoria*	1968	United Kingdom	1992–present	BA	Miyazaki	JET, private lessons, junior high school, kindergarten
Andrea	1976	United States	1992–93, 2002–present	BA, MA	Chiba	Conversation school, high school, university
Theresa	1977	Scotland	2000–2003, 2009–present	BA, MA, PhD**	Chiba	JET, high English school teacher***, university
Carrie	1988	United States	2008–09, 2011–present	BA	Saitama	JET

* I use Victoria's true name in this study with her permission. As she is something of a local and national celebrity, she would be easily identifiable regardless of a pseudonym.
** Currently working on degree
*** In New Zealand public schools

Japan. I knew everyone (except for Carrie, whom I met at a teacher's conference) before the study because of our shared membership in AFWJ (which was briefly discussed in Chapter 4). Through the association's e-mail groups and Facebook pages, I solicited volunteers from three educational contexts (private and corporate *eikaiwa*, secondary and tertiary) living throughout Japan. I also approached some participants directly if I knew they were teaching in a particular context that I wanted to explore.

Interviews

Interviews with the participants, which are described in Table 5.2, occurred over a two-year period from the end of 2012 to the end of 2014. I loosely followed Seidman's (2006: 17–18) method for in-depth interviews of teachers. He suggests that three 90-minute interviews are optimal for obtaining meaningful data to understand teachers' lives: the first interview solicits the participant's life history, the second focuses on the participant's current lived experiences and the third asks the participant to reflect upon their previous experiences and to consider their present and future lives. Taking into account my participants' busy schedules and their distant locations, not all participants were interviewed three times, but the interviews nonetheless followed Seidman's three-stage protocol. All of

Table 5.2

Name	Interviews	Total Minutes
Sarah	August 2014 (one interview)	150
Annie	January–March 2013 (three interviews)	240
Louisa	Jan–Sept 2014 (three interviews)	240
Margaret	Aug–Sept 2014 (two interviews)	180
Lisa	August 2013 (two interviews	180
Pat	August 2013 October 2014 (three interviews)	240
Victoria	January 2014 September 2014 (two interviews)	180
Andrea	Nov 2012–Dec 2013 July 2014 (four interviews)	330
Theresa	Sept–Oct 2014 (two interviews)	180
Carrie	July 2013 October 2014 (two interviews)	180

the first interviews were held face-to-face in my home or my office, in the participants' homes or offices, or in local coffee shops. For convenience, follow-up interviews with Louisa, Margaret, Pat, Theresa and Victoria were conducted via Skype.

Prior to the first set of interviews, I had prepared a loose interview guide based upon data provided by a 2011 questionnaire survey used for my previous research (Nagatomo, 2014), upon my knowledge of the Japanese context and upon my prior personal knowledge of the participants. In nearly all the interviews, the participants were eager to speak and needed no prodding. Although interviews are by nature asymmetrical modes of interaction with the interviewee holding power over the direction of the interview (Briggs, 2002; Kvale, 2006), this was not the case here. The interviews were conducted in English, which was the native language for all of us. However, nearly every participant, myself included, engaged in various degrees of code switching into Japanese, drawing upon our shared knowledge of the linguistic and cultural context in which we were both situated. Some participants seemed to enjoy talking about themselves and expressed eagerness for the next interview.

The face-to-face interviews were video recorded using my laptop computer's camera. The Skype interviews were also recorded by my laptop camera, which was placed on my desk facing my desktop computer. Some researchers have found 'technical hitches' (e.g. Hanna, 2012: 241) while using the Internet to engage in synchronous interaction with participants, but this was not the case during my Skype interviews. There were, however, problems with my computer not recording properly during several face-to-face interviews. I noted that problem immediately after the interview and wrote down from memory what was said. After that, I always used a back-up recording device, such as my tablet computer and/or phone.

In addition to the face-to-face interviews, data was also collected via e-mail as well, particularly in the later stages of the writing when questions and confirmations were asked of the participants. Some participants also provided documents for me to examine as well, for example, materials published by their schools or their own written reflections on their teaching.

Transcription Method

Each interview was uploaded to a transcription software called Express Scribe (see http://www.nch.com.au/scribe/) and was transcribed in its entirety immediately after each interview. I first arranged the transcriptions on lines according to phrases or thought sequences. I did not punctuate the utterances, and I retained most of the fillers (such as 'ah' and 'um'). Long pauses were noted with an ellipsis, the participants' gestures (such as 'finger quotes') were noted in brackets, and words that the participants emphasized were written in capital letters. An example of this comes from Andrea's third interview, wherein she describes the different roles Japanese and foreign teachers have in supporting her school's ESS (English Speaking Society) activities:

> Well there are Japanese teachers
> who are the OFFICIAL coaches
> of the ESS club.
> And we are NEVER,
> native teachers
> are never allowed
> to be the official coaches
> just like we are not allowed to be
> official homeroom teachers
> We have to do all the work
> for the ESS club
> and they hardly do anything.

I sent each participant a version of these transcripts with an explanation that final versions would be 'tidied up' for readability. One seemed horrified by 'how inarticulate' she was in the interview, but I reassured her (and others as well) that spoken discourse, which is usually ungrammatical and filled with stops, starts and fillers, always appears like this when it is written down.

Throughout the writing process of this study, I reorganized the participants' verbatim accounts into a more readable format that included appropriate punctuation and grammatically correct sentences, and I removed and/or edited details that could identify the participants. An example of how a final version of a participant's narrative might be presented in this book is as follows:

> Well, there are Japanese teachers, who are the OFFICIAL coaches of the ESS club. But we, the native [English-speaking] teachers, are NEVER allowed to be official coaches, just like we are never allowed to be homeroom teachers. We have to do all of the work for the ESS club, but they hardly do anything.

Process of Analysis

All of the interviews were read thoroughly. The first type of transcription data described above was uploaded to a qualitative software analysis program called NVivo (2002) to 'make sense of the data' (Silverman, 1993). First, I created chronological biographical profiles of each of participant because, as Seidman (2006) argues, such profiles can greatly enhance the analysis and interpretation of interview data. Then I examined the interviews line by line in order to generate theory from the data (e.g. Glaser & Strauss, 1967; Strauss & Corbin, 1990). I coded each line into categories NVivo calls 'free nodes' and 'tree nodes' that are conceptually linked to each other (see Bazeley, 2007; or Gibbs, 2002, for comprehensive explanations of NVivo software). Through this process, main tree nodes, dozens of subnodes and analytical memos were created, which enabled me to become thoroughly familiar with the data and to link various themes to each of the participants. An example of the tree node of 'Teaching' with some of its subnodes is shown below:

- Teaching
  - Learning how to teach
    - Trial and error
      - That didn't work
    - On-the job
      - Told to do what she liked
      - Observing other teachers
  - Attitudes toward English teaching
    - Fulfilling a community service
    - Boring
      - No other career available
    - Helping others
    - Good way to make money
      - Helps the family
  - Beliefs about students
    - What students need to learn
      - Pronunciation
      - Communication for real world
      - Culture
        - Cultural activities as a window
  - Difficulties with teaching
    - Collecting money from private students

- Don't pay on time
- Methods of collection
- Negative attitudes by Japanese
  - *Eikaiwa* is only fun and games
  - Not useful for real study
- Burnout
  - Getting bored
  - Too repetitive
- Balancing work and family life
  - Childcare issues

Participant Confirmations

During the interviews, the participants spoke about issues not only pertaining to English language teaching but also those pertaining to their private lives as well. As I mentioned earlier in this chapter, I knew many of the participants in a capacity outside of my research, and therefore what they talked about during the interviews might have been more personal than if we had had only had a researcher–interviewee relationship. One of my greatest concerns in writing the results of this research was to not only ensure the participants' privacy but also to make sure that none would have regrets about having taken part in my study. Therefore, I gave each participant drafts of what had been written about them, starting with the interview transcripts and later those that contained my analysis. Several participants asked me to delete and/or change some information that they had found embarrassing. The participants corrected my misinterpretations, and in some instances, they elaborated further on what I had written. In other words, the data for this study was constructed and co-constructed between the researcher (me) and the participants.

The Theoretical Frameworks: Gee (2000) and Wenger (1998)

In this book, I employ two complementary and overlapping theoretical frameworks to interpret how my participants' identity has formed. There are various theoretical threads that have been utilized in examining identity in the past. First, identity was viewed as an individual and innate sense of self (Erikson, 1968; Mead, 1934), but later, beliefs, attitudes and values came to be seen as important forces in shaping not only how people see themselves but also how the world sees them in what Bourdieu (1991) calls *habitus* engaging in what Goffman (1959) calls playing roles. Identity is also established by how people position themselves as compared to others (Davies & Harre, 1990, 1999; Harre & van Langenhove, 1999) as well as membership in groups where common traits hold people together (Hogg & Abrams, 1988; Tajfel, 1978).

In this study, I follow the theoretical framework of Gee (2000: 99), who simply defines identity as 'being recognized as a certain kind of person in a given context' and offers four useful perspectives for viewing identity. I also follow Wenger's (1998) Community of Practice (CoP) theory, (see also Lave & Wenger, 1991) which views identity as developing through belonging to and engagement with various types of groups to which people belong. These two frameworks will now be described in detail.

Gee (2000)

The first theory comes from Gee (2000: 99–100), who argues that identity develops through *Discourse* (a word he capitalizes to distinguish it from *discourse,* which refers to text longer than a sentence), which reflects how people think, speak and act. It provides a 'sort of identity kit that comes complete with the appropriate costume and instructions on how to act, talk and often write so as to take on a particular societal role that others will recognize'. He offers four overlapping and interrelated perspectives to view how identity is constructed: (1) Nature-identity (N-Identity); (2) Institution-identity (I-Identity); (3) Discourse-identity (D-Identity); and (4) Affinity-identity (A-Identity).

The first perspective is N-Identity, which comes from unchangeable characteristics that people have bestowed on them naturally and are only considered important *if* importance is attached to them. Mere biological traits (such as, to use Gee's example, having a spleen) do not have an influence over identity, but other biological traits, such as race, gender and/or age, do. Identity develops from these natural forces and shapes how people see themselves and how others see them, which can sometimes lead to stereotypical and/or ideological ascriptions of people. According to Gee (2000: 102):

> N-Identities always collapse into other sorts of identities. Of course, when people (and institutions) focus on them as 'natural' or 'biological,' they often do this as a way to 'forget' or 'hide' (often for ideological reasons) the institutional, social-interactional, or group work that is required to create and sustain them *as identities.*

The two areas of N-Identity that are of particular interest for my study are the participants' biological traits of being non-Japanese and of being women. In fact, as we shall see, their professional and personal lives in Japan are solidly built upon an identity of 'non-Japaneseness'. Because Japanese people place great importance on learning English from native English speakers (e.g. Duff & Uchida, 1997; Heinrichson, 1987; Kubota, 2011; Kubota & McKay, 2009; Lummis, 1976), these women, all from inner-circle countries (Canagarajah, 1999; Kachru, 1985, 1992), were recruited to come to Japan as English language teachers or they obtained English teaching work after they arrived. Although native English speaking teachers in ESL contexts have advantages over those teachers for whom English is a second language (e.g. Braine, 1999a, 1999b; Kamhi-Stein, 2004; Rampton, 1990; Tang, 1997), native English speakers in Japan, as shown in both Chapters 2 and 3, experience both advantages and disadvantages.

The second biological trait influencing the participants' N-Identities is their female gender. As discussed in Chapter 4, foreign women's experiences as English language teachers and as spouses of Japanese may be significantly different from those of their foreign male counterparts. In Japan, women are primarily viewed as wives and mothers (Liddle & Nakajima, 2000), and because they are married to Japanese men, these women must conform to or they must resist Japanese gendered norms as members of families and of local communities. Thus, gender, together with their status as non-Japanese people, shapes their employment status, interaction with people in professional and personal situations, and the degree of alignment with the communities to which my participants belong.

The second perspective is I-Identity. Unlike identity that is the result of natural occurrences, I-Identity is bestowed upon people by authorities, and it is rooted in institutions that create rules, laws and traditions giving people the right to claim membership in a particular group or institution. For example, this study focuses on teachers. The participants are able to claim identities as teachers because society treats them as such and they have the appropriate qualifications to do so. However, the participants' N-Identity of being non-Japanese is closely connected to their membership in these institutions, even though additional authorization in the form of undergraduate and graduate degrees and certifications is also essential. I-Identity, according to Gee (2000: 103) can be a 'calling' or an 'imposition', because a person can cultivate and develop an institutionalized I-Identity (such as being a professor or a doctor), or a person can be forced to assume an I-Identity (such as a prisoner in a prison). In this study, I-Identity refers to the capacity in which my participants are employed, namely through the conditions of their employment status and through the degrees and certificates that shape that status.

The third perspective is D-Identity, which is identity that develops through interaction and negotiation with others. Certain characteristics or traits that people are believed to have will shape how interaction with others occurs. According to Gee (2000: 104), these characteristics can be seen 'negatively as an *ascription* or positively as an *achievement*', and it is people's discourse that creates 'a site of negotiation [where people are] recognized in a certain way, and fashioning themselves in a particular way'. This is what maintains the identities that are shaped through their I-Identities. Much of my discussion that follows in the subsequent chapters focuses upon the participants' D-Identities.

Gee's fourth perspective is A-Identity, which evolves through shared experiences as members of groups and communities that help create feelings of belonging. Here people develop feelings of affinity if they feel connected with the community to which they belong, or they can develop feelings of alienation if they feel disconnected from it. In this study, the degree of belonging within the participants' places of employment, local communities and even within their families will be examined.

These four perspectives of identity are not discrete categories. They interrelate with each other in complex ways and, when teased apart, can highlight the complexity and fluidity of identity development.

Wenger's (1998) Communities of Practice (CoP)

The second theoretical framework used in this study to examine the participants' identity is that from Lave and Wenger (1991) and Wenger (1998). They conceptualize identity as that which develops through the day-to-day experiences of participation in groups called 'communities of practice' (CoPs). These CoPs can be officially organized (such as an English department) or they can be informal and unnamed (such as a group of teachers who always sit together in a teachers' lounge). CoP members are implicitly aware of the degree of involvement or 'modes of belonging' (Wenger, 1998: 188) that determine acceptance or marginalization in the groups to which they belong. In other words, identity forms amid the 'tension between our investments in various forms of belonging and our ability to negotiate the meanings that matter in those contexts'. In studies of language-teacher identity, the CoP has been used as a useful theoretical framework to investigate the process of identity development (e.g. Morita, 2004; Nagatomo, 2011, 2012a, 2014, 2015; Simon-Maeda *et al.*, 2006;

Tsui, 2007). These studies have mainly focused on Wenger's (1998) three modes of belonging that influence identification and negotiation in groups, and a brief description of this aspect of the theory of CoP follows.

Wenger says that identity forms through a dual process of *identification* and *negotiation*. Identification is a physical process that occurs while participating in a community with other members of that community. Negotiation determines the degree to which members have a voice within their communities and how they are positioned in relation to other members. I focused on Wenger's three modes of belonging under the categories of identification and negotiation: *engagement, imagination,* and *alignment*.

Identity formed under engagement involves 'doing' things that are typical and accepted for that community. Imagination is people's internal picture of their role within a community and can range from marginalization to affinity. Alignment, related to power, determines the degree of allegiance given to a community. Wenger also argues that people's experiences in their CoPs depend upon various trajectories: *peripheral trajectories*, where people will not have full participation; *inbound trajectories*, where newcomers may eventually have full participation; *insider trajectories*, where full members negotiate their identities; *boundary trajectories*, where members of one CoP are linked to another CoP; and *outbound trajectories*, where members leave one CoP for another.

In this book, although there is some overlap, Chapters 7 and 8 consider the participants' narratives through Gee's (2000) theoretical lens, and Chapter 9, in which all the participants' are full-time employees in one context, uses Wenger's (1998).

My Position Within the Study

Before proceeding further, it is necessary to reiterate my own position within the research context. From an insider perspective, I too am a foreign woman in Japan married to a Japanese man. I have also spent many years building my career. Like some of the women in this study, I arrived in Japan in the 1970s with merely an undergraduate degree and no concrete plan for my future. My career in Japan evolved as my personal life in Japan took root. I taught for an *eikaiwa* school and a technical college in the 1970s. I made good connections that enabled me to obtain a part-time university position in the 1980s, and I was hired with tenure in 1988. During my early years in Japan, I taught private lessons to neighbors and their children. I raised my own children in the Japanese school system and struggled to keep them bilingual and bicultural.

As a foreigner who has lived my entire adult life in Japan, I could relate to the struggles and triumphs the participants described. My insider position is likely to have influenced how I approached this project in the first place and how I re-storied (Josselson, 1996) the data provided by my participants, and it is possible that I might have imposed my own subjective interpretations upon the participants' lived experiences. As Bell (2002: 210) warns, narrative study researchers must be cautious in interpreting the data because the 'analysis illuminates the researcher as much as the participants'. In other words, my interpretations of the participants' narrative stories are likely to be a reflection of my own stories as well.

A Word of Caution

Finally, it is important to emphasize that the stories told by my ten participants presented in this book are reflections of their own individual personal and professional lives. If I had had ten different participants, the stories that they would have told me could have been entirely different, resulting in an entirely different book. Certain issues that the participants considered important may not be important to others. Struggles that are related to the environment in which the participants live might not be issues for participants living in other areas. Some people experience a pleasant working atmosphere and others do not, and some people struggle with family issues (particularly those related to in-laws) more than others.

Despite the uniqueness of my participants' experiences of living and teaching in Japan, I believe that the themes that emerged through my analysis of the participants' stories share a number of commonalities with other women living and teaching in Japan – especially those married to Japanese men. Therefore, the stories told here may reflect the lived experiences of others as well.

Organization of Discussion Chapters 6–9

Finally, I would like to present the organization of the following chapters and provide a brief description on how they are approached. The participants of my study are introduced in detail in Chapter 6 wherein I describe all of the participants' backgrounds, what brought them to Japan, their early lives and careers in Japan, and their families' reactions to them entering a biracial and bicultural marriage. Chapters 7–9 cover various aspects of the participants' current professional lives: Chapter 7 describes the work engaged in by the two participants who operate *eikaiwa*

(English conversation) schools; Chapter 8 discusses three participants who juggle multiple jobs to piece together a living; and Chapter 9 focuses on three participants who are employed in full-time positions.

In Chapters 6–9, I mainly describe the participants' personal and professional lives by using the narrative data obtained through the interviews. I keep analytical metadiscourse to a minimum and mostly include it at the end of each section, following Geertz (1988: 2), who advises, 'Good anthropological texts are plain texts, unpretending. They neither invite literary-critical close reading nor reward it'. Wolcott (2000: 76) also agrees that qualitative researchers should allow the data to speak for itself rather than imposing theory upon 'data already collected'. He strongly suggests that

> [i]nterpretive remarks belong in the summation of your work where you situate your study in broader context. That is the place to draw upon the work and thinking of others....Be selective in how deeply you delve. Theory ought to be useful, not simply for show.

Now, let us enter the participants' world and discover Japan from their personal and professional perspectives.

6 Destination Japan

Introduction

This chapter is the first of four that examine the participants' narratives in order to see how these women have discursively constructed and presented their lives as foreign female English language teachers in Japan. In this chapter, I first look at reasons why these women came to Japan and consider their early teaching experiences. The only participant in this study with prior experience and qualifications in teaching English as a foreign language (EFL) was Sarah, and yet all (with the exception of Andrea, who married before moving to Japan) came to Japan with the intention of teaching English. Some of the women had been to Japan earlier as students because they were interested in Japanese language and culture, and this interest brought them back. Others came to Japan because of the poor economic climate in their own countries and because they had unclear long-term career plans.

Then I describe their first teaching experiences and the reasons why they decided to extend their contracts and remain in Japan, intertwined with how they met their husbands and their early years of living in Japan. I conclude the chapter with a brief description of the degree of acceptance of that the families on both sides had toward these couples' interracial and international relationships.

Deciding to Come to Japan

The only participants to come to Japan entirely on their own were Annie and Sarah, who arrived in the 1970s when Japan was well known as a destination for travelers and those seeking adventure to find work teaching English. English teaching was a lucrative way to fund further travels, and native speakers (and especially Caucasian people) were in demand (e.g. Lummis, 1976).

Sarah arrived in Japan in 1974 on a tourist visa with a few years of ESL teaching experience under her belt in the United Kingdom. Although she had qualified to be a secondary-school teacher, she liked teaching foreign students better than unruly British teenagers. She enrolled in several courses related to teaching English as a second language (TESOL) and decided to go out and 'see the world' while getting paid for it. She chose Japan because it seemed to be a safe choice for a single woman, and also because her Japanese students had arranged a place for her to stay upon arrival. Sarah, having had previous language-teaching experience and qualifications, found a good job at an established academic institution within a few days, obtained a work visa and began living in Japan.

Annie came to Japan one year later, in 1975. She was what Thornbury (2002) calls a 'backpacker teacher', who planned to travel around the world before returning to the United Kingdom to settle down with her Scottish boyfriend. To fund further travels, she worked for a while in Hong Kong – first as a secretary and then as an English teacher. She *wanted* to come to Japan, though, not only because of its financial opportunities but also because she had an interest in Japanese culture and literature. Annie loved Japan from the start and said, 'Japan for me – it was a kind of brave new world. It was really lovely to come here. I felt instantly at home.' At first she lived with friends and worked in a pub, but she began teaching English to children and studying Japanese at a language school. She obtained a cultural visa, which she renewed every six months by going to the Japanese embassy in Korea.

The other eight participants came to Japan under the umbrella of study or work. Margaret, Victoria and Theresa – from the United Kingdom – came to Japan as teachers on the Japan Exchange Teaching (JET) program. Louisa, Pat, Andrea and Carrie – all Americans – first came to Japan as students, and while Andrea returned to Japan ten years later with a spouse visa, the others returned to teach as Mombusho English Fellow (MEF) or JET teachers. Lisa came to Japan as a volunteer missionary, sponsored by her church.

The American women, from diverse backgrounds and from different states, all had a desire for travel or adventure that had been sparked by childhood experiences. Andrea, for example, was from rural Wisconsin, and she had hardly ever crossed the state border until she decided, on a whim, to apply to become a Rotary Club exchange student at the age of 16. She wanted to 'escape her small town', and from an early age she envisioned a future abroad, perhaps in a place like Australia. However, she said she had always been interested in Japan:

> I had always chosen Japan for some reason for research projects in school and stuff…I don't … I never, never really knew why… and when I was told I was going to go to Japan, I was like, oh, this is destiny [laughter]. I'm supposed to go there.

As a child in the 1960s, Louisa lived in one of the first areas in Michigan to be racially integrated, where she struck up a friendship with a Japanese child whose father was attending the university there. This motivated Louisa to study Japanese at university before Japanese studies gained popularity, and she spent her junior year abroad in Tokyo, where she met her future husband.

Pat, from Ohio, studied Chinese in high school because it was 'exotic and interesting' but switched to Japanese in university because her university did not have a Chinese language program. She spent a semester abroad in Iwate with her school doing volunteer EFL teaching at a high school (which fulfilled her teaching practicum requirements) while staying with a Japanese family. After graduating from college, she had not settled into any teaching job and could only find work as a substitute teacher, so she decided to apply for the JET program. She said, 'The idea of going back to Japan hit me. I thought I might as well do that now. Go back and have an adventure and teach for a few years.' Coincidentally, she was placed back in Iwate.

Carrie also studied Japanese at her high school in Nevada. She liked it so much that she double majored in Japanese and creative writing at college and spent a year in Osaka where she had a 'wonderful experience... and fell in love with Japan even more'. She returned to the United States to complete her studies, but she felt she 'had to come back to Japan'. She returned as a JET in 2011 and was placed in a private school in an urban suburb of Saitama.

Andrea, the participant who came to Japan at the youngest age (16) in 1992, took more than ten years to return. She studied Japanese in college and upon graduation worked for a few years. Her on-again-off-again relationship with her Japanese high-school sweetheart from her exchange student days took a serious turn, and in 2002, she quit the job she hated, got married and moved back to Japan to the neighborhood where she had gone to high school as an exchange student. She worked for a year at an *eikaiwa* school, but then she was offered a job at her Japanese alma mater.

Interestingly, the three participants in this study from the United Kingdom who came to Japan as JET teachers had little or no prior knowledge of or interest in Japan, and none of them had ever met or associated with any Japanese people before. Both Margaret and Victoria decided to teach English in Japan because they were unable to find good employment after graduation. Victoria, who had interviewed at numerous companies, describes how she stumbled across the JET program by accident:

I just met this woman who was applying. I went to the seminar and I thought 'Oh I'll apply for that, too.' I had no desire to go to Japan. I had never met a Japanese person before. Knew nothing about it. But I was interested in going abroad and that was the only thing. And also, the JET program is all set up, and it has a safety network thing – find you a flat and you get the flight and you just have to turn up. And it was well paid.

Margaret had a degree in library science but was unable to find work in her field due to a hiring freeze related to the poor economy. She worked for a few years as an office assistant but felt she had gone as far as she could at that company. While looking at job advertisements, she came across one about teaching in Japan:

There was a little article about this big [made little square with fingers], and it said teach English in Japan. There was a telephone number and nothing, nothing else. It might have said JET program but it didn't mean anything to me. I thought that I'd telephone and if it sounds dodgy I'll just hang up the phone. But when they picked up the phone they said 'Japanese embassy' (laughs) so I thought that was all right.... I thought that sounds quite interesting and it is only a year – so even if I hated it, I thought I could stand anything for a year. I wouldn't be unhappy every day even if it was a mistake. It'd still be interesting in itself. So I applied.

Theresa also was unsure of what to do after graduating from college with a degree in English literature, so her brother, who was living in Japan at that time as a researcher, encouraged her to apply for the JET program. Theresa's first exposure to Japan was through the Haruki Murakami novels that her brother had sent her as a means to convince her to come to Japan. Before that, she had never even spoken to a Japanese person.

Victoria, Margaret and Theresa all expressed surprise at being selected for the JET program because they felt that the other applicants were avid Japanophiles. Although they did not originally have a deep desire to go to Japan, after having 'studied up' for the interviews, they became keen to go, at least for a few years for an adventure. Margaret was sent to Hokkaido in 1991, Victoria to Kyushu in 1992 and Theresa to Shikoku in 2000.

Lisa came to Japan for different reasons. She had wanted to become a pastor but found out halfway through her university course that women were not allowed to be pastors in her conservative Lutheran sect. Instead, she became a missionary and was sent to Japan in 1989 as an OVYM

(Overseas Volunteer Youth Minister) to teach English. Unlike the other participants who began working immediately after arrival, Lisa was given three months of intensive Japanese lessons and an equal amount of teacher training. Then she was sent to Fukushima, where she taught English at the language center run by her church.

The JETS

This section describes the experiences and the early years of living in Japan for the six participants who came to Japan on the JET program (or, as in the case of Louisa, as an MEF). Each participant's narrative is intertwined with the stories of how they met their husbands, which ultimately influenced their decision to remain in Japan. Although each participant's story is unique, there are some commonalities shared by those who were sent to remote and/or rural areas where foreigners rarely visited.

Louisa

Louisa came to Japan as an exchange student in 1981 and returned to Japan immediately after graduating from university. She became an MEF teacher from 1983 to 1985 and traveled to 43 junior-high schools in Ibaraki as a 'one-shot teacher' (McConnell, 2000: 2). She was treated like a superstar, and huge banners displayed with her name on them welcomed her upon arrival. She was served tea and cakes in the principal's office – sometimes several times on the same day. She laughs, 'I did this whole song and dance...everybody had their clown act...I could probably do it for you right now because I did it so many times' in front of 400 students in gymnasiums. Half of the time, she attended individual classes where each student would ask one question such as, 'Do you like sports? Can you use chopsticks? Do you like Japanese food?' At the end of the day, she was pressed with gifts that included cookies, chocolates, fruit, gift certificates and, oddly, handkerchiefs. At first, she thought her job was fun, but she soon became tired of being an English 'superstar':

> Because I was just at the school once a year, it was not really teaching – it was more like I was a human tape recorder. Their one token foreigner. When I would arrive at some of these schools in the countryside, there would be a huge banner spread across the whole outside of the school with pink flowers saying welcome 'Miss Smith.' And I'd walk into the auditorium and they'd break out into applause. After my speech they were rushing me with their sign pens like a movie star. Like

I was a movie star and I'm signing people's things. Signing their arms. Surprised they didn't have me sign other body parts! Signing all kinds of things all the time. And just for being me. And it was so (pause) bizarre and I really came to hate it because I had done nothing to deserve this adoration or anything. I just arrived there.

Nevertheless, Louisa knew that she had 'a good thing going'. She earned more than 300,000 yen a month and paid no taxes or health-insurance fees. Her subsidized rent was only 4000 yen a month, and she had plenty of money for traveling back and forth to Tokyo. She had reconnected with her boyfriend from her exchange-student days, who had not yet graduated from college. When her contract as an MEF ended, she wondered where their relationship was heading, so she asked him whether she should stay in Japan or 'go back to America to get [her] life back on track'. They decided that she should stay in Japan, and so she got a job at an academically high-level private high school in Ibaraki. Unlike her time as an MEF, she had to 'do things' and 'expand on the things I had done in the speeches and games and things [while an MEF].' Unsure of what and how to teach because she was a classroom teacher for the first time, she consulted teachers' manuals and books on applied linguistics. She taught the students communicative activities, such as how to play scrabble, and because of her proficient Japanese, she helped some university-bound students in a writing seminar with their English-to-Japanese translations.

After Louisa and Toshi married in 1986, she moved back to Tokyo and got a job at an *eikaiwa* school, where she enjoyed the camaraderie of other foreign teachers and enjoyed socializing with the students. She was provided with rigorous training and given detailed explanations of how to use the materials and how to evaluate the students. Louisa said, 'I felt like I was learning the ropes and actually learning how to teach while I was there.' After Toshi contracted tuberculosis and went on sick leave for six months, their income was somewhat reduced. She asked for a promotion at the *eikaiwa* school because she had had the most experience, but the Japanese manager

> [b]asically laughed and said, 'Three years in Ibaraki doing the song and dance thing was not teaching.' You only have whatever experience you got here.... He was like (making a spitting sound) MEF is *not* teaching experience and the high school doesn't count.

Louisa came to feel that she was in a dead-end job and wanted to quit. She laughed, remembering how got her next job at a translation company 'without having to do a translation or anything. They just handed me something and said can you read this? Understand this? I looked at it and it looked like Chinese and I'm like... yeah...' Louisa became pregnant shortly after starting that job, but when she asked about maternity leave, which had recently been made available for women by law, her boss was very 'dead set against it', and told her, 'That's only for Japanese. Go check it out. That doesn't apply to you. You're a foreigner. Go check it out.' Louisa believed him and worked in the office until delivery and then worked from home until her baby was a year old. When her husband was transferred to Ibaraki, she saw that as a good opportunity to quit as it was becoming increasingly difficult to translate while caring for a toddler.

In Ibaraki, she gave birth to two more children and she taught English to friends and neighbors in a few casually operated classes. After moving to Saitama, she began teaching more classes at her kitchen table to earn extra money to offset the higher cost of living. After using all their savings to build a house, she realized she would have to bring in more income. In 2001, she rented a space at the nearby station and opened a language school. Several years later, when that building was slated to be torn down, she built an addition onto her home and moved her school there. Eventually Louisa became tired of teaching at home, so she obtained a CELTA (Certificate of Language Teaching to Adults) and became a BULATs (Business Language Testing Service) examiner and a university part-time teacher. Louisa will be discussed in more detail in Chapters 8 and 9.

Margaret

Margaret, who was a JET teacher in Hokkaido, also came to hate being a 'one-shot' teacher, or what she called being *'gaijin* on parade'. Having to visit 32 schools twice each semester made it impossible to develop meaningful relationships with the students or the teachers. She spent Fridays with teachers discussing the lesson plans for the following week, and in many instances, those with low English proficiency, few pedagogical skills and a lack of confidence returned to their schools and 'rehearsed the students' through the plan she had discussed with them. She complained,

> Students had obviously been thoroughly drilled in advance – probably seven or eight times before I even set foot in the classroom. So they would just chant. It was manic, mad, and it was like – you know, Soviet Era.... And when I got there they would do the lesson *at* me and it was awful.

Six months after arriving in Japan, Margaret began having trouble with her new boss, a sexist whose first words to her were, 'I wouldn't let *my* daughter go abroad to work.' According to Margaret, he withheld necessary information from her and treated the male ALT very differently from her. He was allowed to take paid holidays for various reasons, but she was told she could not, not even a few years later when she applied for time off for her wedding. She said that her application was refused with 'work is more important than play' written across it in red ink.

Although Margaret did not particularly enjoy being a JET teacher, she enjoyed Hokkaido, especially since she met 'Kenji' the week she arrived. She extended her JET contract for the third year 'for the visa' to give them the time to 'decide whether or not to get married'. Kenji was a public servant, and in the last year of her contract he was sent to Kyushu for further training, and then he was transferred to Nagano Prefecture. Margaret completed her contract, they got married, and they moved to Nagano into company housing. Immediately after that, her husband was sent to an intensive English school in another city for several months. Because of Margaret's JET contacts, she interviewed for a position as a CIR (Coordinator for International Relations) in Nagano to help assist with the preparations for the 1995 Winter Olympics:

> All these guys asked how I'd look after my husband if I work. They didn't ask about my qualifications, [and didn't care] that I didn't speak enough Japanese or anything. All they wanted to know was if I had to work late or weekends how I would accommodate my husband (sighs). Anyway, so I managed to not be rude – obviously because I got the job – And I said, he was a big boy. He could cook by himself (laughs).

Margaret completed her work as a CIR and then the couple moved to Shizuoka in 1996 where she became pregnant. Because the hospitals there were 'disgusting, dirty, and old', she returned to Kenji's parents' home and gave birth there. The family moved to Nagano again, where she found a part-time job teaching for the economics and geology departments of a university. Unfortunately, she became pregnant again only a few weeks after starting; moreover, there were serious complications with her pregnancy and she was hospitalized for ten weeks and missed most of her classes the first semester. Her son was born in 1999 after the second term was over, but when her husband was transferred to northeastern Hokkaido, she had to resign. In Hokkaido, with her children in tow, Margaret taught a few mother–child English classes at the community center. They decided to purchase a home near Kenji's parents so that the children would have more continuity in their education by going to just one school, and so they started living a *tanshin-funin* (couples living separately because of husband's job) lifestyle. They chose that house in particular because they saw its potential as a place where Margaret could run an English language school. This will be discussed in more detail in Chapter 7.

Victoria

Victoria, also a JET teacher, was placed in a remote mountainous region in Miyazaki Prefecture in Japan's southern island, Kyushu, in 1992. She was based at the *Kyoiku Jimusho* (Education Office) and traveled extensively to the 11 schools in her district. After arrival, she was shocked to learn that the men in the education office expected her to wait on them:

> They brought me along [to the kitchen space in the office], and I remember he forced my hand on the pot, saying 'this is how you make tea with the hot pot' and I was crying and crying. And he said, 'you are a woman; this is what you do.' It was awful. I phoned CLAIR, which is the support organization and boo hoo hoo. And then I got the contract out and I said, 'I was here to do like international whatsit teaching and (pretend sobbing)... It doesn't say I have to make the tea!' I showed it [the contract] to the man [in the board of education], but they thought I was a real troublemaker and they made my life really, really difficult there. They were awful to me.

Although Victoria was unhappy with her work life, she liked the town and she liked the people. To many people's surprise, she renewed her JET contract. She explained, 'I didn't have anything better to go back to. I was still young and I thought it was better to hang around in Japan.' Life improved in her second year after her request for a transfer to the town's high school was accepted. As the sole ALT for that school, she no longer travelled all over the countryside. She felt like an important part of her school's community from her first day, when they provided her with her own desk and a stack of business cards with her name engraved on them. This was in stark contrast to her first year, where she felt like a 'traveling clown' and was only given a corner of another teacher's desk to work from. She began socializing with her colleagues – during work and at social gatherings – and her Japanese skills improved. The nicest colleague was a Japanese language teacher, 'Kenta', who was substituting for a woman on maternity leave. Because neither had the nonteaching responsibilities of regular teachers, they had much time to chat. Two months later, even before their first date, Victoria knew she wanted to marry him.

When they first began dating, they kept it a secret, meeting in parking lots outside of town and driving together to neighboring towns for dinner or a movie. Their secrecy was not only to avoid ordinary small-town gossip concerning teachers but because of his family background. He was a Buddhist priest who was expected to take over his family's 440-year-old temple with a *suitable Japanese* wife. With great difficulty (which will be discussed later in this chapter), they received permission to marry just before Victoria's contract as a JET teacher ended. Victoria's personal and professional life will be discussed in greater detail in Chapter 9, which deals with those women who are working in multiple contexts.

Pat

Pat, who became a JET in 1992, was assigned to several junior-high schools and one high school in Iwate. Instead of doing the 'one-shot' teaching as experienced by Margaret and Louisa, she did a series of six-week stints at junior-high schools and went to the high school once a week. She felt that her schedule was unproductive because as soon as students became accustomed to English lessons, she moved on. She assisted in 12 classes at the high school, and she had one full day per week in the board of education's office, which she felt was 'a waste of time sitting in the office with guys doing paper work all day while I'm just sitting here twiddling my thumbs', so she requested to spend an extra day at the high school instead. Only after a thorough discussion of whether or not the existing budget could allow for the extra minimum-fare bus ride that the extra day would entail was her suggestion accepted.

Pat liked Iwate and her job, and she felt well prepared for living in Japan because of her Japanese language ability. She met 'Joji', who had just returned from working in the tourism industry in Argentina, in her second year. Because he wanted to change careers, he was studying to enter physical-therapy school. To avoid local gossip, they dated secretly at first, mostly staying home, watching videos and playing cards. Joji's mother, who was a peace activist, had Joji drive her to meetings in a nearby city, so when she learned about Pat, she suggested Pat join them. This enabled them have 'normal' dates in restaurants and theaters while his mother attended her meetings.

Joji was accepted into physical-therapy school when Pat's contract as an ALT ended. She moved closer to his school and began teaching at a newly opened and understaffed *eikaiwa* school for children so she could get a working visa. She worked there for two years but was unwilling to sign a contract for a third year since Joji, who was about to graduate, had obtained a job as a civil servant and they were uncertain as to where they would live. When the school refused her request for a six-month contract, she quit. They registered their marriage eight months before their church wedding to avoid visa problems. Thus free from visa worries, she began working for another *eikaiwa* school, which gave her more prestigious classes and even dispatched her to a local university.

After their wedding, they lived in public servant's housing near Joji's workplace. They wanted to start a family immediately, but Pat did not get pregnant. Five years later, she quit the *eikaiwa* school to have more free time and less stress. By then, the university had asked to employ her as a part-time teacher directly, and people who were leaving Japan passed other good jobs, including more university ones, on to her. She could teach fewer hours for more pay, but with much less stress. In 2003, Pat gave birth to her first daughter, and in 2006 her second was born.

Theresa

Theresa joined the JET program in 2000. She was placed in a large city in Shikoku where she lived in an apartment building with all the city's JET teachers. She did not do 'one shot' teaching, but taught at one school for an entire year. She met 'Taki', a first-year PE teacher at her second school, and when her JET contract expired the two of them went to the United Kingdom to study. After Theresa obtained a teaching license, they moved to New Zealand on the working holiday visa program. Theresa taught high-school English and history and Taki taught math and *kokugo* (Japanese language) to Japanese children and worked as a Japanese language ALT in public schools. They got married in 2008, and they decided to return to Japan where there would be more career opportunities for Taki. To prepare for this, Theresa obtained an MA in Applied Linguistics and was hired from New Zealand to teach in the language center of a university in Chiba, and Taki began teaching at a nearby international school. Theresa gave birth to two children, and with those two maternity leaves, her five-year contract has been extended until 2016. Hoping to avoid working from contract to contract and to obtain a tenured position, Theresa enrolled in a distance British PhD program to study the merging of EFL teaching with literature.

Unlike the other participants in this study, whose careers have centered solely on EFL teaching, Theresa has had five years of experience as a secondary-school teacher teaching first-language students, and she is also teaching content courses based on literature and poetry to her Japanese students who are learning English. Despite the difficulty of combining the teaching of literature with the teaching of language, she enjoys her Japanese university students. She feels they are generally more interested in learning poetry and examining literary texts on a deeper level than her students in New Zealand, who were mainly interested in knowing what they would be tested on. She explained in a follow-up e-mail,

> In the two different contexts of teaching literature to first language students in high school and literature as a content-based elective in a liberal arts program, one point of difference is the reason for studying. While high school students are rightly concerned with the examinations they must prepare for related to the content, ESL students are looking beyond the current text to applications of language outside the classroom. That itself can be a positive side to content-based teaching in an L2 context.

Theresa, who is still in her thirties, may obtain tenure once she finishes her PhD, but she is limited to searching within a commutable distance from where her family has put down roots. Luckily, since they live in an urban area near Tokyo with numerous universities situated within an hour's commute, Theresa might be successful.

Carrie

Carrie is the youngest and most recently married person in this study and the final JET teacher to be discussed in this section. Her experience differs greatly from the others for several reasons. First, she came to Japan more than 20 years after the JET program began, and many of the difficulties that it faced in its early days (McConnell, 2000) had been ironed out. Although Carrie, 'being a country girl at heart' had requested placement in the countryside, she was sent to an urban area of Tokyo. Just one month after arrival, she met 'Yuya', a PhD student living in the same apartment building. They began dating and got married in March 2013 while Carrie was about halfway through her JET contract.

The most significant difference between Carrie's situation and that of other JET teachers is that she was placed in a *private* high school and not a public one, and the implications of this will be discussed later in this section. Like most JETs, Carrie had had neither previous teaching experience nor pedagogical training beyond a several-day seminar provided by JET. She was told that she could 'do whatever she wanted' in the classes, but she panicked at such freedom, and said, 'I thought, "Ohmygod, what does *that* mean? What do you want me to do? Give me some clues!"' After observing several classes, she realized those courses focusing solely on grammar did not need her. She asked the head of the department if she could hold a class of follow-up activities to reinforce the listening exercises covered in the students' book, and that became the starting point for Carrie's teaching.

Carrie learned how to do her job through ongoing discussions with the English teachers and the principal, through researching EFL teaching sites on the Internet and, importantly, she says, from a useful 300-page resource book of activities compiled by former JET teachers, *Planet Eigo* (Cohen, 2010). Carrie developed fun classes and created extracurricular English-related activities for the students, such as an 'English newspaper' with quizzes and online practice, and she broadcasts a weekly lunchtime music 'radio' show over the school's intercom.

As an ALT, Carrie is supposed to *assist* Japanese teachers and give lessons together with them to the students, but she says that sometimes she does and sometimes she does not. Some teachers enjoy working with her, while others 'kind of sit there [in the back]' and only take part in the class to discipline students if necessary. Unlike many JETs who complained that they were mainly used as human tape recorders, Carrie was given increasing autonomy to *teach* at her school. Although this was difficult at first, she appreciated being given the opportunity to learn and grow as a teacher.

As discussed in Chapter 3, private schools are not subjected to the same hiring restrictions as public schools. Carrie's school asked her to stay after her JET contract expired. In September 2014, she signed a 6-month contract to bring her into sync with the Japanese academic year, which starts in April. However, Carrie's husband completed his PhD in 2014 and was offered a postdoctorate position in Ishikawa Prefecture, and so Carrie resigned. Carrie is sad to be leaving her students and colleagues, but at the same time she is 'ready for a new challenge' and wants to move on before 'getting burned out'. She explains,

> I worked at JET for 3 years. They [her high school] wanted to keep me forever. I could have stayed as long as I wanted. I really liked my job and I liked my school, but in a way I'm kind of glad that we are moving on. Sometimes I think I could have this job forever (makes a happy face) or 'oh I'm stuck here' (makes a sad face) (laughs). I feel I've done it now and I'm ready for something else.

The four years that Carrie has lived and taught in Japan (including her year as an exchange student) have helped her transform from a shy girl who, as a child, was afraid to use the telephone because a stranger might answer, to a confident woman standing in front of a class. Her family was stunned by her initial decision to study in Japan because it was so 'out of character, *very* out of character'. Despite their fears, Carrie thrived in Japan and became determined to return after graduation. To overcome her shyness, she said that she adopted 'fake it till you make it' as her motto, which helped her become the type of person she wants to be:

> Part of me, another part, is I *like* to be in front of people. I'm a little scared about it, but I like kind of acting. So once I'm up there, it all melts away and YAY! That's not me. I wear my teacher hat – or whatever it is.

One of the main reasons why Carrie came to Japan was to 'to reinvent' herself, which she says she was able to do successfully.

The Other Teachers

In this section I discuss the initial career paths of those women who were not JET teachers.

Annie

As mentioned earlier in this chapter, Annie came to Japan in 1975 on a tourist visa to earn money. She liked Japan so much she put down roots and decided to stay. She began teaching children and gradually developed the connections to run her own classroom in a neighborhood community hall. Her life was enjoyable, and she made many friends in the foreign community. Annie moved into a shared house with other yoga enthusiasts, where they would have yoga sessions and dinner together with friends, including 'Kazu', whom she met in 1976. He became her 'rock' – a person she could depend on, and their relationship developed gradually.

Kazu helped his family run their small milk-delivery business in an upscale residential area in central Tokyo. Since there was not much future in this, with Annie's encouragement, he went to night school to learn electronics. Despite his parents' initial opposition to their relationship (which will be discussed later in this chapter), they moved in together and married in 1981.

In 1984, Annie began teaching in the elementary school of a private girls' escalator school close to her home. At the end of a one-year maternity leave in 1987, the principal suggested that she should stay home with her baby instead of returning to work. Her friend, who taught in the school's junior high, saw this as the opportunity to bring Annie in as the school's first native English-speaking teacher. With the emotional and physical support of her husband and his family, Annie returned to work.

Annie and the Japanese teachers engaged in team teaching, which was still unusual in the 1980s. To ensure smooth classroom delivery, Annie spent hours scripting every detail of every lesson. The school expanded its English program and hired several more teachers, but Annie was shocked to learn that that these new teachers were being paid more because they held ELT certificates, even though she had seniority and was preparing all of the teachers' classes.

In 1990, she took a semester's leave of absence and went to England with her daughter to obtain the RSA (Royal Society of Arts) certificate. With her new qualifications, she became a full-time teacher in 1993. The school's foreign-language program continued to expand, and innovative programs were introduced, which included greater collaboration between teachers of *other* subjects, English-only policies, and regular classroom observations. Annie was an insider at the school where she helped coordinate the program, traveled abroad with students on school excursions, and had her ideas considered and accepted.

Annie reduced her workload (particularly nonteaching duties that consumed holidays and weekends) and semiretired in 2010 at the age of 60. At first, she taught as many courses as before, but she has gradually cut back. She says, 'I'd like to continue doing a little bit of teaching as long as I still have the enthusiasm, because the enthusiasm is the most important thing of all. If you can't bring joy into your teaching then you shouldn't be there, in my view.'

Annie's work at her high school will be discussed in greater detail in Chapter 10.

Andrea

As mentioned earlier in this chapter, Andrea began teaching at the same high school she had attended a decade earlier as an exchange student. She was the only foreign English teacher hired for the newly established Intercultural Course (IC). Because of a government grant, more foreign teachers were hired to teach in the General Course (GC). These teachers were not ALTs, and they were allowed to teach without Japanese teachers present because of short-term teaching licenses granted by the board of education.

Andrea's duties included teaching 19 classes, supervising student clubs, proctoring exams, attending meetings, translating documents, attending school events and even supervising students during their daily cleaning activities.

In 2002, when the program began, Andrea was given free rein to teach what she wanted, and despite having little pedagogical experience, she helped coordinate a systematic curriculum that ultimately included presentation, debate, discussion and other communicatively based classes. She felt respected by her Japanese and foreign colleagues for her organizational skills and for her teaching.

Andrea's standing began to change after her year-long maternity leaves in 2007 and in 2009. Because public-school teachers undergo transfers every five to ten years, those that knew of her history with the school and of her contributions to the school had been transferred out and new teachers transferred in. Little by little, she lost the courses that she had taken pride in teaching and that she had considered to be hers. She attempted to regain respect and status by enrolling in a TESOL MA program. Unfortunately, this did not improve her situation, and in 2014 she resigned and began teaching at a university. Her years at the high school and her new position at the university will be discussed in more detail in Chapter 10.

Lisa

As mentioned earlier, Lisa came to Japan in 1989 on a two-year contract as an OVYM (Overseas Volunteer Youth Minister) with her church. She was sent to a small city in Fukushima Prefecture where she enjoyed teaching and socializing with her students. When her contract with the church ended, Lisa did not want to return home, but she did not want to continue volunteer teaching either. Tired of being 'so poor', she got a 'regular job in regular society' at a nearby *eikaiwa* school.

Lisa was surprised to find that the friendships she had developed with her students no longer continued, and they had befriended the new missionary teacher instead. That was quite a painful 'eye opener', but she made different friends. In 1992, she met 'Yusuke' at a party and liked him because he spoke to her like she 'was a regular person' and not just a *gaijin*. Even though his English was proficient, he was a 'you're-in-Japan-you-speak-Japanese old-fashioned kind of guy'. He waited while she used her dictionary, and she said that they somehow 'talked and talked and talked and talked'.

Before committing to marriage, Lisa said she wanted know if she could commit to Japan, and this commitment involved acquiring Japanese proficiency. She challenged herself to pass the highest level of the Japanese proficiency exam, and to do this she isolated herself by moving in with her father in the United States. There she 'holed up like a hermit' for six months to study seven days a week from morning to night. Her strategy worked, and she passed the exam on her first try.

Lisa and Yusuke married in 1994 and they moved to Osaka, where Yusuke entered a PhD program. Lisa supported them both by working at a large *eikaiwa* school. The 1995 Hanshin earthquake, which killed approximately 5000 people, disrupted their life; they suffered a lot of household damage and needed to move to a different apartment building. During Yusuke's PhD studies, Lisa gave birth to two boys, and they spent a year in England. Unfortunately, after Yusuke completed his studies, he was unable to obtain a job.

They returned to Fukushima, and although the new plan was to open up a language school together, Lisa had growing doubts about the stability of her marriage, and she questioned the wisdom of going into business with her husband. She jumped at the opportunity to teach at a local medical technical college, and even though she hated to leave her baby with a friend, she knew that they needed the stable income that such a job would bring. In 2003, Lisa was hired at a nationally known private high school after the national English curriculum placed greater emphasis on communicative English. Although Lisa worked full time, she was responsible for all of the housework and childcare as well as teaching in the evenings at their own school.

She decided to divorce Yusuke, but to gain full custody of her children she kept the divorce proceedings amicable by accepting half of what is generally given as child support, and she agreed to live locally with the children. The divorce was finalized in 2007, and Lisa now lives with her teenage sons in a comfortable townhouse near rice fields and natural hot springs several kilometers away from their father.

Lisa struggles to support her children by teaching 30 lessons a week in the high school, a technical college, several preschools, an *eikaiwa* school, and privately. The way that she juggles all the demands in her life will be discussed in more detail in Chapter 8.

Sarah

The last teacher discussed in this section is Sarah, who was the first participant to come to Japan and who has had the longest teaching career.

Although she had initially planned to stay in Japan for only two years, she never considered returning home:

> Everything was going so well. Of course not only the romantic side of things but earning lots of money. It was going very well. So it never occurred to me to go back. I didn't consciously make a decision to stay at that time, but who is going to give up all that money to go back teaching part time at a language school in England? I don't think so! (laughs)

Sarah became attracted to Japanese culture and she began *shorinji kempo* (a type of martial arts) classes because she wanted to do something she could not do in England. It was there she met 'Yoji'.

By the time Sarah and Yoji married in 1977, her career was prospering. She had a tenure track position at a two-year college, and she taught private lessons at home. Yoji persuaded her to quit the college so that they could open up an *eikaiwa* and *juku* (cram school) together. He argued that a home business would provide better income and that it would be easier for her to balance work with the children they had hoped to have. They rented a large house that could double as a domicile and as a school, and the plan was this: Yoji, who was a graduate of a prestigious university, would teach college preparation courses, and Sarah would teach English conversation. Although many students signed up for *eikaiwa*, none did for the college prep classes, and so Yoji began teaching at another *juku*.

Between 1978 and 1983, Sarah gave birth to three boys. By the time the youngest was born, she had approximately 50 students (from preschoolers to adults) and was teaching daily. Exhausted, she quit teaching to spend more time with her children and to do the 'wifely thing'. They moved to a smaller house and tried to live on Yoji's salary. Unfortunately, Yoji was an unreliable breadwinner, because he quit every job for 'trivial' reasons. The family was short on cash, so Sarah needed to return to work. Luckily, she obtained several part-time university classes.

After Yoji failed her final ultimatum about 'hanging on to a job', she left him in 1986. With her savings, she moved into a tiny apartment with a shop below it in a commercial district with her three sons. There, she planned to open up a language school again. Terrified that the 100,000 yen per month she brought in from her university classes would not cover food and rent, she inquired at the city ward office about welfare benefits for single mothers. She could not qualify for benefits since her earnings were slightly over the limit, but the ward office put her in contact with single-parent organizations and even offered her a loan. Luckily, as soon as she opened her school, the 'students kept pouring in'. She soon became financially self-sufficient, but she worked long hours teaching and raising her children.

Although she had hoped to reconcile with her husband, their divorce was finalized in 1989. When she accumulated enough part-time university classes to live on, she closed her school and moved to a larger apartment. In 1990, Sarah hit the EFL teaching jackpot: 'Kawa University' (KU), where she had been teaching since 1987, offered her tenure. Her friends and acquaintances told her how 'lucky' she was, but this annoyed her somewhat because she felt it was a well-deserved break ending years of personal and financial struggle. With a guaranteed and stable income, she obtained permanent residency and qualified for a housing mortgage. Sarah's story will continue in Chapter 10.

Reactions to their Marriages

Before proceeding any further, it is important to discuss the participants' relationships with their husbands' families because, as discussed in Chapter 4, most interracial marriages between Japanese and Westerners have occurred between Western men and Japanese women, and this is still the case (Yamamoto, 2010). Whereas positive images of Western men as spouses for Japanese women have been absorbed into Western and Japanese discourse, images of Western women as spouses for Japanese men have been, and still tend to be, negative. Western women are seen to be too loud, too abrasive and too opinionated to be appropriate matches for Japanese men, and Japanese men are seen too chauvinistic and physically unattractive for Western women (e.g. Appleby, 2014; Kelsky, 2001; Ma, 1995; Oguri, 2002; Shibusawa, 2006; Takahashi, 2013). Such attitudes are likely to have colored the perceptions of the families on both sides. This section thus examines the degree of opposition toward some of the participants' marriages and how such problems were resolved.

The women's families

None of the participants reported strong opposition from their own families, although some said their families had expressed feelings of concern due to the distance involved (in the case of Margaret) and due to their youth and lack of experience (in the case of Carrie). Margaret worried that some of her elderly relatives, who had experienced World War II, might have had prejudicial attitudes toward Kenji, but that was not the case. Her uncle, who had fought in Burma, said upon meeting him, 'Welcome to the family. As you know, YOU have nothing to do with what happened. If you marry her, you'll be one of us. Without question I accept you completely.'

The husbands' families

The fact that the participants' families accepted their marriages, even if hesitations existed, is probably because adult children in the West choose their own spouses. In Japan, marriage is often seen as a family affair rather than an individual choice. Three of my participants – Annie, Margaret, and Victoria – faced strong opposition from their husbands' families, and attempts were made to separate them from their Japanese boyfriends/fiancés.

Annie's husband's parents, for example, were so concerned about Kazu's involvement with a foreign woman that they sent their friend's English-speaking daughter to find out 'what designs she had on their son'. They thought Annie was a bad influence, and they wanted him to marry a traditional Japanese girl who would live with them and help run their business. Instead, Annie encouraged Kazu to go to school, to move out and, most alarmingly, to take an extended trip abroad. A few days into their trip, he called home to find that 'his father had taken a turn for the worse, and collapsed in some way'. Annie felt that this was 'psychosomatic', 'not intentional', and that it happened because of stress over their relationship. Kazu agreed to return home after visiting Annie's parents in Scotland and to cancel the remainder of his trip. Ultimately Kazu's parents accepted Annie as their daughter-in-law. Although she refused to live together with them, they lived close by, shared many meals together and ultimately became very close.

In Hokkaido, Kenji's family 'staged an intervention' at a family gathering. 'They hijacked him and said, "you can't date this foreigner [Margaret]. You can't marry this foreigner."' After that, he would not speak to them for six months. Finally, his elderly grandmother, who had the 'final say' concerning family matters, asked to meet Margaret, and in her strong rural dialect asked, 'Will you give him enough to eat?' The old lady seemed satisfied with Margaret's answer and consented to their marriage. Although Margaret and Kenji would have married regardless of his family's support, plans went ahead for a wedding. His father, in trying to look on the bright side, announced, 'It could have been worse. She could have been a Korean.'

Margaret soon learned that Kenji's mother, in 'traditional mother-in-law fashion', was determined to control as much of their lives as she possibly could, starting with insisting on her way for the wedding and eventually snooping through their possessions. Margaret adopted a strong stance against her in-laws that she has maintained over the years:

> I decided to be nasty to start with and soften up later...I drew my line and never went over it and if they came over my line I fought back hard until they retreated. I didn't know how else to do it. They were so overwhelming. And you know, would just ignore everything [Margaret's opinions] and I realized they would just agree, and then do what they wanted....Even if you stated your case and you think it was OK, it never was. If it [any decision] wasn't ok for *them*. So I just decided that I had to be brutal.

Margaret needed to establish firm boundaries. For example, when Kenji gave his mother a key to their front door, she entered when they were out, opened their bills and later criticized their credit-card usage. Margaret learned to put the chain on the front door and go in and out of the back door, which required a different key. Despite these difficulties, they became very close over the years. Margaret knows that they would do anything for her or their grandchildren, and now that they are quite elderly, she looks out for them.

The opposition Victoria faced when she wanted to marry Kenta was complicated due to him being the heir of a 440-year-old Buddhist temple. He was expected to take over as head priest with a 'proper' Japanese wife. After secretly dating for almost a year, he introduced Victoria to his family. His siblings (who, according to Victoria, have great power over him) declared, 'No. You cannot marry her [Victoria].' After Victoria learned that, she thought they would have to break up.

Despite *omiai* (marriage meetings, which nowadays are like blind dates) arranged by Kenta's mother, Kenta continued to call and see Victoria. As their relationship became more public, his mother attempted to 'scare' her away by having her friends warn Victoria that she was going to be 'a real bitch mother-in-law'. Finally, his parents asked to meet Victoria once again. During that meaning, Kenta's father leaned forward and hissed, 'Well, do you need a ring?' Victoria felt a little like she had just been proposed to by her future father-in-law, but she was happy that they seemed to finally accept her.

Victoria believes the main reason why their marriage was finally accepted was because Kenta, who was 37, needed a wife, and there were no other candidates. The family and the congregation must have also realized that 'This [their relationship] can't be just a flash in the pan kind of thing. He must be really serious about it.' After their wedding, which was a media event with helicopters hovering over the temple, Victoria settled down as a temple wife. She found that the life was difficult and filled with numerous unwritten rules and regulations. After giving birth to two sons, she felt others assumed that she had fulfilled her usefulness and from then on, she should spend her life doing temple chores. Victoria complained, 'It was like my life didn't have any purpose. It was like my life was over. You can just shut up and serve tea.'

Victoria decided to take the test for the basic priest license, a qualification that approximately one-third of temple wives obtain to be able to help more with temple business. When Victoria's husband developed cancer after they had been married for seven years, however, she decided study for the highest-level priest license, motivated by fears that if he should die, her son could lose his inheritance and she could be pushed out of the temple. We will learn more about Victoria the priest and English teacher in Chapter 8.

Acceptance from the husbands' families

The other participants said they did not face opposition from their husbands' families at all. Pat's husband's parents had resigned themselves to the likelihood of a foreign daughter-in-law when he had lived in Argentina for several years, and they supported their relationship from the beginning. Theresa's husband's parents were relieved that they finally got married after dating for so many years, and they were particularly happy that the couple decided to move back to Japan. One reason why there was little opposition could be that their husbands were *second* sons and not required to continue the family name and traditions. Carrie's husband's parents, the youngest in this study, are quite cosmopolitan after having lived overseas, and for them, a foreign daughter-in-law was not a problem at all.

Summary of Chapter 6

The purpose of this chapter was to introduce the study's participants in detail by explaining their motivations for coming to Japan, their initial teaching circumstances, how they met their husbands and how they came to remain in Japan permanently. Some of the women had an interest in coming to Japan that was motivated by their personal experiences and/ or their educational backgrounds, but others ended up in Japan almost by chance. Had Victoria, Margaret and Theresa not heard about the JET program, their lives might have gone in an entirely different direction. The degree of initial job satisfaction differed among participants and depended upon the type of work they did, the colleagues they had and their students. All of the women *liked* living in Japan and they wanted to stay. Some felt that they had some unfinished business there and wanted to return after initial visits as students, but others met their future spouses and decided to remain permanently. None of the participants' careers, as we shall see in the following chapters, remained static. They all took numerous twists and turns, and they are likely to take even more twists and turns in the future.

Although Pat's, Theresa's and Carrie's stories will not be analyzed in the next three chapters, they will reappear briefly in Chapter 10 when I conclude this book. Next, we will look at how Louisa and Margaret operate their *eikaiwa* schools.

7 Running an *Eikaiwa* Business

Introduction

This chapter, which focuses on *eikaiwa*, is the first of three chapters that examine the teaching contexts of my participants in this study. In Chapter 3, I described issues surrounding informal English education in Japan, in particular that which takes place in *eikaiwa* schools. The ideologies of *eikaiwa* have been criticized for promoting the ideas that white native-English speakers are the ideal conversational partners for Japanese, and that only through *eikaiwa* can Japanese people become internationalized global citizens. Furthermore, what is learned in *eikaiwa* is often said to be far removed from the realities of Japanese people's lives (e.g. Kubota, 2011; Lummis, 1976; Mizuta, 2009). This may be true, but without a doubt, it was the ideologies of *eikaiwa* (which also extend to other areas of English language teaching carried out by non-Japanese in Japan) that provided not only a source of income but also a career for the participants in my study.

In the previous chapter, for example, we saw how *eikaiwa* teaching shaped Sarah's early career in Japan. In fact, she operated a successful *eikaiwa* school twice in the 1980s, once upon marriage (believing such teaching would be ideal while raising a family) and again as the sole supporter of herself and her three sons after separating from her husband. Although it is implied in criticisms of *eikaiwa* that any white native speaker can hang a sign outside their door and instantly become an English teacher, operating a financially successful and high-quality school is not a simple matter. Sarah, in fact, closed her school entirely when she accumulated sufficient income from stable outside sources, even though her school was successful.

In this chapter, I look at the issues surrounding the operation of *eikaiwa* schools experienced by two of the participants who have recently engaged in such enterprises: Louisa and Margaret, whose schools were established in the 2000s. In fact, as we shall see in this chapter, Japanese people's attachment to studying *eikaiwa* may have shifted somewhat (but not entirely) since then.

Louisa and Margaret both operate their *eikaiwa* schools from their homes as legally registered businesses. Although their circumstances differ, they share many similarities. In this chapter, I describe the steps that both women took in opening up their schools, followed by a discussion of the types of students they have and the social and economic problems associated with them. This sometimes presents conflicts, as we shall see, because in reality, an *eikaiwa* business is a *business*. When money exchanges hands, the quality of the relationship between the teachers and the students changes. Louisa and Margaret's futures as *eikaiwa* school owners will also be considered and, finally, I describe how Louisa and Margaret's personal and professional identities are formed by using Gee's (2000) four perspectives of identity, which were described earlier in Chapter 5.

Getting Up and Running

As discussed in the previous chapter, Louisa and Margaret had had some years of English teaching experience: Louisa was a Mombusho English Fellow (MEF) and Margaret was a participant in the Japan Exchange Teaching (JET) program. After their contracts ended, they taught for various schools and businesses, and Louisa had even worked as a translator. After having children, however, they curtailed their work and taught casually in loosely organized lessons. Margaret, for example, who taught in a community hall where money was not supposed to change hands, only charged 500 yen for 'snacks'.

After purchasing homes, however, both families needed more income, and so they decided make a business out of teaching to help defray their increased expenditures. Louisa first taught from her kitchen table. This was unsatisfactory and 'made for bad family dynamics' because her children needed to wait upstairs until the lessons were over. Sometimes her students misbehaved by 'walk[ing] in my kitchen and get[ting] a drink of water in the middle of the class like they would do if they were playing [with Louisa's children], and they got into everything and broke things'. This made it difficult to maintain a professional atmosphere, and some parents did not view her as a *real* and *experienced* teacher but just as another *yochien* (kindergarten) mother.

After her youngest child entered elementary school, Louisa decided to move into an inexpensive rented space near the local train station. She officially registered her business with the tax office in 2001 and began recruiting students. She soon had 15 children's classes and six adult classes weekly. At her peak, students came from eight different elementary schools, and she earned approximately 500,000 yen per month.

The building in which her classroom was housed was slated to be demolished in 2005, so she decided to relocate her business. As a registered business owner, she borrowed seven million yen from the bank to build an addition onto her home with a separate entrance and toilet. Although the loan repayment was less than the rent she had been paying, it was not tax deductable, and so even though her income was the same as before, her taxes rose. To cover the cost of the increased taxes, she added more night classes. Despite her busier schedule, though, she was close enough to 'home' to be there in case of an emergency and to be able to cook dinner for her family.

When Margaret and her husband purchased a house in Hokkaido in 2004, they selected one that could function as both a residence and as a conversation school. There was a downstairs room suitable for a classroom, but some immediate and long-term renovations were necessary, which were carried out in three waves and cost approximately five million yen. The most urgent was a sturdy fence to protect future students from the next-door neighbor's vicious dog. It soon became clear that an extra toilet was necessary as well to ensure the family's privacy:

> There was one woman who EVERY SINGLE WEEK would want to go to the toilet. She would disappear for ages to go to the toilet. To go to the toilet they [students] would have to walk through my kitchen, through my living room, to the *genkan* [front hallway], past my stairs, to the toilet. She would be gone for 15–20 minutes at a time. And I couldn't find out what the hell she was doing, because I was teaching other people, and I KNOW she was riffling upstairs or in my living room. She was one of the odd – you know you get odd people – she was an oddball. And when I had the toilet made I said, 'You can use this now.' And she said, 'I don't want to.' I said, 'I don't care what you want. That's it.' She used to make attempts to go through my kitchen ANYWAY.

Other improvements Margaret added were parking spaces, road heating (essential for a snowy area like Hokkaido), an outside deck for mothers to wait on and shelving for the classroom. It took Margaret several years to get her first 40 students, after which she hired an office assistant. In 2012, she reached her peak with 100 students, and she teaches nearly every weekday morning and afternoon.

The Students

This section examines issues related to *eikaiwa* students. Louisa and Margaret decided early on to hold only group lessons because they had learned from previous experience that private students are often problematic. Even though private students pay more money per hour, they cancel lessons and want to reschedule at times that are not always convenient. In contrast, group lessons, with a permanently set time, provide more income per hour *if* the classes are fully subscribed. Louisa and Margaret's daytime classes are comprised of housewives and retirees, while afternoons and early evenings are made up of children and students. Margaret only teaches 'ladies and children' to avoid potential gossip 'if men are coming and going at all hours', because her husband is often away on business.

Children versus adults

A successful *eikaiwa* school must have a sufficient number of fee-paying students to exceed expenses and to provide income. Adult language learners, particularly those who study as a hobby (Kubota, 2011), might be fickle and soon quit. Therefore, it is necessary to have a steady influx of students and to keep those already enrolled from quitting. Children, who rarely quit immediately, are the financial super glue holding together *eikaiwa* businesses like these. Parents are eager for their children to gain an academic and cultural edge, and children are the most reliable students. Children sometimes begin learning English from as young as three or four years old and continue until secondary school, if not longer, providing a long-running steady source of income. Both women agree that parents try to keep their children enrolled as long as possible, even when having financial difficulty.

Dwindling enrolment

Both Louisa and Margaret report a noticeable decline in incoming students, particularly kindergarteners, after having reached peak enrolment several years ago. One reason for this might be because they have fewer connections with the preschool and kindergarten world now that their own children and their children's friends and siblings are older. As they are no longer interacting daily with children in this age group and their mothers, direct connections have weakened and there are fewer word-of-mouth applicants. In addition, many kindergartens now offer English classes (as well as other types of lessons) as after-school daycare packages, in which parents can leave their children in kindergarten for longer hours. This, Margaret believes, is the main reason why she had no incoming kindergarteners at all in 2014.

In addition to there being fewer incoming students, some students quit. An ideal children's class is one with the maximum number of students studying and progressing together at the same rate for many years. Unfortunately, with every withdrawal, the class size shrinks, because neither teacher adds new children to existing classes due to differences in the children's proficiency levels. While this policy maintains the quality of their lessons, it results in less hourly income. Unfortunately, this means that some classes, Margaret says, have shrunk in size by a hefty 50%.

Reasons for fewer students

Students quit studying English for numerous reasons, which include economic difficulties, shifting interests and parental attitudes toward academic study. Some students' families can no longer afford to pay for their children's extracurricular lessons. Margaret, for example, lives in a town where 30% of the residents are employed in one industry. When the economy worsened and salaries were widely cut, she lost ten students. She says that parents still believe in the long-term benefits of English study for their children, so they try to keep them enrolled as long as possible, but now they will delay enrolment until after children enter elementary school. In addition, some children simply lose interest in English over time and wish to join some other after-school enrichment activity instead.

Parental attitudes toward *eikaiwa* for their children also shift as the children become older. They often want their children in the upper elementary-school grades or in junior high school to study English in the 'Japanese' way; they have them quit *eikaiwa* and send them to *juku* (cram schools) instead. This is partly because of beliefs that foreign teachers only teach fun and games, which will be discussed in detail later.

Problem students

Sometimes students in *eikaiwa* schools are asked to leave, even though this results in a loss of income. Usually, this decision is made to protect the school. For example, Margaret learned that some siblings had been enrolled in her school to spy on her. She would have never known this had the father had not directly told her that he had recently bought a franchise *juku* and his children were to report back to him about her teaching methods so that 'when [he] employs [his] English teacher, [he] can tell them to do what you do'. Shocked, Margaret told him, 'Here is the door,' and refunded his money.

Margaret also terminated a student's contract for what she felt was rude and unreasonable behavior. Margaret suddenly cancelled a class because of a life-threatening medical emergency involving her son. Although the other students accepted the cancellation without question, this woman demanded an apology, complaining about Margaret's 'unprofessional behavior' for failing to notify her directly. Instead of apologizing like the woman wanted, Margaret refunded her tuition and told her that she never wanted to see her again.

Louisa needed to expel a poorly behaved child who disrupted the class to such an extent that the other mothers 'ganged together' and said it was 'either him or them'. Although Louisa felt bad for the child and his mother, she said 'I couldn't afford to lose that [other] chunk of students. I was buying groceries with their money'.

Fighting Against the Ideologies of *Eikaiwa* and *Eigo*

In Margaret's town, there are few children, so competition to attract students into educational businesses is fierce. A recently opened chain school franchise nearby has attempted to 'steal' Margaret's students. The philosophy of this school promotes learning through the repetitive filling out of worksheets. According to Margaret, the school owner has advertised that communicative English is not only insufficient for Japanese children but is also potentially harmful. By drawing on the competing discourses surrounding *eigo* and *eikaiwa* (Nagatomo, 2014a), the owner of that chain school has positioned himself as qualified to teach Japanese students in the Japanese way and positioned the only native English-speaking conversation school teacher in town, Margaret, as unqualified. She says,

> He actually advertises that we are NOT the [NAME] English *gaijin* school. We [the other school] don't play. We teach PROPER English with proper grammar. We know how to teach because we are Japanese. And they actually use *my* name and another school's name and say how bad we are. I'm serious. So I get quoted to by mothers. They'll say, 'Oh you don't teach grammar, do you?' and I say, 'Yes, I teach grammar.' [They reply] 'But the [name of school] man says [NAME] English doesn't teach grammar. She does games. *Gaijin* don't know grammar.' He says FOREIGN teachers [in his advertisements]. I'm the only foreign teacher in my area. So yeah, it's me.

As a result of such aggressive advertising and negative publicity, one of Margaret's long-term students quit. His mother rationalized, 'But you don't teach grammar. I want him to do the EIKEN [an English proficiency[1]] test.' Margaret was understandably upset because her students had been preparing for that exam for months. Immediately after the boy switched schools, he passed the exam, and so 'The guy [the teacher] gets to say, "look at MY students." But he did nothing.' Even though the boy passed the exam, Margaret feels his communicative skills will come to a 'grinding halt' because that new school only focuses on writing worksheets. Nevertheless, Margaret will never take him (or anyone else who quits) back if they are dissatisfied with her school or with her teaching methods. Margaret, who has pride and is unwilling to compromise, says, 'You have to be ruthless I think. You don't lie down and say "kick me."'

Is *Eikawa* just fun and games?

Margaret holds regular class observation and parental meetings to explain her curriculum. Despite such activities, one mother, whose child has been studying with Margaret for more than ten years, exclaimed when she noticed the file of lesson plans on Margaret's desk, 'Oh you have a plan!' It seemed that this mother (and possibly other mothers as well) believed that Margaret does not teach but plays instead.

Louisa found that some parents believed English classes taught by foreigners should be conducted *only* in English, because that is how *eikaiwa* classes taught by foreigners are *supposed to be taught*. Louisa, who is fluent in Japanese, uses both languages to teach. Classes for younger children are conducted bilingually and, as children develop English proficiency, her use of Japanese decreases. Despite this being a well-stated policy, one parent informed Louisa that she was planning to withdraw her son because he could not understand what was going on in what she believed to be an 'only English' class. Louisa asked her observe, and once she realized the class was bilingual, she had him stay. He ultimately became one of Louisa's 'success stories' and stayed until high school and passed the second level of the English proficiency exam.

More Than English Lessons

Running an *eikaiwa* school entails more than teaching language; teachers also provide knowledge of the English-speaking world to their students, which is why many students enjoy attending such schools in the first place (e.g. Duff & Uchida, 1997; Kubota, 2011). Cultural events and activities contribute to enrolled students' satisfaction and can attract prospective students. Margaret organizes three annual events: one at Halloween, one at Christmas and a spring party. The spring party and the Halloween party are held with all students (and their friends) in attendance, and Christmas parties are held in individual classes. The Halloween party has become a neighborhood affair with the neighbors taking part in it as well. A local baker makes special Halloween cakes, and neighbors distribute them to her trick-or-treaters. Some neighbors enjoy this event and even 'go whole hog and decorate the house and dress up [in costumes]'. This event is good publicity for Margaret's school, and it makes her feel connected with her neighbors.

Teaching Adults

Teaching *eikaiwa* to adults presents different challenges from teaching children. Adult students attend *eikaiwa* lessons for various reasons. Sometimes students have a concrete desire to improve their English skills, but many adult learners enjoy the social aspect of *eikaiwa* (e.g. Bailey, 2007; Kubota, 2011; Takahashi, 2013). Adult classes are easier to manage because unlike children's classes, which merely shrink in size when enrolment drops, adults can move more freely between classes. They have more flexible time schedules, and most adults do not mind being in mixed-ability groups if the differences in ability are not extreme.

Socializing at *eikaiwa*

Some students have been attending Louisa and Margaret's classes for years. Margaret, for example, has one close-knit group of ladies who travel domestically and internationally together. Margaret believes that their weekly gathering is more of an opportunity for them to meet than for them to actually study. The textbook, which she calls a prop, has taken four years to complete:

> If I'm not careful it [the lesson] would degenerate completely into Japanese. But nobody would seem to mind. I would feel guilty about that. But they don't want to do exams, and they don't want to be pushed and they don't want to turn the page in the textbook. So fair enough. Why are they coming? I think it's the social thing they like.

In addition to studying English with friends, some adults, who may be lacking in social skills, enjoy having a ready-made group of friends they can socialize with on a regular basis. Margaret explains,

> I have a lot of students that are bizarre. The *eigo* [English] nut brigade is always with us. Well, there are always people who are inadequate, and they are looking for friends. And nobody will be friends with them. So they have to go to organized jollity to get their friends. And obviously English is one of those, isn't it? There is always one oddball. I have got two at the moment (laughs).

Friendly with students, but not really friends

The atmosphere of successful adult English classes should be warm, welcoming and friendly. No matter how friendly the atmosphere may be, however, students pay money for these lessons and, when money is exchanged, the relationship is more of a business one than an actual friendship. *Eikaiwa* teachers, especially school owners or independent teachers, develop friendly relationships with students, but there is a line that cannot be crossed. Louisa said she used to be friendly with students and mothers, but once she began teaching them, friendships became impossible. She felt that some took advantage of their friendship by asking for favors (such as getting refunds or rescheduling classes). Others complained when their children failed EIKEN tests or had fallen behind, and they became 'offended' by the candid explanations Louisa, as *a teacher*, provided. Her comment below highlights the differences between friendly *eikaiwa* relationships and real friendships:

> I'm really glad a few of my Japanese friends never decided to take lessons from me. Because they knew that once you move into that student–teacher dynamic that our friendship might suffer. The women who are my friends have never been my students. And most of my students are really good friends, but they are not GOOD friends. You know what I mean? Although they know every aspect of my life, there is a line there. Once I'm not teaching them, we never meet. And we are not friends really.

Another example of how relationships can deteriorate when lines are crossed is illustrated below. A friend from Margaret's former neighborhood moved nearby and wanted to study English at her school. Although Margaret had reservations about this, the woman insisted. Unfortunately, both the personal friendship *and* their *eikaiwa* relationship ended:

> She quit after three months and I was more than glad. I felt very uncomfortable. And she was naughty about it [their former friendship] as well. She'd say, 'Oh do you remember the time dah dah dah?' It let me down a bit. She has a photographic memory and she would say [during class] 'Oh you used to say blah blah blah...' Oh that was 10 years ago! Can't I change my opinion?... I didn't like the fact that she would drop little zingers in. I think it ruined the friendship. She wanted to show off. I'm not a PET and I'm not a TOY. I didn't like that. I'm sorry she fell over [an accident that forced her to quit the class], but good riddance.

Money Matters

Although money was briefly discussed earlier in relation to loss of income when students quit, this section describes the financial aspect of *eikaiwa* in more detail. It first focuses on how the women became financially independent, and then it describes difficulties of collecting money from students.

Financial dependence/independence and taxes

One decision that dependent spouses of Japanese salaried workers must make is whether or not to earn over 1.3 million yen per year, because going over that limit entails a loss of spousal benefits that include monthly allowances, health insurance and pension payments. Such corporate benefits were established to support the ideology of the nuclear family headed by one salaried worker, but they have been criticized as career obstacles for women that contribute to the gendered wage gap in Japan (e.g. Abe & Oishi, 2009; Sakata & McKenzie, 2006). By earning more than 1.3 million yen, wives not only lose these benefits, they are also required to pay hefty resident taxes as well as pay for their own insurance and pension plans. To compensate for the loss of these benefits and the increase in taxes, an annual income of more than 3 million yen is necessary. This amount can be difficult for self-employed workers (such as English teachers) to achieve and to maintain.

Margaret earned over 1.3 million yen in her fourth year of operation, and that created a tremendous financial burden for her family, because when her husband's company deemed that she was financially independent, her spousal benefits were removed retroactively. As usual, she submitted the documentation for their jointly filed taxes to the company's accounting office before the March 15 tax deadline. In July of that year, they were surprised to find that her husband's take-home salary was 'next to nothing'. After he inquired why, the accounting office told him,

> 'Oh, we realized that she [Margaret] should have been independent of you since April. So we took everything off of you that you had gotten [from April onwards]. And she went to the hospital so many times.' That was like 130 thousand yen.

The company had reduced his salary, removed her from his insurance and held her financially accountable for all hospital visits she had made since April 1. What was even more frustrating was that while the local tax office considered Margaret's earnings to be below the 1.3 million yen dependency limit, the company accountant did not. He had calculated her teaching materials as assets that 'could be sold' to students. Margaret complained that that reasoning was 'as logical as a chef selling the knives to the customers'. Margaret's own accountant later told her that he had 'never heard such stupidity' in his life after he consulted with the company accountant about this. Her husband complained to the head office in Tokyo, but that resulted in the implementation of new regulations concerning self-employed wives of the company. 'They said to him, "From now on, thanks to you, if your wife is self-employed – the second she is self-employed, no matter *how little* she earns, she will be independent of her husband".' Although it is unlikely the company can legally carry out such a threat, it does illustrate a corporate attitude that wives should not work. The following year Margaret earned below 3 million yen, but she became more determined to expand her business:

> OK. I'm full time and I'm going to work as much as I can. Why not? Workers [at her husband's company] have to retire at 54, so I always knew that there would be no guarantee of work for my husband after that. So I would have to be the main breadwinner until he found something.

Although Louisa had been earning a substantial under-the-table income through her home teaching, she had not filed or paid taxes since leaving the translation company. Because of this, Louisa and her husband were unable to apply her income toward their home mortgage. After she opened her *eikaiwa* school at the station, however, she formally registered her business and became financially independent. This financial independence later enabled her to obtain a loan in her own name to build the addition onto their house.

Collecting tuition

Once *eikaiwa* schools move beyond casual teaching and are officially recognized businesses, money must be carefully documented for tax purposes. This means that teachers must devise means to effectively and efficiently collect money from students, who need to pay regularly and on time. Both teachers experienced some difficulties in establishing reliable payment systems for lessons, and through trial and error, they have become strict.

Louisa first had a 'pay-as-you-go' system and allowed students to make up missed classes. However, this resulted in students constantly trying to renegotiate schedules and payments. Some would say, 'Oh we're going to be taking a trip so we're only going to be here half a month. Could I pay for half of the month?' Although she accommodated such requests at first, she quickly realized that her school expenses remained the same whether or not the students attended. She also realized, through her own children's experiences with extracurricular activities, that other schools require advance payment and do not provide refunds for absences. Louisa decided to follow suit, telling parents,

> If your kid comes down with the flu for three months or if it snows and you don't want to bring them in the snow or if your kid has a temper tantrum and decides not to go to school that day...you have to pay.

Louisa and Margaret initially collected tuition in *geshabukuro* (envelopes specifically designed for paying for private lessons such as piano, art and/or English). Unfortunately, students, even adults, often forgot to bring them. When adults asked if they could pay the following week because they had 'forgotten' their envelope, Louisa complained, 'I was like – I don't care about the fricken envelope! Just give me the cash. But they were "Oh no. I forgot the envelope. Can I bring it next week?"'

Such payment delays can interfere with the schools' operating budgets and with tax paperwork. Both women then began requiring students to pay through automatic withdrawal systems from bank and/or postal accounts. Although this system was more efficient, some students still insisted on paying cash. For example, a single father of one of Margaret's students has refused to open an account. His cash payments are usually late, or he insists that he has paid already. Margaret hesitates to push him because he seems to be having a 'rough time' so she decided to 'let it [the past missed payments] go'. To solve this problem, however, she recently began requiring those making cash payments to sign a receipt book.

Some students (or their parents) have insufficient funds in their accounts on the days withdrawals are to be made. Margaret's assistant spends one morning each month contacting those students, and if payment is not made the following month, she asks them for the money directly. Louisa's bank attempts a second withdrawal in ten days if a student's account has insufficient funds, but if there is still no money, she asks the student for it directly. Such students seem slightly embarrassed and make excuses: 'Oh I don't use that account for anything.' This, however, irritates Louisa. She claims, 'Hey I pay MY monthly bills. I put money in the accounts that need to have things withdrawn from them.'

Misunderstandings about *eikaiwa* teachers' incomes

Despite the challenges that have been described thus far in this chapter, people might see *eikaiwa* schools as financially lucrative businesses. Some students have complained that the fees for the *eikaiwa* classes are too high. These complaints may be rooted in beliefs that native English-speaking teachers (especially *mothers*) do not make need to make much effort to teach English, because they are doing just what comes naturally. Louisa now realizes she had undercharged students when she first began teaching, because the mothers got together and told her that her fees were too high. Later, students assumed that she is 'rich' from teaching. Unaware of the school's operating costs and taxes, they believe that all that tuition money is her disposable income:

> So many people think that all this money is just my pocket money – you know like 'oh you have a working husband and so any money that you earn is...' I felt lots of times – I felt hostility from mothers about 'you're earning all this money and charging all these high prices and so'... This was money I NEEDED. My husband was not making as much money as they thought because 'Oh he graduated from [top university name].' No he is NOT. We were paying off our house that we bought on a full mortgage. We borrowed 100% of the money, so our monthly payments on just the house ate up his salary – a big chunk of his salary. And braces. I paid for braces I was paying for you know.... And when the children were younger and I wasn't really doing it [teaching] full time and I was buying diapers. I was buying

extras – but we never took any trips. We never did anything. Once every three years we might go to America, and once every other year we'd go to his hometown in Aomori. But we never took family trips. We never did anything.

Louisa and Margaret's Futures

As this chapter has shown, operating *eikaiwa* schools is difficult because of the unpredictability of student enrolment, the unstable income, and complicated student–teacher relationships. Many teachers, such as Sarah, quit *eikaiwa* businesses and, as briefly mentioned in Chapter 6 and which will be discussed in more detail in Chapter 8, Louisa has recently quit as well.

Margaret, on the other hand, may be unable to do that, no matter how low student enrolment becomes. She lives in the countryside, where few teaching positions are available. She is not averse to taking on outside work if such an opportunity arose. For now she will continue to teach at home, even if only a few students enroll in her classes, because 'low income is better than no income'. Her husband must retire soon, and her sons still need to go to university. Margaret is seeking ways to increase her income to cover the loss of her husband's salary and to pay for looming educational costs. To do this, Margaret says,

> I'll do anything even if I think it is over the top. I'll do it because I feel like I have got to be the English prostitute you know. Sell myself to anyone who will have me, but I don't like that feeling. Three or four years ago I was over [the allotted number of spaces for students] and turning people away and that actually made people want to join more and it was really nice and a good feeling, and now with the economy tanking it's not good...if another school opens up with the next teacher being young or pretty or handsome, I've had it!

Margaret is not only worried about money but also whether or not she will remain physically capable of *eikaiwa* work:

> I don't want to be teaching 24 hours a week, and on the floor [with the children]. I have a bad back, a herniated disc, and the kids sit on the floor and a little kid jumps on my back or yanks my head down. I'm not built to withstand it any more. As time goes by, I'd like to reduce my workload. Not now, not for the next ten years. Because I can't. But I'd

like to. But I don't want it to be reduced because nobody comes! I want it to be my decision.

Examining Margaret and Louisa's Identities Through Gee's (2000) Theoretical Lens

To conclude this chapter, let us now examine Louisa and Margaret's narratives in relation to Gee's (2000) perspectives of identity. At the heart of these women's identities lie their N-Identities of being non-Japanese, being native English speakers, and being female. These three characteristics enabled them to develop lucrative businesses in Japan while also taking on roles as wives and mothers.

At first glance it may appear that their I-Identities are weak because they are not affiliated with larger educational institutions. However, their I-Identities have evolved from being owners of professionally run language schools, a fact that is not only symbolized by having many satisfied students but also by having dedicated spaces for teaching (which are not part of their families' living quarters), by legally registering their businesses and by hiring assistants and/or accountants. As tax-paying business owners, they are authorized to demand appropriate payments from students. These measures indicate they are not just casual *eikaiwa* teachers but *eikaiwa* professionals.

D-Identity, according to Gee (2000: 103), can be *achieved* or it can be *ascribed,* and this perspective of identity develops in people through the way that others 'treat, talk about, and interact' with them. Louisa and Margaret's D-Identities thus develop from having fully subscribed classes and/or classes that continue for many years, symbolizing their pedagogical capabilities and their popularity. At the same time, however, we saw how these women encounter preconceived beliefs concerning non-Japanese teachers, who are seen to be monolingual (which they are not) and who only teach fun and games (which they do not).

In addition to the D-Identities that ascribe qualities to the teachers because of their N-Identity of being non-Japanese, the expectations they hold of themselves, many of which are shaped by the years they have been living in Japan, causes mixed feelings of pride and guilt. The women are proud that they were able start a lucrative home business and they are proud that they can substantially contribute to the family finances. All of this has been done by carefully balancing their work lives and their family lives. Once Louisa moved her school back to her home, she extended her lessons into the evening hours, cooking dinner between her afternoon and evening classes.

However well organized the women were with their teaching schedules, they spent most afternoons and evenings with other people's children, causing some feelings of guilt. Margaret regretted that she was unable to take her own children to extracurricular lessons because of this. Instead, they were expected to behave quietly while she taught and never interrupt for any reason unless 'there's blood'. As the children grew older, such problems decreased, but evening time spent with the family still remained limited.

Louisa and Margaret's A-Identities are related to the degree of affinity they have toward their students, which is also related to student enrolment numbers. Both Louisa and Margaret seemed to have had the greatest feelings of affinity toward their schools when they reached their peak number of students. Margaret remembers how good she felt when she had to turn away students. Her affinity toward her business has become slightly reduced, but she says she will do what it takes to support her family through times ahead.

Through Louisa and Margaret's narratives, we also found that *eikaiwa* is about more than studying English; it is also about the social relationships that are formed through such classes. Those students attending the classes cannot really be friends, because in reality they are paying for a service. Nonetheless, positive social relationships with students do develop, and these relationships contribute toward feelings of affinity on the part of the teachers who teach the class and on the part of the students who attend them.

Summary of Chapter 7

In this chapter, I described the opening and operating of two *eikaiwa* schools in two different areas of Japan, and I examined the issues and concerns that accompany such a business. I also analyzed Louisa and Margaret's personal and professional identities according to Gee's (2000) theoretical framework, and found that their N-Identities as non-Japanese and as women have greatly influenced the other three perspectives of identity.

Although there has been negative discourse surrounding *eikaiwa* teaching, which is seen to be rooted in Japanese people's unattainable desire to become a '*kokusaijin*' (international person) (Mizuta, 2009: 47), there is also a discourse that believes such teachers, particularly native English speaking teachers, are not quite capable of teaching in ways that are in the best interest of Japanese. This was most evident in the negative advertising by Margaret's competitor.

Furthermore, it is also commonly assumed that most *eikaiwa* schools are in the business to make money, even at the expense of the students. News stories of large conversation schools going bankrupt, leaving many students who have already paid their fees (and the *eikaiwa* teachers who had not been paid their salaries) dominated the media in the early 2000s and are still in people's memories. Of course, Louisa and Margaret's businesses do need to earn a profit, but it is clear that they also keep their students' best interests at heart. A good example is that neither teacher combined children of different levels into one class, even though it would have been more cost effective for them to do so. Instead, they taught classes that were undersubscribed and thus lost money.

The stories told by Louisa and Margaret and analyzed in this chapter are, of course, their own experiences, but it is very likely that they are similar to those of other female teachers engaged in similar *eikaiwa* businesses who balance work with family. In the next chapter, we look at those participants who teach in multiple contexts.

Note

(1) The EIKEN Foundation of Japan assesses the four skills of English proficiency of Japanese. The test is taken by more than 2 million examinees annually in 18,000 locations throughout Japan. Established in 1963, the EIKEN test is now one of the most common proficiency exams taken by Japanese (EIKEN, 2015).

8 The Jugglers

Introduction

This chapter examines the lives of those participants who piece together their living by teaching various kinds of students in multiple contexts: Victoria, Lisa and Louisa, all of whom live in different areas of Japan. Having spent more than 20 years in the country, they are fluent in Japanese, and they feel integrated into their local communities to various degrees. Such integration, however, is not without struggle. In continuing my discussion of Gee's (2000) theory of identity that was brought up in the previous chapter, we shall see how these women's female and non-Japanese N-Identities shape how they are viewed as wives, mothers, teachers and neighbors. When they are ascribed with D-Identity characteristics that are not in harmony with their own self-perceptions, they are resourceful and they take measures to achieve their own identities, which has led them toward personal and professional change and enabled them to develop their I-Identities.

These women seem to put in more hours teaching than the full-time teachers (who will be discussed in the next chapter). However, as we shall see, their careers are precarious and depend upon a wide range of external factors, including the whims of students, the local economy, institutional regulations and even Mother Nature. Although some have substantial incomes, they still must arrange for their own insurance and pensions. All of the women consider their income as essential to maintain their families' standards of living, and for Lisa, her income provides the sole support for herself and her two children.

Victoria: Priest and English Teacher

I begin my discussion with Victoria, who was described in Chapter 6. She came to Miyazaki Prefecture as an assistant language teacher (ALT) in 1995, and despite strong opposition because she was a foreigner, she married Kenta, the eldest son of a 440-year-old Buddhist temple. She moved into the same compound as her in-laws, and as the *yome* (bride) of the eldest son, she became the lowest-ranking member in family's hierarchy. As a newlywed, it was difficult for her to learn all the unspoken rules in the family and in the temple, and she realized that her small monthly stipend as a temple employee was insufficient to cover daily necessities, small luxuries and, most importantly, her annual visits to the United Kingdom.

Luckily, Victoria was still in high demand as an English teacher after her contract as a Japan Exchange Teacher (JET) ended, because 'everyone thought we [the village] would become international'. She could earn her own money and had a good excuse to 'get out of the house'. Kenta's family supported her teaching, because they thought it was a 'kind of *fureai* [good community relations]', but when her mother-in-law (who had been a career teacher herself) began to feel that Victoria was more interested in *income* than in promoting the temple, she warned her to never let it be known that that she 'teaches for the money' but that she teaches because she 'wants to'. This caused some conflict because, as Victoria said, 'I wanted to get paid!'

Victoria's husband was diagnosed with cancer when their eldest son was very young, and she was afraid that if her husband should die, her son would lose his position at the temple to a distant relative and that she would be pushed out of the family. With Kenta's support, she studied for the highest-level priest exam to qualify as a head priest. This, the two of them believed, would enable her to keep the temple operating until their son was old enough to take over. She memorized long lists of 'Buddhist patriarchs and stuff while pushing the kids around in their push chair'. Her studies were challenging, but they provided her with escape 'from the daily grind', and she enjoyed the seminars and examination sessions held at the sect's main temple in Kyoto.

She had believed that Kenta's family would respect her more after obtaining the license, but she felt that they 'resented' and 'became wary of [her]', and they acted like 'she had become too big for her boots'. Instead of being congratulated for passing such a difficult exam, insinuations were made that it had been specially 'made easier' for her.

Victoria's schedule

Now, 15 years later, the family's future at the temple is secure. Kenta completely regained his health, and Victoria and Kenta work together as head priests. Their eldest son is a university student at a Buddhist university and is preparing to take over the family business one day. Victoria's main responsibilities lie with the temple, but as mentioned earlier, she also teaches English. She teaches as an ALT in the public schools as well as in private kindergartens and in daycare centers, and she holds private and group lessons in the temple's mausoleum. She juggles a full teaching schedule of approximately 25 classes each week and, as Table 8.1 indicates, she runs back and forth between neighboring schools and her home within a single day.

School bus driver

Sandwiched into Victoria's teaching schedule are unpredictable temple duties (which will be discussed later) and her participation in her children's school activities. For example, when her eldest son was in high school, he belonged to a nationally competitive martial arts club, which involved a strict traditional *sempai–kohai* (senior–junior) hierarchy among the members. These rules of behavior transferred to the mothers, with the mothers of older students bullying the mothers of younger ones. Victoria's positions as a priest and as an English teacher were useless in this hierarchy. Unwilling to wait for her turn to be a senior parent at the top, she saw a means of escape. The club owned a full-size bus but had no qualified bus driver; grabbing the opportunity, Victoria obtained a bus-driving license and became the team driver. Although her weekends were filled with driving the students to events, she no longer needed to remain in the gyms' drafty bleachers at the beck and call of the senior mothers. Instead, she stayed in the bus, read books and napped.

Thus far we have seen two separate examples of how Victoria resisted ascribed roles based on her N-Identity as a woman and as a non-Japanese and how she achieved new I-Identities (Gee, 2000). In the following sections, let us examine in detail how Victoria juggles her multiple I-Identities as a priest and as a teacher.

Identity conflicts as a priest and a teacher

As mentioned earlier, Kenta's family was not congratulatory after Victoria successfully passed the priesthood exam. In doing so, they would have needed to reshape their perception of her as a *foreigner* and as a temple *wife*. If the head temple had, as the family believed, 'made things easier for her', then her achievement could not be considered the same as theirs. Although her qualifications technically give her the same official status as 'all the bigwig priests in town', she says that she is still excluded from their parties and gatherings, most likely because she is a *woman* and because she is a *foreigner*.

Despite not being treated quite equally in the local temple community, her status among the congregation improved, and she felt she was no longer seen as her husband's 'bit of foreign fluff'. She explains,

Table 8.1 Victoria's Weekly Schedule

	Morning	Afternoon	Evening
Monday	Tea ceremony in Kumamoto with husband	Free afternoon	
Tuesday	One class at an elementary school	Go home. Sleep. Make copies to prepare for classes	
	Two classes at the kindergarten (5 minutes from the elementary school)	One lesson at a different kindergarten	
	One class at the elementary school		
	School lunch at the elementary school followed by planning session with teachers	One class with elementary-school girls in the mausoleum	
Wednesday	One class at daycare center	Drive home, make copies, prepare	
	Then drive to the next village	Drive back into town	
	Three classes at the elementary school there	Two classes in the mausoleum	
	Lunch at school		
Thursday	Five classes at the largest junior high in town	One class in the mausoleum	One 90-minute Adult English conversation at the community center
	One preparation hour		
Friday	Teaching at either of two village junior high schools (eight times a year, three classes each)	Two classes in the mausoleum	Relax with friends and family
	Daycare centers/kindergarten		
Saturday	Temple work/family activities	Temple work/family activities	
Sunday	Temple work/family activities	Temple work/family activities	

As a priest, people saw me differently. [Before] I'd be serving people in the evening and drunken guys would touch me and stuff. I'd complain to my husband but he'd say we can't do anything because they are the congregation.... Nobody sexually harasses me now when I'm wearing my robes.

Victoria's I-Identity as a priest is now no longer under question, and she works hard for the temple. But as we saw in Table 8.1, much of Victoria's week is filled with English lessons in various places. Although her schools understand her need for a flexible schedule because of the unpredictable nature of temple business (particularly funerals), her family often conveniently 'forgets' her weekly teaching schedule (which is determined months in advance), and they schedule in routine temple work at times when she is teaching. This causes conflict, because if she refuses to cancel her lessons, she is viewed as selfish, but if she cancels her lessons, she resents giving up her paid work in order to conduct temple business. Being forced to choose like this irritates Victoria, because many temple events, such as memorial services, are suggested by the temple and not by the family that needs them. Victoria's lessons end in the late afternoon so she would be able to teach *and* perform memorial services if they were scheduled for 6:00 pm, but Kenta and/or his parents often schedule them for 5:30 pm, and then they become angry when she refuses to do them.

This disregard for her teaching schedule, she feels, trivializes her work outside the temple, and it shows that her family disregards her professional status as a teacher. Interestingly, Victoria's mother-in-law was a career public-school teacher herself (although she had never taken the head priest license), and yet she seems to be the most unwilling to acknowledge Victoria's status as a teacher and unwilling to make allowances that were likely accorded to her during her own career. One reason for this may be related to common assumptions that *eikaiwa* teaching is not *real* teaching, that therefore Victoria is not really a *real* teacher, and thus she is less deserving of respect.

Victoria's teaching

After the town stopped hiring the more expensive and high-maintenance JET teachers, Victoria began working as a direct hire for the *kyoiku inkai* (education committee) and not for the board of education (see Chapter 6 for a description of her struggles with the board of education). This constitutes her most stable income, and she fills in the time gaps with lessons at local kindergartens and daycare centers. In the afternoons, she holds private small-group lessons in a room at the family mausoleum, which is situated within walking distance of some of the schools. She pieces together her weekly schedule like a 'jigsaw puzzle' to 'maximize [her] earning potential'. In this section, I first discuss the teaching that Victoria does in schools as an ALT and her relationships with her colleagues before examining several issues surrounding her private lessons.

Being an ALT

With 20 years of teaching experience behind her, Victoria is not the 'fresh-off-the-boat *gaijin*' she was when she arrived in 1995 as an ALT. Now she is older and more experienced than many of the teachers she is hired to assist. She is also more familiar with the students and with the local community than many of the Japanese teachers who transfer into the school district from elsewhere. Because of preconceived notions generally held about foreigners and ALTs, an annual negotiation and renegotiation of her teaching position needs to be carried out at the onset of each academic year. There is sometimes a struggle for linguistic, symbolic and actual power, especially with recently transferred teachers who are unaware of Victoria's standing in the community and with those teachers Victoria says suffer from English linguistic and pedagogical inferiority complexes. Drawing upon her pedagogical knowledge and her understanding of the local context, she wishes to be the 'alpha teacher' who controls 85% of the class. She says she doesn't want to 'steam roll them but [she] doesn't want to play second fiddle to someone who can't do their job'.

Nevertheless, at the schools, everyone's official I-Identities are clearly delineated, and Victoria's position as an ALT (as discussed in Chapter 3) places her symbolically and legally on a lower level in terms of status than the classroom teachers. Concurrently, however, everyone's identities are also relational and positional. Through this process of negotiation, some Japanese teachers are unwilling to give Victoria free reign in the classroom, but others are. Her D-Identity as a teacher is enhanced when her suggestions are taken. Sometimes she feels that this occurs because the teachers have confidence in her as a *skilled teacher*, but in other instances she feels they allow her to take charge because they are 'just lazy and happy to sit in the back'.

Victoria has taught at the local elementary schools for years, but since English became a part of the official elementary school curriculum in 2013, she has been repositioned below the Japanese teachers in terms of status, because these teachers are legally obligated to ensure that students complete the official curriculum. However, compared to what Victoria had been teaching, the new curriculum moves at a 'snail's pace' and introduces far fewer language items to the students. Therefore, she must renegotiate the English curriculum with each teacher, trying to get them to 'go outside the box' and at the same time trying to reestablish herself as the 'alpha' teacher. Because Victoria feels that the Ministry of Education, Culture, Sports, Science and Technology (MEXT) has placed damaging restrictions on students' learning, she convinces the teachers to move quickly through the officially approved textbook to free up more time for in-depth teaching of language items as well as for more communicative activities.

During her negotiations with the teachers, she draws upon her teaching expertise and her extensive knowledge of the students in the community as her bargaining chip. When teachers agree with her proposals, the curricular guidelines are followed and students' English skills progress rapidly. However, problems develop after students advance to the next grade, because not only must Victoria negotiate the yearly syllabus with new teachers, she must also 'go backwards' with the same students and 'teach' them what they have already learned in order to follow the prescribed textbook. When the children graduate from elementary school, Victoria meets them again at the junior high just 100 meters away. There, the students take another linguistic step backwards to follow the prescribed junior high school curriculum. All of this, it seems, is a waste of time – time that could be better spent moving forward with English language learning.

One of the strongest attitudes shaping language instruction in Victoria's schools (as well as elsewhere) is the importance attached to classes taught by Japanese teachers. Foreigners, especially those who are ALTs, are often positioned as outsiders and temporary sojourners in Japan, whose primary function is to act as linguistic and cultural representatives (e.g. Browne & Evans, 1994). As discussed throughout this book, long-standing beliefs exist that English suitable for Japanese students must be taught *by* Japanese teachers and *in* Japanese. *Eigo* (English language) classes, taught by Japanese, are accorded greater importance than *eikaiwa* (English conversation) classes taught by foreigners.

This attitude is also evident in a teacher who had recently transferred to one of her schools. She says he is the 'worst teacher' she has ever worked with and complains that he 'can't understand and he can't speak English'. Apparently, he has no interest in working together with her and even refused to meet her prior to their first class. As a result, the first time they met face to face was in front of the students. Then, he attempted to position Victoria as the outsider:

> He said [to the students], 'Shall we get her [Victoria] to do a self-introduction?' The kids looked at me, and I looked at them. And I looked at the teacher. I said, 'The only self-introduction needed is between *you* and *me*. I've known these kids since they were babies.'

According to Victoria, 'things went downhill from there.... There is no team teaching, absolutely no team teaching with him.' He continues to refuse to meet her to discuss class plans and he glowers in the back of the room while she teaches.

Another teacher, who is considered to be a 'super teacher' because of her linguistic and pedagogical skills, positions Victoria in class as a monolingual English-speaking linguistic representative for students, even though Victoria is fluent in Japanese and has been teaching bilingually for years. Victoria believes that that teacher wants to maintain power as the teacher in charge by directly and indirectly positioning her as the *assistant* and not as a knowledgeable teacher. Victoria complains, 'She is a control freak because she doesn't let me do anything.... She always tries to put me in my place, so that I'm lower. Absolutely lower.' The teacher admonishes Victoria for speaking Japanese in the classroom by saying, 'Only English; only English.' She feels the teacher not only fails to acknowledge her instinctive knowledge of what students can and cannot understand because of her years of experience, she also ignores the needs of the students, who may or may not need bilingual assistance.

These two teachers seem to have ascribed to Victoria characteristics commonly associated with ALTs, namely those of being temporary sojourners and foreign outsiders with little or no knowledge of the local context. Whereas the first teacher disassociates himself entirely from her class, the second teacher maintains control over the class by enforcing a projected monolingual English-speaker identity upon Victoria. In other words, neither teacher makes effective use of Victoria's strengths, which is a pity for everyone.

The Japanese teachers Victoria works with must not only reconsider their own preexisting attitudes towards ALTs when they begin working with her; they must also accommodate her other I-Identity as a temple priest, which does, from time to time, interfere with school schedules. The town's *kyoiku inkai* (education committee), which has hired Victoria to teach for the school district, knows and accepts this, but new teachers may be surprised by temple-related disruptions to their class schedules.

At the elementary schools, time changes can be easily accommodated, but at the junior high schools, where different teachers teach different subjects in assigned time slots, this cannot be so easily done. An interesting example of how Victoria's teaching life and her temple life overlap with each other is as follows: last winter, she taught her morning classes at a junior high, changed into her priest robes in the staff bathroom during lunch, performed funeral rites nearby, returned to school, changed back into her work clothes and then taught her afternoon classes.

Private teaching

As shown earlier in Table 8.1, Victoria also teaches group lessons in the afternoon in a room at the family's mausoleum, which is, admittedly, an unusual place for an English conversation school. Some, but not all, of the children are aware of their surroundings. Mourners come and go during lessons to pay respects to the deceased upstairs. When the children express curiosity, she asks them if they want to 'go and have a look' and says the children are all 'Ohhhh!' when she takes them upstairs. She assures them that they (the deceased) are 'not scary or spooky and that we are good company for them. They are just dead. They are not like maggoty and they are just dead.' The children then return to their English games and activities.

The payment method for these English classes is conducted much more casually than the methods described by Louisa and Margaret in the previous chapter. This is because of the likelihood of cancellations, which occur not only because of Victoria's temple responsibilities but also because her classroom space must sometimes be used to hold funerals. As Victoria says, 'I can't teach English next to the dead guy in the room'. Rather than refunding money for untaught lessons, Victoria finds it easier to charge for those that were actually taught.

Unfortunately, this system also works to the parents' advantage and sometimes puts Victoria at financial risk, because students' parents do not feel obligated to pay for lessons that their children do not attend. For example, one group of mothers 'ganged up' and said they would not pay when schools officially close because of influenza outbreaks. During that time, children are required to stay home, but not all schools close. Therefore, some children continue to come to the lessons while others stay at home. Without the classes being fully subscribed, Victoria loses 20,000–30,000 yen per month during flu season.

Although Victoria feels she has no choice but to accept those mothers' demands, she does require payment for classes that are missed for other reasons. Although she maintains some flexibility by considering students' individual economical cases, she remains firm when parents try to make excuses for their child's absences by rationalizing, 'Oh, you know my daughter was sick for so long...', and she tells them, 'You can't negotiate it after the fact.' Parents are 'kind of grumpy after that' but they 'generally pay'.

Although there are few foreigners in Victoria's town and not so many *eikaiwa* teachers, there is some competition from several *juku* (cram schools) that teach academic skills for children to get ahead. Despite her already busy schedule, she decided to open up a language academy in a space at her friend's kindergarten and to teach a few more classes in an attempt to prevent a rival kindergarten, which has just started a *juku* for 6–12-year-olds, from snatching both current and prospective students.

Victoria: In conclusion

Victoria's narratives clearly show how she managed to reshape her ascribed lower-status identities as a temple wife and as an ALT into higher-status achieved identities as a head priest and as an accomplished English language teacher. Her determination not to accept the discursive practices of others, which would have relegated her to subordinate positions, enabled her to create her own identity. Such resourcefulness is not only evident in how she became a head priest but also how she briefly became a bus driver for her son's school's martial arts team.

Victoria's A-Identity is rooted in her insider membership status in the community. As a teacher, her relationships with the students she has been teaching longer than any Japanese teacher have much importance for her. She knows that she is not merely a linguistic representative or a cultural referent for them; she is a part of their lives.

Nonetheless, Victoria says that she would like to have a 'teaching home' that she could be permanently associated with. She would like to rekindle that strong sense of belonging that she had during her second year as an ALT, when she was treated like a member of the faculty (see Chapter 6). A full-time job would provide such an identity for her, but this, she explains, would be impossible under her current circumstances:

> I don't have any 'home' anywhere I can call 'home' you know. An education home I'd like to be a member of staff somewhere, but I can't. I can't work full time because of the – you know – dead bodies popping up (laughs) I just balance and balance. I'm like a jigsaw puzzle, each day is a jigsaw puzzle of slots....It's juggling in the extreme.

Lisa: A 30-Lesson-a-Week Teacher

The next participant discussed in this chapter is Lisa, who also lives and teaches in a rural area where there are few foreigners but which is up north in Fukushima Prefecture. Instead of having a large family network like Victoria, Lisa struggles as a single mother. To make ends meet, she works every day, and she pieces together a schedule that includes about 30 lessons per week in an *eikaiwa* school, daycare centers and kindergartens, a private high school, a technical college, and several private lessons. Lisa's weekly schedule is shown in Table 8.2.

Lisa's stable income comes from the private high school and the technical college, which she supplements by teaching at four different daycare centers/kindergartens and at an *eikaiwa* school. She takes on private students not so much as to increase her income but to help someone who is struggling with English.

She is chronically exhausted but says cheerfully, 'My schedule is very doable because I don't have to prepare a nice supper for my [ex] husband and my kids aren't picky and they help out.' Examination week, however, is particularly exhausting with 'a couple of sleepless nights' because she marks papers well into the night. She cannot do this work on campus like most of the other teachers because she must leave campus immediately after school to head for her afternoon classes. Unlike her married foreign male counterpart, who 'doesn't have to worry about making dinner and doesn't have to do laundry during test corrections', Lisa must tend to her children during exam periods as well.

Table 8.2 Lisa's weekly schedule

	Morning	*Afternoon*	*Evening*
Monday	Tech college	Technical college Daycare center until 4:30	
Tuesday	High school	High school (till 3:30) Daycare center till 5:00	
Wednesday	High school	High school (till 2:30) Daycare center 3:30–5:30	
Thursday	High school	High school (till 5:00)	Private lessons
Friday	High school	High school (till 3:30) *Eikaiwa* school (4:30–7:00)	
Saturday	*Eikaiwa* school (9:30–12:30)		
Sunday		Private lessons	

Teaching in the aftermath of the earthquake

It is impossible to tell Lisa's story without discussing the impact that the Great Tohoku Earthquake and the consequent tsunami and nuclear disaster has had on Lisa's personal and professional life. As mentioned in Chapter 6, Lisa experienced the 1995 Hanshin Earthquake in Kobe, but the disruption from that earthquake was minor (even though her apartment building had become unlivable) compared to the aftermath of the earthquake that took place on March 11, 2011. After the 1995 earthquake, she said she 'just cleaned up the stuff and moved. Life went on'. But she says, 'for the people that had to be evacuated [because of the tsunami or the nuclear disaster], their lives are not going on'. Lisa was luckier than many others in her area; even though she had no electricity or water for several days following the earthquake, and even though there was extensive breakage of all her crockery and damage to her appliances, her family was safe and her home remained structurally sound.

For this research, I interviewed Lisa over a period of two days in the summer of 2013, which was more than two years after the earthquake. As we drove through her area, she pointed out parking lot after parking lot and described the structures that used to stand on them. We visited parks and playgrounds that were empty of children. Instead, they contained notice boards with the day's radiation levels displayed on them.

Many of Lisa's friends moved away after the earthquake, but she is obligated to stay, not only because this is where she earns her living and where she has put down roots, but also because her divorce agreement with her ex-husband prohibits her from taking the children out of the area. For Lisa and those who have remained, life has irrevocably changed. The town is surrounded by rice paddies and lush vegetable fields, but only the elderly, the brave or the ignorant dare to consume their contaminated produce. Bottled water must be used for drinking and cooking, and Lisa 'no longer plans a recipe' but decides what to cook after seeing what vegetables from distant cities are available that day at the supermarket.

The way of bringing up children in the area has also changed. For example, after the earthquake, her sons, like all children in that area, were only allowed to go outside for 15 minutes a day, and they had to give up playing baseball until an 'empty-ish factory', donated to the city by a wealthy owner who financed its conversion into an indoor playing field, was completed. For now, the problem of radiation has been eased somewhat, but she is concerned for all the local children's futures, and says, 'One of the saddest things is that nobody is going to want to marry the kids that grew up here' because of the potential health problems caused by radiation.

Despite the permanent changes the earthquake has had on her life, Lisa says she does not think about it constantly, but it 'blip[s] in and out [of her head] at least several times a day', and these thoughts now guide her teaching methods and how she interacts with her students. She no longer covers serious topics in her high-school and university classes, because she feels her students' lives have become serious enough. She explains,

> I have to be really careful what I say to students. Like I don't want to talk about death in any shape or form any time. I don't want to talk about painful things. I don't want to talk about the future in certain ways, because I don't know how hard the students have been hit. Losing family members. Even in [her city] there was some death. But some of my students are from other areas now [mostly evacuees from the coastal areas], so I tread very lightly in the way I speak, and there are topics I don't approach any more. They have enough pain in their lives. I want them to be happy in my class. I don't cover some critical issues. Maybe I am a bit more sugar coated.

Lisa censors her dialog and avoids seemingly simple conversational topics such as 'vacations' or 'families', which could cause painful feelings. She no longer asks students if they plan to return to their hometowns for the holidays, because some students no longer have hometowns to go to. She no longer asks if they are going to visit 'Grandma' because Grandma might have died in the tsunami. She is also less strict with poorly behaved students than before, believing that their poor behavior might be due to posttraumatic stress disorder. *Because of these issues* that seem so bleak, however, Lisa is even 'more motivated than ever before to give them new skills for the challenges that will be facing them'.

The disaster has also influenced the way that Lisa teaches at the daycare centers and kindergartens, and it makes her determined not to quit these jobs even though they are so physically demanding. She puts her energy into these afternoon lessons to help alleviate the children's stress. They are not allowed to play outdoors any more, making them the 'chunkiest' kids in Japan. Lisa feels that daycare centers and the parents have 'only so many tricks up their sleeves' to occupy children, so they allow them to watch more TV and to play more video games than before. Lisa hopes that the hour they spend with her in energetic English lessons will provide some relief for the children, for the daycare teachers and for the parents:

I want them to have so much fun in my one hour that they wouldn't even want to go outside and play. The little guys – I think the five and six year olds – they remember going outside, but by now they are conditioned to know that they can't. The littlest guys have never been able to go outside. Kind of like city kids that know how to play indoors or something. But little kids get stressed out. And I want to be a bright spot and have them run around and have fun singing and dancing and enjoy that hour. And that will make the rest of their day a little easier and they won't be so hyper when they go home. And so mom and dad will have an easier time that evening because they [the children] got to hop and skip and crawl in my class.

The 11 March disaster had an impact on Lisa's livelihood as well, because as a part-time teacher, she is paid only for the classes she teaches. Since many of her classes were cancelled for weeks and some children's classes disappeared entirely, it took a year for her to recover financially. Luckily, she managed to survive without reaching into her 'nest egg' this time, but she fears she would be unable to survive 'another financial hit like that'.

High-school Teaching

The private high school where Lisa teaches 17 classes per week provides her with her most stable income. Being affiliated with this prestigious and well-known school enables her to claim an I-Identity as a teacher at that school, even though as a part-time teacher she receives no social welfare benefits. Nevertheless, she is not an ALT and she is in control of own classes. Furthermore, her contract has no term restrictions, and she believes that the school will continue to employ her as long as it is financially able to do so. She has been teaching there for more than ten years, and she feels respected for the way that she gets along with her colleagues, for the way that she teaches the students and, most importantly, for her struggles as a single mother.

Because of recent budgetary cutbacks, the school reduced her foreign male counterpart's teaching load by two classes, but hers remained the same. Feeling guilty, she offered him one of her classes, hoping that he would have done the same for her had the situation been reversed. Even though this gesture decreased her own monthly income, she explained, 'I couldn't have the desk next to him and do that [have more classes/money]. I couldn't do it. I couldn't do it.' The school's decision to cut back his classes and not hers, however, supports her belief that it sees her as the more valuable teacher. She believes,

> If push comes to shove, they would choose me over him.... His intellectual skills are higher than mine, but my disciplinary skills are better. I play nicer than he does. I'm easier to get along with. Whenever they need to tell him something they come to me and 'can you tell him?'... I think that is why they purposely cut his two classes. They respect me more and they know I'm a single mom. They didn't want to cut my schedule.

Despite the struggles brought by the earthquake and its aftermath, Lisa is an optimistic person and she enjoys her teaching, which she feels provides valuable knowledge for students. The effort she puts into her classes pays off:

> I never ever dread getting up in the morning to go to work. I love my students and I love my job when the bell rings, I have to teach and there are 42 eyes looking at me. I like the challenge. You see it in front of your eyes. You plant the seeds and you water and water and you weed and you weed. And at the end of the school year when they say something unprovoked – they say something to me of their own accord in English with their own creativity – it's...you know, it's better than fresh tomatoes. And that's saying a lot because I love fresh tomatoes. It's like gardening.

The daycare centers/kindergartens

Lisa's students at the daycare centers and kindergartens generally range in age from babies to three- and four-year-olds, but during school holidays older children who are in daycare attend her classes as well. Children participate freely in the classes, in which Lisa teaches through songs, dances, stories, games and crafts. The youngest take part 'as soon as they can crawl over to me if they are interested', but she tries to use the last 15 minutes of a session to 'teach' the older children. It's not easy holding a class with a wide range of students, but she measures her classes' success by the following:

> I know a class is successful if the children are drooling. If they are drooling that means they are interested. And if someone peed in their pants that means I did a perfect lesson because that means they didn't want to go to the bathroom (laughs).

Private lessons

Lisa does not usually like to teach individual private English lessons, but she occasionally makes exceptions. She does not teach these classes 'for the money', but because she wants to make a difference in someone's life. She says,

> Anybody who can make it to a regular school, go to a regular school, I don't want to teach you. But I do take people in under my wings for special reasons. My Sunday afternoon student is a special case for budget reasons. I charge beer.

Although additional income from private lessons would certainly be welcome, her most recent student is a junior-high-school girl who had been having trouble keeping up with English at school. After the mother approached Lisa with her concerns, Lisa realized that, without some intervention, the girl could fall through the educational cracks. She began tutoring her and, knowing of the family's financial struggles, asked for payment in the form of a weekly 'six-pack of her favorite beer', which coincidentally, she laughs, is the 'cheapest beer on the market'.

Lisa: In conclusion

Clearly Lisa has aligned herself deeply with the community in which she has mainly lived in since arriving in Japan in 1989, providing her with an A-Identity that influences both her professional and her private life. She is an insider not only because of her long-term residency but also because she shares solidarity with those who survived, remained and continue to struggle in the aftermath of the 11 March earthquake. Outside of taking her previously planned two-week trip to the United States during her spring vacation in 2011, she has remained in town and, side by side with other parents, weeded and tended to the school grounds that had become contaminated by radiation. As an insider, she also feels empathy toward her students and their families who may have suffered great personal loss. This is reflected in her teaching at the high school and technical college where she teaches academic English and at the kindergartens and the daycare centers where she teaches English through rambunctious play. As a non-Japanese person (her N-Identity), she could have chosen to leave the area rather than stay to help rebuild, but she decided to stay, and this has also given her great respect in the community.

In addition, Lisa's other N-Identity as a woman, particularly a single mother, has shaped the discursive practices of those around her. As discussed throughout this book, women in Japan are viewed primarily as wives and mothers (e.g. Liddle & Nakajima, 2000), but there is also great respect for those who struggle with these ascribed identities. Lisa, a divorced single mother, feels this respect from her employers and colleagues because they 'know [her] situation', and she believes that they will look out for her. An example of this was mentioned earlier when budgetary cutbacks within the high school resulted in a reduction of her foreign male colleague's classes but not hers. She surmised that the reason why this happened was partly because they believe her to be the better teacher, but also because they believe that she needed the income from those classes more than he did.

Lisa also feels respected by her colleagues for her struggles, and this respect is manifested in concrete ways. For example, she needed to bring her son with her to school one day when he was too small to remain at home alone. She 'stashed him in the girls' locker room – a *tatami* room' [Japanese style room with straw mats on the floor] and checked on him periodically. The other teachers knew he was there, and when a male colleague discovered that her son had wet his pants because he did not know where the toilet was, he went to the store to buy him a clean pair of pants. Lisa says that it is 'the little things like that – people working together and respecting each other' that make it easy for her to align herself with her workplace and with her colleagues.

Unfortunately, however, because of her hectic schedule, Lisa has been unable to establish workplace friendships – although she has friendly relationships with colleagues – and she has little time to spend with friends. Her closest Japanese friend is a *'sempai* [older and more experienced person] in the divorced world' who has been a 'source of strength' and with whom she can have 'heart-to-heart' talks. Although she cannot spend as much time as she likes with her, she knows that that friend is there.

Lisa is also a member of the Association of Foreign Wives of Japanese (AFWJ), even though she is divorced and her daily life seems far removed from other members of the association, who generally live far away. She maintains her membership in the group because of the sense of community it provides. She says,

> Just knowing that people are in the same boat [having a Japanese husband and/or living in Japan], just knowing that, makes me feel so much better. Not isolated. I know that I could say, 'OK. I'm coming to Tokyo, I need to meet anybody at Starbucks. Who is available?' And someone would come to meet me. Just knowing that is wonderful.

Lisa works hard and provides a good life for herself and her children. However, unlike the other women in this study who are married, she has no second income to fall back on during tough times. Unlike Sarah (the other divorced woman in this study, who will be discussed in greater detail in Chapter 9), she has not obtained a permanent and secure job. In other words, Lisa's career is dependent upon the local economy and upon the demand for English teachers. Nevertheless, as the following comment shows, she believes that her insider position within the community will help her survive no matter what happens.

> I'm the go-to person, one of the go-to people, and I can pick and choose the best jobs. So I have gotten my fingers in a lot of pots, and the more pots you have your fingers in, the more connections you can make. And if one door closes, another door – you can find something someplace else.

Understandably, she worries about her short-term and her long-term financial future. Her loss of income during the year of the earthquake made her realize that she is walking precariously on a financial tightrope and that she has insufficient savings for any long-term setback. Now, she hopes to increase her immediate income to offset her sons' impending educational costs.

She not only worries about the English teaching market drying up but also about whether or not she will be able to keep up with the physical demands of teaching as she ages, particularly with the children's classes. She says, 'I'm going to have to keep working at something to supplement my pension [that she predicts to be 60,000 yen per month] because there's no way I'll be able to survive on that. It's scary.' Nevertheless, Lisa is optimistic that she can manage by ultimately moving into low-rent housing, by teaching a few classes and possibly by taking on translation work.

Louisa: From *Eikaiwa* School Owner to University Lecturer

The last participant discussed in this chapter is Louisa, whose *eikaiwa* school operations were analyzed in the previous chapter. Although Louisa made a decent living from her school, she began to feel that she was 'in a rut' and she disliked staying home all the time. Her children were growing up and she no longer needed to be at home for them. She looked into becoming an IELTS (International English Language Testing

System) examiner after a friend told her the money was good. However, her application was rejected because she did not have an advanced degree or a certificate related to teaching English as a second language (TESOL). Her years of teaching experience and her efforts in keeping up with the latest developments in English as a foreign language (EFL) by reading methodology books and teachers' manuals did not count. This section focuses on how she remedied that situation and started a new career after the age of 50.

Developing a new professional identity

The first step that Louisa took was to go back to school. It had always 'bothered' her that she did not have a graduate degree like her siblings in the United States. As an *eikaiwa* teacher, an advanced degree was unnecessary, but after she began to want to quit her home business, she found that without one, the plum jobs would be beyond her reach. She first considered attending graduate school, but she realized that the cost and the effort of obtaining an MA at her age might not pay off, especially if she would have had to close down her school to study for one.

Then she looked into the Certificate in English Language Teaching to Adults (CELTA), which she said had not been around when she began teaching in Japan. 'It came into existence in the early 90s for all the upstarts [newly arrived language teachers] (laughs)'. After considering various options, she decided to do a one-month intensive CELTA certificate course in Thailand during August 2012 when her school was closed for the holidays. Despite her initial hesitations about studying in a third-world country, she found that the program was actually excellent, with strict quality guidelines. She explained, '[N]o matter where you get the CELTA [in Canada or Australia], it's the same thing.' While doing the course, she had 'so much fun' studying with the other students and enjoying a holiday because she did not have 'to worry about laundry or food or children or driving people here or there. It was just wonderful!'

Becoming a proficiency examiner

To fulfill the postcertificate teaching requirements of the CELTA, Louisa needed to teach at a school for a year after completing the course, so she taught a few part-time classes at a private high school. In October 2012, after some in-house training, she became an oral examiner for the Business Language Testing Service (BULATS), which involves visiting companies and conducting 12-minute interviews with examinees to determine the level of their English proficiency. She enthuses, 'getting the CELTA was the best thing' because it enabled her to make this professional change:

> It [BULATS testing] pays very well and it has gotten me out of the house and going into various corporations around Tokyo. Back into heels and I feel like an adult! I feel like I have a high paying job. It's like you walk in there in your suit – I had to buy a suit! I didn't own a suit! I bought a suit last November and walk in, and you know – you get this ID card and I'm beeping in and using all these high security areas, and had to beep to get out of the room to go to the toilet and beep to get back in. It's all very interesting. A big difference from teaching in my kitchen and I really, really loved it. It was fun getting out and I still enjoy it!

Not only was Louisa enjoying this new professional lifestyle, she was making good money that was relatively 'hassle free'. When she realized she had potential to earn more from BULATS, she resented having to turn down assignments due to her teaching commitments at home. She reduced the number of classes and consolidated them into two days to free up blocks of time in case she would be called for testing. She became fed up with her home business, but she still needed its steady income.

Teaching in tertiary education

The opportunity to teach at a university came, like it does for so many others, via a personal connection. A friend from AFWJ told her that 'University A' was looking for someone to teach basic English to nursing students. Apparently, the previous Japanese teacher's classes had 'been really boring'. The university wanted their students to have a pleasant, but not overly taxing, oral communication course. They believed that someone with experience in teaching children would be able to provide such a course and that an MA was unnecessary. Louisa was apprehensive about her chances of being hired, but halfway through the interview, when they began telling her, 'This is where you put your bags. This is where you check in,' she realized that she had been hired.

Her first semester at the university was challenging. Although she had been keeping abreast of the EFL field through reading pedagogical materials, and the CELTA had provided her with the confidence to teach large classes, it was nonetheless necessary for her to adapt to an entirely new educational system. At first, she was consumed with class preparation. The school requested her and the other foreign teacher (who had been hired at the same time) not to use a textbook. They developed a syllabus to use with the students, whom they had divided into two groups. First, Louisa made detailed keynote presentations for each class so that she would not have to spend time writing on the blackboard. Second, she spent much time evaluating students:

> I had them do assignments, little tests. I had them turn stuff in. I videotaped all the assessments, but rather than grading on the spot – I was afraid I [might] miss stuff, so I could replay and replay and if I asked them to repeat something during the conversation. There were certain things they were required to do in their speaking assessment, and to make sure that they did it, I taped it all. I went back and watched it. It took a lot of time.

By the summer of 2013, Louisa had quit teaching children entirely. Her second semester at the university was easier because she had 'ironed out the kinks', keeping what worked well and eliminating what did not.

With her foot in the university door, Louisa was hired to teach at 'University B' in April 2014. Although that university generally requires its teachers to hold an MA, there were no other applicants for that position. Once again, she realized halfway through her interview that 'it [being hired] was basically a done deal'. That was when she quit all of her *eikaiwa* classes and deregistered her business.

That year, she taught at the two universities on Wednesdays, Thursdays and Fridays and kept Mondays and Tuesdays open for BULATS testing. University B has a more rigorous academic program than the nursing college, which made her 'feel like [she's] at a *real* school now. Because the other school isn't really a university. It is really more of a *semmon gakko* [technical college]. This [the new school] is a *university.*'

Understanding the hierarchy of university teaching

As discussed in Chapter 3, there are many advantages to teaching in universities, including a stable income, paid holidays and greater prestige. As also discussed, there is a hierarchy within the university system that influences those who work in that context. Louisa is, of course, very excited to be a part of this world, but at the same time, its hierarchy is becoming more apparent to her. She is beginning to see how she is positioned as a part-time teacher in relation to full-timers. In both schools, she experiences an '"Oh, you are a *hijokin* [part-time teacher]" kind of comment' that puts her in her place and makes her 'fully aware that [she is] at the bottom of the totem pole'. These comments range from offhanded remarks about salaries or other perks received to the different regulations for part-time and full-time teachers. For example, one school strictly limits the number of photocopies part-time teachers are allowed to make, and the other has separate photocopiers of unequal quality for the two groups of teachers to use. Only full-timers may use the 'huge, brand-new state of the art photocopier, but part-time employees are relegated to the printer-type *insatsu-ki* (a more economical type of copier) machine' which, according to Louisa, produces poor quality handouts and is prone to breaking down.

In both schools' there is a separate lounge for part-time and full-time teachers, again with different (and better) facilities, even though full-time teachers have private offices as well. At the larger University B, full-time teachers have practical perks that make their daily lives easier, such as being able to purchase cafeteria coupons enabling them to sidestep the student line during lunch hour. Louisa asked if she could purchase those coupons but was told they were *only* for full-timers.

Although these examples might seem insignificant, they represent a myriad of factors shaping the lives of part-time teachers as permanent peripheral members of the community of practice (Wenger, 1998) of university teachers in Japan. Louisa has noticed these concrete smaller discrepancies of not having the same access to facilities as in her first year, but as discussed in Chapter 3, the larger discrepancies between these positions may become more apparent to her later.

Finding her own way as a university teacher

Another interesting theme from Louisa's narrative concerns her positioning among those teachers who have had greater experience teaching Japanese university students. It is true that Louisa is a newbie in this world, but she is not an inexperienced teacher. Yet, people are quick to point out to her the huge gap between small-group teaching and university teaching. Other teachers have told her that the students 'are this way or that way', but Louisa did not appreciate hearing this and explained, 'I'm a new teacher. I don't have any preconceived ideas. I want to try! Let me get discouraged a few years down the line! (laughs).' She wanted to make her own judgments concerning students, and she wanted to put her own ideas to work.

Attitudes that students are not entirely capable English language learners may also be behind University A's decision to replace the Japanese teacher (who presumably focused on traditional means of language instruction) they had with one who had had experience *teaching children*. The nursing students are, of course, not children, but the school did not want to tax their students with language study so that they would be better able to concentrate on classes related to their majors. It seems that, more than anything else, the English classes are supposed provide a pleasant interlude for the students. Yet, as mentioned earlier, Louisa began teaching with enthusiasm and spent many hours preparing for class and evaluating students. She also engaged in weekly self-evaluations by keeping track of every activity she carried out, which has enabled her to create an ongoing system that seems to be working for her.

Teachers at University B also informed Louisa that she should not be overly optimistic about the students' abilities. However, Louisa has found that 'none of the stuff that was told to me about the students is coming true'. By following the pedagogical methods outlined in a textbook called *Marathon Mouth* (2011), she created a class that was in direct contrast to what she had been warned about: No students sleep in her class, hands are raised to answer questions and students voluntarily do their homework. She describes a part of a typical class:

> I ask a question, 'OK, who can tell me... you know... "A", "B", or "C"?' And ten hands go up in class. Kids are like, 'Me! Me! Me!' Actually, I told them to say that [Me! Me!]. At first they were 'Hai!' 'Hai!' 'Hai!' [Yes! Yes! Yes!] Well, I tell them, in the states little kids say 'Me! Me! Me!' (laughs). Anyway, it's been really great.

She is very pleased that her classes have been highly evaluated by her students in the end-of-semester surveys. This is understandably a great source of pride for her, and it gives her greater confidence in herself as a teacher.

Louisa has also become more involved with professional development activities, and she has recently attended and presented at language teachers' conferences. Importantly, she has become involved in the revision of a popular conversation book that she enjoys using and its accompanying teachers' manual. Working together with the author and publisher, she is helping to design communicative activities to bridge the two books with a mid-level book. Louisa is making some smart moves as a part-time teacher without an MA. She is establishing herself as a teacher in her field in concrete ways that will enhance her résumé and open up further university doors. It is unlikely that Louisa will obtain a full-time job, but she does not particularly want one. Instead, she is establishing herself as a competent university teacher, who, with her increasing experience and professional connections, will probably be able to become selective in choosing where she teaches.

Differences in running an *eikaiwa* school and being a part of larger organizations

Unlike when she was operating her *eikaiwa* business, where she was in charge of everything, Louisa now is a part of several large educational organizations, each with various rules and methods of operation, some of which are difficult for her to comprehend. For example, in her first semester at University B, she taught extra classes for several months to cover for a teacher who was on sick leave. Instead of receiving monthly pay for those classes, she received a lump sum at the end, putting her into a higher tax bracket. The take-home pay thus reflected one month's worth of teaching rather than three. After complaining to the university's accounting office, she was told she would be eligible for a tax refund at the end of the fiscal year, but the reasons as to why remuneration was carried out in this manner were not offered.

She also had difficulty understanding the regulations concerning travel allowances. Louisa commutes to both universities by car, which enables her to carry all her teaching materials with her and to comfortably wear 'a suit and heels' for the professional image she is trying to create. The allowance for train travel at University B is significant, with some teachers commuting from as far away as Tokyo. However, the university's allowance for those driving to work is far less, and in fact, Louisa found that what she received was actually insufficient to cover gas and toll fees. It seems somewhat unfair that if she had received full coverage for driving, it would have still been less than had she been commuting by train from Tokyo.

Louisa is finding that the administrative cultures of her two universities are somewhat complicated to navigate, but she feels she has good rapport with the administrative staff, which actually can go a long way in creating a good reputation at a school. Her proficiency in Japanese means she can submit necessary paperwork by the deadlines and she does not need to be 'coddled' like teachers who cannot speak Japanese. Week by week, her confidence grows, and she admits, 'I feel like I've been able to smoothly just kind of get into their system.'

You can't go back

Louisa had invested much of the past 20 years of her life in her *eikaiwa* school, and as discussed in the previous chapter, some friendly relationships had developed over time. Although Louisa had closed down her school entirely, a group of women who had studied with her for 18 years had contacted her and asked if she would teach them again. She agreed, saying that she 'kind of missed them', but only in a casual, friendly and unofficial way.

The plan was to be this: students would pay for the lessons in cash on a lesson-by-lesson basis (enabling Louisa to cancel freely if something else came up). Now that her family was using her classroom for private purposes, the lessons would be held in a *karaoke box* (a private room rented by the hour where friends usually gather to sing *karaoke*) next to the gym they all belong to. It seemed like an ideal place to meet, chat, drink coffee and go their respective ways at the end of the hour.

Unfortunately, 'That first lesson after the nine month break at the karaoke place was a disaster,' and Louisa thought to herself, 'Oh crap! Why did I decide to do this again?' The students 'obviously felt the same' because they called before the second lesson (which was going to be held at a McCafé since the *karaoke* box did not work well) saying they had decided against any further lessons. Although she had enjoyed seeing the women that she had known for many years, she was 'not sad' when those lessons had definitely come to an end. She had physically and emotionally moved away from private teaching entirely. Furthermore, more doors in the university world were opening up anyway. From April 2015, Louisa took on more classes when she was hired at 'University C'.

Louisa: In conclusion

In Chapter 7, we saw how Louisa's I-identity was rooted in her professionally operated *eikaiwa* school. She had become tired of working from home, and a decrease in the number of students had resulted in a decline in income. She discovered that without an advanced degree, however, making upward changes would be difficult. With the support and encouragement of her family, she obtained official recognition as an English teacher in the form of the CELTA certificate. This provided entry into tertiary education and enabled her to expand her I-Identity into that of a university teacher.

We can also see how the discursive practices of others have influenced this developing I-Identity. University A wanted their students to have an easier time in their English classes and purposely looked for someone with experience in teaching children, indicating popular beliefs that *eikaiwa* taught by foreign teachers is fun and easy, while *eigo* taught by Japanese teachers is hard and stressful. Those beliefs, however, opened that first door for Louisa, which subsequently opened the doors to Universities B and C.

We can see how attempts had been made to shape Louisa's forming A-Identity as a university teacher through the stories of the old-timers, which (according to Wenger, 1998) are often a means to create solidarity and unity within a community. The purpose of these stories on the one hand was to 'warn' her about the students but also, on the other, to bring her into their group in a sort of apprenticeship position. Nonetheless, she resisted adopting those teachers' discourse concerning student ability as her own and created a new D-Identity as a teacher who was able to turn the tables, so to speak, in the classroom. This identity is reinforced through the students' enthusiastic behavior in the classroom and by their positive evaluations at the end of the semester.

Louisa's identity as a university teacher continues to develop through imagination and alignment with the community of practice (Wenger, 1998) of university teachers in Japan. As a part-time teacher, she is on a permanent peripheral trajectory where although she *is* a member of the universities she works for, she will never be a full participating member. Her A-Identity at these institutions is somewhat weak. While she may not fully align herself with them, she continues to strengthen her I- and D-Identities as a university English teacher. With only one year of experience in this new world, her identity development (as it is for everyone) is a work in progress.

With more than 30 years of teaching experience, Louisa has taught in nearly every type of EFL context in Japan: as a Mombusho English Fellow (MEF), a high-school classroom teacher, a private *eikaiwa* instructor in her own home, an *eikaiwa* school teacher, an *eikaiwa* school owner and a university teacher. She has also engaged in nonteaching work as well, such as translation work and language proficiency testing.

Louisa's weekly schedule is now fully booked. At the onset of the academic year in 2015, she had 10 university classes and taught four days per week. Her weekends are consumed by class preparations. Her daily schedule is not as hectic as those of Victoria and Lisa because she does not move to multiple sites within one day. Louisa has developed a schedule that is manageable and comfortable for her with the maximum rewards in terms of time, effort and money.

Summary of Chapter 8

In this chapter, I have described the personal and professional lives of Victoria, Lisa and Louisa. These women are extremely resourceful and focused. They juggle their careers by stringing together various types of jobs that fit their lives. Victoria, as we saw, juggles multiple roles as a Buddhist priest, English language teacher and even a bus driver. Living in a conservative area of Japan like she does, it would be easy to become swallowed up by the larger and demanding personalities of her husband's family. With great resourcefulness, she resisted having I-Identities ascribed upon her and, through a series of smart steps, she has made an independent professional life for herself, one that is, for the most part, quite comfortable.

Lisa struggles to support herself and her two children by teaching nearly 30 lessons per week, and yet she feels optimistic and enthusiastic about the work she does. Other teachers might experience burnout from such a hectic and physically demanding schedule, but Lisa knows she cannot afford to do this. She carries on, and she feels respected within the community because of how hard she works. She also feels that the work she does benefits her local community, especially as it recovers from and adjusts to the aftermath of the disasters of 11 March. Because of her insider position, she can emphasize with students and teach accordingly. Being appreciated as an important hardworking member of the community is one way to sustain and maintain such a grueling schedule – making her life so much more than just *earning* a living. It *is* living the life that she has to the fullest.

Louisa has been very successful at reinventing her career as a teacher in Japan multiple times. Unlike Victoria and Lisa, however, she lives in the Kanto area (the areas surrounding Tokyo), where numerous opportunities for teachers exist within commuting distance. It is likely that over the next dozen years, Louisa's schedule will shift and there will be changes in where and when she teaches as well as shifts in her BULATS examination schedule.

These three women's stories have illustrated much resourcefulness and resilience in creating, developing and maintaining a self-managed English teaching career in Japan. They experience much more freedom than they would have had they worked for one institution for a monthly salary, but at the same time, they need to be vigilant as to changing trends and local developments, especially since their income is dependent upon factors that are often beyond their control.

9 The Full Timers

Introduction

In this final analytical chapter of the book, I describe three participants who are or who have been employed full time and who have developed a strong sense of belonging to their workplaces: Andrea, Annie and Sarah. All three of these women's alignment toward their workplaces differs because of the responsibilities they have been given, their feelings of acceptance and their relationships with their colleagues.

In this chapter, I am mainly looking at *how* these women fit in at their workplaces. To do that, I examine the participants' narratives in this chapter by using Wenger's (1998) theory of identity (see Chapter 5) in addition to that of Gee (2000) used in Chapters 8 and 9. Wenger's theory of identity was described in detail in Chapter 5, but a brief recount of it follows.

Wenger (1998) says that identity evolves through the day-to-day experiences of participation of groups called communities of practices (CoPs); that the degree to which members can identify with their groups develops through a dual process of *identification* and *negotiation*; and that this process includes three modes of belonging: *engagement, imagination* and *alignment*. Identity formed under engagement involves 'doing' things that are typical and accepted for that community (which is similar to Gee's I-Identity). Imagination is people's internal picture of their role within a community and can range from marginalization to affinity (which is similar to Gee's D-Identity), while alignment, related to power, determines the degree of allegiance given toward a community (which is similar to Gee's A-Identity). Wenger also argues that the trajectories on which people are placed also shape how they identify as members of their group. These trajectories are *peripheral trajectories*, where people will not have full participation; *inbound trajectories*, where newcomers may eventually have full participation; *insider trajectories*, where full members negotiate their identities; *boundary trajectories*, where members of one CoP are linked to another CoP; and *outbound trajectories*, where members leave one CoP for another. As we shall see from Andrea, Annie and Sarah's narratives, these trajectories have influenced their identification within their communities.

Andrea: From Public High School to Private University Lecturer

The first participant discussed in this chapter is Andrea, who taught for 11 years at the public high school in Chiba she had attended as a high-school exchange student. She joined Central City High School (CCHS) (a pseudonym) in 2003 after having only one year of EFL employment at an *eikaiwa* school. She felt welcomed there despite her relative inexperience. Through trial and error, she helped create and coordinate communicative courses with her foreign and Japanese colleagues. She was proud to be *the* native teacher behind the Intercultural Course (IC) program, which was well known throughout the city, and she was thought of as a competent and popular English teacher who 'organized and managed everything.... and they [colleagues] were quite respectful'.

When she left for a year-long maternity leave in 2007, Andrea's colleagues worried how they would cope when she was gone, and they gave her such a hearty welcome upon her return that she felt that this job was 'her calling in life'. Unfortunately, she found that it was not easy balancing housework, childcare and a full-time job. Andrea also began to feel that a newly hired foreign male teacher ('Mike') was vying for her position, which was permanent and not related to the availability of grant monies like the other foreign teachers' positions were. Her fears increased when she unexpectedly became pregnant again. Distraught, she concealed her pregnancy at first and when she finally revealed it to the head of the English department, she cried and begged her not to let Mike take over while she was gone. Despite being reassured that her position as the IC teacher was secure, Andrea nonetheless felt uneasy during her second maternity leave.

She was not met with the same enthusiasm when returning to work the second time. She felt that eyes were on her and that people were wondering how she could 'take care of children while working'. She also realized that her earlier fears concerning Mike were not unfounded. While away, a powerful Japanese teacher named 'Jiro' 'took him under his wing' and had asked him to be his assistant teacher for his students going through the IC course. For Andrea, that was a sharp blow:

> That's MY job [points to her chest]. I'M supposed to do that. That is what I DO. For every teacher in the IC [voice becomes tearful]. Up until that point that is what I did. All of a sudden, Mike was doing it for him. And I thought maybe it is just a one-time thing you know, but I felt like all of a sudden my job was being dissipated.

Work that had previously fallen under Andrea's domain was now being turned over to Mike, and she was told:

> You can do this and this, but you can't do that, because that's Mike's thing.... It was like, well, you're no longer going to just do the IC. You have to do other stuff, too.... At first it was very difficult for me to let that go. I really took a lot of pride in what I did. And then it was kind of slowly taken away from me.

A final blow was the elimination of a popular drama course that Andrea had developed. Third-year students engaged in dramatic activities throughout the semester and then performed for other students and faculty. Although all of the students looked forward to the class, Jiro had decided it was frivolous and replaced it with a discussion course with 'serious topics [finger quotes]' to be taught by Mike.

Going to Graduate School

Andrea realized that despite her long history with the school, she could no longer maintain her insider status. Many of the teachers who knew her from before had been transferred out, and incoming teachers only saw her as 'just one of the foreign teachers'. Losing her earlier identity as an alumni and as the teacher who helped develop the IC program, she attempted to create a new one based upon pedagogical and linguistic knowledge by going to graduate school. She believed an MA would protect and raise her status at the school, but when she and another foreign female teacher ('Mary') announced their acceptance into graduate school at a faculty party, they were was met with 'stunned silence', followed by 'heckling' from Jiro and Mike, who jeered,

> How are you going to manage grad school and coach the debate team next year? You're not going to be able to handle both! You have to work, you can't study all the time! You have to actually work and stuff!

Feeling disheartened by their colleagues' lack of enthusiasm for what they had felt to be exciting news, Andrea and Mary left the party early. Later, Andrea was informed by another foreign male colleague that after leaving the party that night, Jiro and Mike drunkenly mocked them by saying, 'Those fucking bitches, who do they think they are?'

Negative attitudes attached to their graduate-school attendance continued. Just one month after starting graduate school, Andrea learned that the vice principal had been investigating complaints that had been lodged against her. After questioning the head of the English department as to why, she discovered that the complaints were trivial, but he warned her that some teachers who were 'really upset' were scrutinizing her behavior. He advised her,

> In order to not make them upset, you should never talk about graduate school while you are at work and you should NEVER work on anything related to graduate school while you are at your desk. You should keep it very quiet... If you want to talk about it with Mary you should leave the room or talk about it after work, because you don't want to upset them.

She followed her department head's advice, even though she felt it to be unfair that she and Mary were prohibited to study at their desks during free periods but other teachers, particularly Mike and Jiro, could use that time to gossip and talk about trivial matters, such as sports, instead.

Deciding to leave

Although Andrea had always understood that she was hired and worked under different conditions from Japanese teachers (see Chapter 3), limitations and regulations for foreign teachers at her school were becoming increasingly stringent. They were no longer allowed to travel with students on day excursions outside of the city, and the number of nonteaching duties, for example the proctoring of numerous exams for all subjects, was increased. She also discovered how little her voice mattered. When the principal sought recommendations for a new foreign teacher, she introduced someone with much teaching experience and an MA. When she asked the principal why he had selected a relatively inexperienced candidate without a graduate degree instead, he told her that 'he had looked at all the résumés and he is the MOST qualified candidate'. This statement convinced Andrea that he had never even examined the résumés but instead had selected the candidate the powerful teachers wanted.

This was when Andrea began to envision a professional life outside the school, and she became determined to quit after finishing her MA. She physically and mentally distanced herself from the IC course. First, she (and Mary) moved to a different English department office, which was considered an 'undesirable' place by the 'powerful teachers' because only 'unwanted' teachers such as 'newbies' and/or 'scapegoats' had their desks there. They were warned that if they moved they would be unable to return, but Andrea and Mary were determined to distance themselves from what was increasingly becoming an unwelcome atmosphere. Andrea relinquished many of her IC classes and began teaching more for the General Course (GC) program, but both she and Mary found that they enjoyed working with the new teachers in their new office. Once again, Andrea established an identity as a valuable and knowledgeable teacher but with different colleagues. Although she enjoyed teaching in the GC, that transition was nonetheless painful:

> So it took a long time for me to let go of it and to be OK with it. I don't think I'm still really OK with it, but I found that spreading myself out and working in the General Course more – I found I really enjoyed working with the general course students. I guess if I didn't enjoy it I would be really upset. But because I enjoy it so much, I don't mind any more.

Andrea earned her MA in the fall of 2013, and she resigned from the high school[1] after being hired for a contracted full-time position at a private coeducational university.

Moving to a university

I interviewed Andrea again at the end of her first semester at 'Yama University' (YU). Although it is still too early to determine how her identity as a university teacher will develop over time, three areas of change thus far are worth noting: her identity as an employee of an institution, her identity in relation to her colleagues and her identity in relation to her students.

Not surprisingly, there are great differences between the two teaching contexts, and one of the greatest differences is the freedom offered to university teachers in enabling them to determine how and where to work. YU trusts teachers by not regulating their daily schedules beyond the specific classes they are to teach, their conversation-lounge duties and occasional meetings. Even though Andrea had had the most seniority at CHSS in terms of years of employment and education (even among the Japanese teachers who worked there), she felt deprofessionalized by always being under the watchful eyes of colleagues, bosses and/or administrators. Now, even though she is 'starting at the bottom of the heap', she feels that it 'might be a fairer playing ground' because she believes she will be judged by professional standards rather than personal ones. Her comment below indicates such optimism. Not only does she feel like a valued professional, but her family life has also improved:

> I just feel so happy to have that kind of trust relationship, and I feel like I have a lot more freedom. I'm practically bouncing in my shoes. I can go home now. I know I'm going to go home and work, but I can work at home and I don't have to feel guilty. At CCHS I always felt really guilty because I did a lot of work at home on weekends and mornings, but people just assumed that 'oh she's leaving at 4:30 – that means she's going to a party or something.' Of course I wasn't!

Work no longer conflicts with family life. Teachers at CCHS, both foreign and Japanese, were perceived to be shirking their duties unless they devoted an extraordinary amount of time to the school in addition to teaching their classes. Without watchful eyes on her at her desk (to make sure she is not studying) or checking the time when she leaves to pick up her children at daycare, she is much happier. The biggest difference is feeling that the university assumes that she *is doing her job properly* as a teacher, unlike her former colleagues, who were assuming *that she was not*.

Collaboration and camaraderie

Despite being generally happier in her new workplace, Andrea is learning to adjust to various differences, especially that of collegial collaboration. At the high school, teaching was largely a group effort; teachers bounced ideas off each other, and decisions concerning curriculum, materials development and student assessment were often made in pairs or in groups. At YU, however, teachers teach whatever they like as long as they follow minimal guidelines. Andrea mainly teaches required speaking classes for first-year students, and she is expected to develop her own teaching materials and to assess students based on topics covered in the required listening textbook used by all students in their freshmen year in a class taught by Japanese teachers. At first she assumed that there would be more collaboration, or at least *discussion*, among the teachers to develop some kind of standardized teaching program and testing methods. Instead, she found that she was left alone to devise her own curriculum and system of evaluation. She then realized that university teachers' independence is not only related to self-scheduling but also to determining what to teach. She says

> Everyone is trusted to just do what they need to do and you don't have to tell people what you are doing and ask them what they think,

because they don't care. They are not going to take the time to talk to you really, because they are busy with their own stuff.

This independence in the workplace, however, has created a slightly lonely atmosphere, because Andrea was accustomed to the camaraderie and social banter that resulted from spending many hours working together with other teachers. Now, she usually works alone in her office because most of her office mates have entirely different schedules.

She has also discovered that, unlike at CCHS where teaching materials were developed together and shared freely, some teachers at YU seem guarded about their materials and with whom they shared them with. This implies that ownership of the teaching materials lies with the individual teachers rather than with the school for the benefit of the students. Andrea felt surprised by this, because before leaving the high school she digitalized and filed her materials for current and future teachers to access. Andrea feels that one reason why teachers hesitate to share materials at YU could be that in the past, some colleagues might have taken advantage of the pooling of resources by not reciprocating in return. This is not to say, however, that no collaboration exists between colleagues at YU, but that collaboration seems based on trust relationships rather than on workplace proximity. At first, Andrea was baffled and unsure of how to proceed, but now, after one semester, she feels that she has established good relationships with a few colleagues, and she feels optimistic that the second semester will be easier.

University students versus high-school students

One reason why Andrea had difficulty developing appropriate teaching materials during her first semester at the university was because of the academic differences between her high-school students and her university students. Although she knew that the YU students would have lower English skills than those at CCHS, she was unprepared for exactly how low that would be. Her former students were 'expected to be more autonomous' in carrying out tasks and assignments. They knew they would attend high-level universities, and they were capable of holding discussions and making presentations in English. Now she teaches basic sentence-level grammar:

> They have very little vocabulary, very little grammar. They can't even... I don't think they ever listened for the last six years they were in junior and senior high schools. So basically, I'm starting from scratch.

The dialogs we are doing are like, 'Do you like movies? Yeah, I like movies. Do you like sports? No, I hate sports.'

These students, who are more accustomed to academic failure, 'require constant attention, direction and praise', and she feels she 'is holding the students' hands just to get them through a 90-min class'. She no longer occupies the front of the room as a lecturer; she moves around the classroom and checks on the students. She found that consistency is important, and the students appreciate the routines that she has established. One routine involves opening every class with a dictation exercise, which 'settles down' the class and introduces the material to be covered that day. She also prepared her students carefully for the final speaking exam, hoping that they can experience success. She wants them to discover that they *can* communicate, even if it is in basic English.

Some teachers might feel that they have taken a step downwards when moving from capable and motivated students to lower-level and less motivated students. However, Andrea has chosen to see this as a 'challenge' and 'something new' that takes her out of the 'rut' she had been in. She explains, 'Now I am actually using my brain again and trying to think of ways to teach them and ways to engage them and ways to think of classroom management strategies. So it's good for me.'

Andrea and CoP

Andrea began teaching at CCHS with little prior experience, but she developed pedagogical expertise through trial and error and through the encouragement of her colleagues. Andrea was, of course, aware of her peripheral trajectory as a foreign teacher in relation to Japanese teachers who are hired and work under different conditions. However, she did not feel marginalized because of the 'mutual engagement in shared activities', the 'accumulation of a history of shared experiences' and the 'development of interpersonal relationships' (Wenger, 1998: 184). Her sense of value as a teacher was reified when teachers from other departments and from other schools came to observe her classes; when students in lower grades looked forward to doing the drama projects she had established as a tradition for third-grade students; and when her students did well in city-wide debate contests.

Her voice was heard, and she had fully developed an identity of participation despite being on a permanent peripheral trajectory as a non-Japanese teacher (e.g. Houghton & Rivers, 2013). She gained expertise and experience while she *did her job*, and she *invested herself in her relations with her colleagues*, which are two necessary conditions to develop identity through engagement (Wenger, 1998). Imagination enabled Andrea to adopt an identity as a competent teacher and as an inside member of CHSS. This alignment toward her school was also an essential part of her identity. However, when her position within the school shifted, her identities of participation became those of identities of nonparticipation (Wenger, 1998), and she experienced a great sense of loss.

The shift from being an insider to being an outsider was related to the ongoing changing interpersonal dynamics due to personnel changes. Japanese teachers transferred in from other schools to replace those who were transferring out, and foreign English teachers quit and new ones were hired. When Andrea returned from her second maternity leave, many of her old allies – those who knew her when she was 'at her prime' – were gone, and she came to feel that she 'didn't know who they were and they didn't know who she was either'. She felt more and more marginalized when the work she believed was *hers* was allocated to others. Her ideas were no longer adopted, and as a result, she developed an identity of nonparticipation.

Andrea attempted to renegotiate her identity at CCHS by increasing her educational capital through obtaining an MA. She imagined that by doing this she would be able her to realign herself as a valued insider at CCHS, but this did not happen. The pedagogical and theoretical expertise acquired through her studies was unrecognized by those holding power and, contrary to her expectations, it did not give her a greater voice. Instead, it marginalized her further. She became even more aware of the asymmetrical power relationships within the school, which led to feelings of 'marginality, disengagement, and nonparticipation', an experience much like that of Mingfang, the teacher in Tsui's (2007: 678) study.

Then Andrea began to move her alignment away from the school and to see a future for herself as a member of the wider EFL community instead. Such negotiability, as Wenger (1998: 197) argues, enables people to 'take responsibility for, and shape the meanings that matter within a social configuration'. By distancing herself from the IC course (and those who made her feel marginalized) and by aligning herself with the GC, Amanda was able to reestablish herself as a knowledgeable teacher and gain the respect and admiration of the new teachers, some of who had transferred in after 'the whole graduate thing blew up'. The theoretical knowledge obtained from her MA course empowered her because it enabled her to 'theorize [her] personal practical knowledge' and 'gain confidence in [her] own pedagogical approaches' (Tsui, 2007: 644). She began giving presentations at conferences and was making connections with teachers outside the school. Although Andrea's initial motivation for obtaining the MA was to reestablish her insider position at the school, when it was not possible for her to do so, she voluntarily placed herself on an outbound trajectory, which ultimately led to her current employment in a university.

Now, as a contracted full-time teacher at a university, Andrea is once again on a peripheral trajectory within the university in which she is employed. This time, however, the boundaries of the trajectory are clearly laid out in the time frame of her contract. At the moment, she does not feel marginalized by her position at the university because of the freedom and trust given to her, which enables her to see herself as a professional teacher. This is in stark contrast to her final years at CCHS. Now, Andrea's modes of belonging are not completely aligned with the university itself but with the students that she teaches there and with the wider profession of university EFL teachers in Japan.

Is Andrea better off as a university teacher? For now, the freedom and trust she has is welcome; the teaching is challenging, and she enjoys her students. She seems to be constructing a teacher identity that is based on her own internal criteria through her newly acquired academic knowledge and through her interaction with students. At the time of this writing, only four months have passed since Andrea left CCHS, and she is optimistic about the future. She is also aware that she must use her time well for the duration of her contract. She is *becoming* a university teacher in that she is also adding research to her work life and hopes to develop her academic skills by publishing in her university's journal and by presenting at conferences. This will not only enhance her professional standing at the school; it will boost her résumé when she must begin looking for her next job.

Even though it may be difficult to obtain a permanent position, Andrea is no longer limited to teaching in *eikaiwa* schools or secondary schools as she would have been had she not gone to graduate school. She now has the necessary minimum qualifications to teach at university, where even contracted positions command more respect and offer greater benefits (Fraser, 2011), despite dangers of eventual 'burnout' (Murray, 2014). Unfortunately, not all teachers are willing to invest in the necessary time and money to obtain a higher degree or to spend time conducting research and publishing articles to improve their employability (Nagatomo, 2014b, 2015). Unfortunately, these teachers might find themselves squeezed out of their positions by younger, fresher and more energetic teachers in similar ways that Andrea felt squeezed out of hers.

In the next section, we look at the professional identity development of Annie, who also worked as a high-school English teacher but, as we shall see, in entirely different circumstances from Andrea.

Annie: A Private High School Teacher

The second teacher discussed in this chapter is Annie, who has lived in Japan for 40 years and taught at an academically mid-level private girls' escalator school for 26 years. She took semiretirement at the age of 60 because she was becoming tired of the nonteaching duties that consumed much of her time. She still teaches a few classes at this high school, as well as several others in a different school.

In the beginning

As mentioned in Chapter 6, Annie was first affiliated with her institution's elementary school, but after her maternity leave she began working at the junior high school, where she helped shaped much of the language-education policy that the school adopted into its curriculum during the 1980s and the 1990s. The Japanese Exchange Teaching (JET) program bringing in assistant language teachers (ALTs) to public schools had not yet begun, and classes cotaught classes by Japanese and non-Japanese were extremely rare. To ensure that the classes proceeded smoothly, Annie engaged in the time-consuming task of scripting every lesson for both teachers to follow. The Japanese teachers were also learning new teaching techniques such as total physical response (TPR) and other communicative activities that they could carry out in their own classrooms. The school's team-teaching program proved successful, and more native English speaking teachers with Royal Society of Arts (RSA) Diplomas and other English-language teaching (ELT) certificates were hired. Although Annie was pleased to have more teachers join the expanding program, she was in for an unwelcome surprise:

> I discovered that they were getting paid more. They demanded more money. I said this is ridiculous and I'm doing the work. I was furious because I was making teaching plans and people were using them and getting paid more because of this piece of paper.

Annie decided to obtain some sort of advanced degree. She had considered an MA but was disinterested in linguistics. She wanted to learn 'practical classroom skills and second language acquisition [techniques] that were going to work', and so she decided upon an RSA Diploma instead. She took a semester off from school in 1990 and went to Scotland with her three-year-old daughter. The program was 'very practical', had 'intensive teaching and classroom practice', and it 'was a lot of fun'. She returned to Japan to write the remaining papers and, to fulfill the diploma's requirements for teaching adults, she taught evening classes at an *eikaiwa* school for a while. She was promoted to full-time permanent status in 1996 and was given increasing responsibilities at the school, which included accompanying students abroad on study trips, working on committees and coordinating the expanding language programs in the junior and senior high schools.

Developing a reputable English program

Annie was her school's first foreign teacher, and by 1991, they had hired three foreign full-timers, and team teaching expanded into the junior and senior high school, making the school a pioneer in language education. It obtained educational grants and published its own teaching materials and teachers' resource books, and it attracted many college-bound students wanting to learn English. Gradually, the English program moved beyond teaching functional situations, which Annie felt were actually far removed from the students' lives, to teaching content materials through English, particularly in the form of project work. The teachers felt that students should have more important topics to talk about than superficial aspects of Japanese culture or celebrity news. After several teachers, including Annie, attended the International Institute of Peace Education (IIPE) in Tokyo in 1992, a team-teaching project focusing on global studies began. The development of this course involved much departmental discussion, because, as Annie says, such a course was not only about language teaching but also about introducing issues that have moral and social implications as well: 'I feel we have to be very careful teaching these issues – that we are not just turning students into [holding] certain positions, and it is very hard because they don't have enough [background] knowledge.'

The strengths of team teaching in a global studies program

In 1994, Annie's school introduced a new systematic team-teaching curriculum that started in junior high school with a basic introduction to foreign cultures and explaining Japanese culture in English and then moved on to discussing world news and global issues in senior high school. Unlike team-teaching in public schools, where the foreigners are merely *assistants*, the method devised in Annie's school utilized the strengths of both the Japanese and non-Japanese teachers to help students become accustomed to learning difficult vocabulary and to reading authentic materials. According to *Go Global: A Global Education Resource Book for Language Teachers* (Tokiwamatsu Gakuen, 1998: 8), a resource book published by her school,

> We think that team teaching with a foreign teacher and a Japanese teacher is a good way to teach global issues. To read authentic news articles in the English newspaper is very difficult for high school students. For the Japanese teachers it is also hard to simplify them into easy English. Foreign teachers can deal with the news easily, but they need the Japanese teachers' help when some vocabulary, or the background to the news, is difficult to explain in English. So we cooperate and help each other, but take a different role in the class.

Annie says that one of her main concerns in developing this approach was teaching students to think beyond problematic global issues. By introducing them to various organizations such as Habitat for Humanity, World Bank and Free the Children she hopes that students would not merely think, 'Oh how terrible. Aren't we lucky to live in a nice rich country like Japan' but that they would consider solutions to such problems instead. She is most rewarded when her students take what they have learned in her class and apply it to their own lives.

> When I hear about students doing things [in the global community] I'm delighted. I went to an amnesty meeting once, and a girl came rushing up to me and said, 'Oh you're Annie! I remember your class! Your global studies class got me really interested.' The student is now a nurse and involved in various NGO activities.

On being a language teacher

Even though Annie places importance on global issues in the language classroom, she considers herself first and foremost a language teacher. There has been some criticism from some non-English teachers when students occasionally watch Japanese videos in the English class to introduce the lesson's content. Such teachers seem to feel, 'Oh you are teaching English. You should show them an English video,' but Annie feels justified in providing schematic knowledge to her students, which helps them acquire the advanced vocabulary necessary for writing summaries and giving presentations in English. She sums up the advantages as follows:

> We are language teachers so we have to always balance what we are doing. I mean, they are learning – through studying global issues they are learning a lot of useful vocabulary. If we were still doing in senior high [communicative activities like] 'Where is the bank?' and 'How much are these apples?' we would be doing them [students] a disservice. I want them to have something important to talk about, and it is easy for them to express. There are big issues about getting them to express their opinions, because they know so little.

Improving Japanese skills

Several years after the global-studies course began, Annie began studying for the highest level of the Japanese proficiency exam. Students were tackling difficult concepts in English and in Japanese, and she was having trouble keeping up with their homework. Students summarized newspaper articles in English, but she felt, 'It is not really so helpful checking the English if I don't really know what is written there [in the newspaper article].' Besides, she felt frustrated at having lived in Japan for so many years but still being unable to 'skim and scan in Japanese'.

She successfully passed the exam but discovered that an additional perk of her intensive Japanese study included learning better ways to express her opinions in Japanese. This improved her relationships with her colleagues because, 'Saying things in a polite sort of way tends to be a sort of Japanese way. So then I was treated differently.'

On being a working mother and raising a bicultural child

Not only was Annie's school progressive in giving a non-Japanese teacher an increasing amount of responsibility, but they also accommodated her as a working mother. For example, when her daughter was young, she was exempted from some work during the summer holidays and later, when she needed to accompany the students abroad on their home-stay programs, she was allowed to bring her daughter with her. Such allowances, together with the emotional and physical support provided by her husband and his parents, enabled her to work and raise her daughter without much difficulty.

Her greatest difficulty was, however, dealing with other mothers at the public elementary school. Determined that her daughter 'would not miss out' on anything, she followed the usual demands made on mothers, such as hand sewing the numerous bags required of first graders and following Japanese cultural holidays.

Nonetheless, she found that there was a sort of discrimination against mothers who worked. Annie explains, 'There was a very interesting sort of culture in the school between stay-at-home moms and working mothers.' Those who worked sent their children to *gakudo* club (after-school daycare), where children of all grades played together and the parents socialized with each other. Children spent afternoons engaging in physical activities such as climbing trees and swimming, and in the summer, there was a camp. In that group, Annie formed strong friendships with the other parents. Such friendships, however, were not as easily made with the mothers who did not work. Annie describes their positioning of working mothers and nonworking mothers, which influenced their relationships, in the following way:

> The mothers there [at the elementary school] were sort of oh *'anata wa ojozu desu ne'* (you are so good at this) and things like *'uchi no ko zen zen dekinai'* (my child can't do anything), and this kind of stupid stuff. I couldn't stand this jostling for this kind of strange reverse superiority thing that goes on. I don't have the language to describe it really, but women play these kinds of games, which feel very false. But in the *gakudo*, everybody is busy and people are very frank and open. There are just none of those kinds of issues. [But at the elementary school] There's a lot of, a sort of 'status' and establishing who you are, establishing your status in funny ways, which is not relevant for working moms who are just trying to get meals on the table and take care of kids and have a good life. It's a very different kind of world and I didn't relate very well with those mothers, I have to say. Some were very nice, but there was this expression, *'gakudo no ko'* (children from the after school club) (laughs), which you know, was kind of discriminatory attitude toward these kids.

Annie's description above is interesting because it particularly highlights sociopolitical attitudes according to which women should devote their entire energy to their family (in particular, to their children) (e.g. Liddle & Nakajima, 2000). There was, and possibly still is, a suspicion that working mothers are not raising their children properly. Those years were 'quite tough' because the nonworking mothers in the parent–teacher association (PTA) would nominate working mothers like Annie for committees and then schedule meetings during their working hours. Annie either needed to bow out of the meeting or make arrangements to be absent from school.

Another area of difficulty in sending her daughter to the public school was her increasing feelings that on one hand her biracial and bicultural daughter was being treated differently from other children, and that, on the other hand, she was not being recognized for her dual background.

> I always felt that when she was in the Japanese school, even though they were very nice and she had friends, there was definitely a subtle, um I wouldn't call it discrimination, but 'otherness' of being different. And in her school, in her class, there was one little Indian girl and a half-American boy, but the school never made any acknowledgement of the fact that these children had other aspects that could be interesting to the school. The curriculum was set in stone and we moved through the curriculum.

Annie wanted her daughter to receive an English education and to be in a school with more international children and internationally minded parents, so she transferred her daughter to an international school from the third grade of elementary school, where she completed the rest of her schooling.

Retired life

Annie semiretired at the age of 60 because she no longer wanted to travel overseas with students and have nonteaching duties during holiday periods. As a part-time teacher now, her relationships with her students are the same but without the day-to-day interaction with other teachers concerning nonteaching activities, and she is beginning to feel like a peripheral member of the school. She feels some 'sadness' about this increasing distance, but she has filled her time by teaching global issues part-time at another high school as well. Annie intends to continue doing a 'bit of teaching, as long as [she] has the enthusiasm, because the enthusiasm is the most important part of all'.

On being an insider foreigner living in Japan

After living and teaching in Japan for 40 years, Annie is happy with her private and professional life, but she feels there is some room for improvement in Japan, particularly regarding social issues. She does not view herself as an outsider but as an insider with the right to speak out on both positive and negative issues concerning Japan, even though she is sometimes criticized for it:

> Sometimes I'm critical of various aspects of Japanese culture. But, basically I love this country. It is my adopted country, my second country. When I defend Japan to people who don't have that deeper connection [particularly that of being married to a Japanese national], I've had that dismissive 'Oh, you're Japanese, are you? You've gone native, haven't you?' (laughs) Comments like that. I just think you [people married to Japanese] do have a deeper understanding. Perhaps you are willing to accept certain things in Japan. That's just the way it is. Even though I feel very negative about some aspects about it, I still want to see some progress. I want my second country to be going in the right direction.

Comparing Annie and Andrea's degrees of belonging to their schools' CoP

Now, let us compare the degrees of belonging that Annie and Andrea have felt at their schools. Both were regular classroom teachers who could teach alone (although both engaged in team teaching as well from time to time). Both women took pride in helping their schools establish and develop innovative curricular programs, which included the teaching of communicative English and the teaching of global awareness through English. They also engaged in nonteaching activities such as departmental committee work and taking care of students. Whereas Annie developed an increasing identity of participation as a full member of her school, Andrea developed an increasing identity of nonparticipation, which ultimately led to her resignation.

These different feelings of belonging are rooted in the hiring practices of the two schools. Annie's school, a private one, has greater personnel flexibility. She was able to move up the ranks from being a part-time teacher to become a permanent full-time one, and her salary was at the same scale as her Japanese colleagues, with annual pay increases, bonuses and social welfare benefits. Although she said that there were some work limitations due to her being a foreigner (i.e. she was unable to be a homeroom teacher and nor could she serve as the head of a committee), she worked the same amount as her Japanese colleagues and had taken on many additional responsibilities.

Andrea, on the other hand, was employed by a public school under entirely different criteria from the Japanese teachers, who are civil servants.

Although Andrea put in the same hours as her Japanese colleagues, she never received a raise. Although she expected to be employed permanently because her contract had no term limitations, the position was not a 'lifetime' one like her colleagues' or like Annie's, for that matter. Whereas Annie was given increasing responsibilities that made her feel more and more a member of the community, Andrea's responsibilities, especially the ones she enjoyed doing the most, were becoming curtailed. This made her feel increasingly like an outsider, and additional responsibilities that she had not been required to do before were being heaped upon her.

A second area of difference concerns the development and sustainment of collegial relationships. Private-school teachers generally work for their schools permanently. Annie's initial introduction to the school was through 'Mariko', who was a powerful, innovative and influential teacher, and of course, on the insider trajectory. By working with Mariko and other like-minded colleagues, Annie could establish long-term relationships with her colleagues through shared experiences that continued over time, which contributed to her strong identity of participation. Annie even interviewed prospective teachers, both Japanese and non-Japanese, asking them about their teaching beliefs and teaching philosophy. This clearly established Annie's position in incoming teachers' minds that she was a complete and important member of the faculty and not just foreign window dressing.

Andrea, on the other hand, taught at a public school, where teachers periodically rotate among schools within the district. Therefore, by the time Andrea had resigned, no teacher remained who had worked with her during the implementation of the school's IC program, and there was no shared history to look back upon or with which to construct current relationships. Instead, incoming Japanese teachers saw her as just one of many foreign teachers. Furthermore, those powerful teachers on the insider trajectory who used to be her allies were no longer in the school. When the power base changed, Andrea lost her privileged standing to another foreigner who allied himself with the new head of the 'power team'. However, there is no guarantee for him that he will be able to sustain his own position at the school as time goes by either.

In sum, to describe these differences in terms of Gee's (2000) perspective of identity, it is clear that the participants' N-Identity of non-Japaneseness shaped the other three perspectives but in different ways. Their I-Identities as English teachers employed in Japanese high schools were clearly shaped by the discursive practices of their colleagues and administrators (D-Identities), which lead to feelings of belonging as in the case of Annie or to feelings of alienation as in the case of Andrea. Annie managed her

A-Identity by remaining with her school until retirement, and Andrea managed hers by resigning and finding a different job.

Sarah: A Tenured Professor

The last participant to be discussed in this book is Sarah, who, like Annie, has been living in Japan for 40 years. She reached the pinnacle of the EFL teaching hierarchy in Japan by obtaining tenure at a university in 1990. Life before tenure was tough, and there were times when she wondered how, as a single parent, she would be able to earn enough to support her three sons. After receiving tenure, people envied her for her 'luck', but she felt that she deserved 'this break' after years of financial hardship:

> As a person teaching in Japan I think I have been extremely lucky with the jobs that I got. And years ago somebody actually said, 'Oh you are so lucky!' And I was annoyed. 'It's not luck. I've been working for bloody years and I finally got the right job!' I was quite annoyed that it didn't reflect on the fact that I had studied and worked my ass off for years and years and years, and was finally getting a cushy [university] job.

With a stable income and a secure future, she qualified for permanent residency and was able to obtain a mortgage to purchase a home. With tenure, Sarah no longer needed to juggle working in different schools, and she no longer needed to teach private English lessons. In the eyes of part-time teachers, however, it often appears that full-time teachers' lives are easier. While it is true that they may be paid more for teaching fewer classes, they are often quite busy because of increased administrative duties and increased responsibilities.

The university's English program

Sarah's university is one of the leaders in undergraduate and graduate social welfare education. Students are required to take general education courses, but in recent years, the importance attached to these subjects has been reduced, and the school offers more courses that will improve students' chances at passing the qualifying exams to become national social workers. Sarah is the only tenured English teacher in the university, and she oversees all of the English classes taught by the Japanese and non-Japanese part-time teachers. Sarah explains that there used to be various classes in English and other languages for students to take 'for fun', but now the school only offers one basic four-skills English class that is required for all 750 first-year students and a one-semester elective English course for second-year students.

Sarah aims to develop a curriculum for the university that would provide a standardized English course for all of the students, none of whom are English majors. She wants them to learn basic English communication skills. In an effort to coordinate the program and at the same time sustain teachers' classroom autonomy she has suggested 'that all the teachers teach the same thing [communication]' but 'the route [method] to take to doing that' can be flexible.

She says the foreign teachers are 'very pleasant and cooperative' and would even agree if she suggested that they use the same textbook. However, there has been substantial resistance from the Japanese part-time teachers (who are in the majority), who do not see the necessity of teaching the four skills of English. Most of these teachers are sufficiently proficient in English to teach conversational English, but Sarah thinks they probably 'feel very nervous about it' and that they mainly want to teach students 'Shakespeare or Hemingway' in the same manner that they themselves studied English as students.

Despite repeated explanations of the English program's curricular goals to these teachers, some still 'barrel on, and the students fail, and they [students] feel sort of miserable'. She describes one recently retired teacher who had 'refused to believe that he couldn't get his students to do this high-level English stuff like he had done in university, and he would fail 50 students a year' because they could not perform to his expectations. Even those teachers who have agreed to follow the curricular goals do not do so. One Japanese teacher, for example, said that she had understood the program's requirements at a job interview, but she selected a typical grammar-focused reading book that is often used by Japanese teachers as her textbook anyway.

Outsourcing teachers

When the university opened a new education department, it decided to no longer rely on the troublesome and more expensive part-time teachers who refuse to follow the university's English education policy but instead to ask an outsourcing company to dispatch teachers instead. This measure, Sarah complains, excludes those excellent part-time teachers who would have welcomed the opportunity to teach more classes in the newly formed faculty. At the same time, however, it 'serves them [those teachers who refuse to cooperate] right' for missing the opportunity to have more classes.

The university has been using dispatch teachers for about four years now and, according to Sarah, many of the previous problems have been solved. She devised the coordinated curriculum that the teachers are supposed to follow, and she selected the textbook the teachers are supposed to use. She explains,

> It's my name that goes on the syllabus, but it is not me that's teaching. It's the guys from this company that come to teach. They use *my* book [a textbook that Sarah had coauthored]. Of course I do everything; I write the syllabus and everything is done. 'Here's the book. Teach it.'

Despite the issues and concerns surrounding dispatched teachers as discussed in Chapter 3, Sarah believes that this system 'works great'. Many are enthusiastic teachers with MAs in fields related to teaching English as a second language (TESOL). Some teach at other universities and come to her school to 'fill up their schedules'. Others may be in between teaching contracts, and for some, working for a dispatch company enables them to get a foot in the door of university teaching. As illustrated by Louisa's story in the previous chapter, it is easier for a teacher to get hired at a university if they already have had some experience teaching at one. Importantly, according to Sarah, 'The students love them [the teachers]. They are no longer suffering through Shakespeare, and they are sort of cool guys, handsome, and tall – you know – Charisma Men [see Chapter 4] entertaining students.'

Despite the teachers' youth and energy, there are occasional problems with those who do not take their teaching responsibilities seriously or those who do not have the necessary pedagogical experience to handle passive university students. Sarah remembers coming across a teacher

> trotting back from the 7-11 [convenience store] when he should have been in the classroom. Some of them don't know the rules, so they have to be taught the rules of behavior if you are working at a university. Rules like, 'show up on time.' 'Don't pop out for a coffee in the middle of class' (laughs).

To maintain academic quality among the classes, Sarah often observes the teachers' lessons. She said that one woman, who had only had prior experience teaching business English at an *eikaiwa* school, was 'to be quite honest, hopeless, and she got angry and said [to students] "Why won't you cooperate with me? You must be stupid then."' Luckily, that teacher quit before Sarah needed to ask her to leave. While observing another teacher, she was shocked that he pointed, snapped his fingers and whistled at students when asking them questions:

> He was treating my students like dogs! But they didn't seem to mind. They probably thought this how they do it in the UK. I was a bit annoyed and I said, 'You really shouldn't do that. That is not really right. You should find another way...tap them on the shoulder, or whatever you want to do. But I don't think you should whistle and snap your fingers at them.' And he was most annoyed and quite angry.

Sarah reminded him that she was in charge by telling him, 'OK. Be angry. That's OK. But don't do it. Do something else.' She said, 'I kept my eye on him. I think he decided he wanted the job more than he wanted a fight with me.'

Unlike part-time teachers who work directly for the school, it is easier for Sarah to 'get rid of' dispatch teachers who underperform or who do not follow the curriculum. She can tell them, 'Don't come back next week,' knowing the company will send a replacement without any problem. The reverse is also true, though. As discussed in Chapter 3, without a sense of affiliation toward an institution teachers work for, they are quick to resign 'if anything better crops up', making it difficult to retain good teachers. However, for the most part, Sarah feels that the problems that exist in the other faculties that still rely upon directly hired part-time teachers have been partially resolved because of the dispatched teachers.

Traveling abroad with students

In addition to overseeing the English program, another one of Sarah's duties is to accompany students to the United Kingdom. The study abroad program, which was established around the time that Sarah joined the university, is one reason why they hired her in the first place. The university realized that they needed a 'responsible full-time English teacher, and the Japanese teachers didn't want to do it'. Furthermore, '[T]hey needed somebody who was at home in England.'

Interestingly, there was miscommunication concerning the expectations the university had of Sarah before her first trip abroad with the students. She recalls,

> They had failed to take into account that I was a single mother (laughs). Or maybe they had and they just thought, 'Oh maybe foreigners are different or something.' I don't know what had been going through their

heads, but the next year they said, 'OK. Now we've got this six-month thing all set up.' And I thought, 'Wow! Great! Six months in England!' And then I realized they WEREN'T going to pay for my children to go. And I asked, 'Did you think I was going to LEAVE them here?' (laughs). They were too young. I argued and sulked and did everything, and in the end they agreed to pay for ONE [child].

Her oldest child remained in Japan with his grandmother, but all in all, while it was a 'good experience' for her children, it was a 'financial disaster' for her.

The teaching

Sarah enjoys teaching most of the time because the students are easygoing and friendly, even though they are 'not geniuses at English'. She tries to make their English lesson as pleasant as possible with pair work and games so that the students can 'have a laugh doing it, without much strain'. Since they do not need English for academic purposes, she hopes that they will be able to be self-sufficient in a simple way and apply what they learn in her class in the real world some day:

> I think the students have a pleasant interlude in their lives in my class but I hope they learn that English isn't scary and if I need to I can talk to a foreign person and communicate some basic needs. If I want to go to England or Hawaii or somewhere you know at least I can go buy myself something.

Sarah also teaches *zemi* (seminar) courses, which are common in Japanese universities. A *zemi* is generally comprised of a small close-knit group of students who study under a tenured professor. The professor and the students discuss and research topics that are often related to the professor's research interests, and the students ultimately write a graduation thesis on that topic. Traditionally, *zemi* teachers write letters of recommendation and help students secure employment upon graduation, and they socialize together outside of class. In many cases, lifetime friendships develop between the members of the *zemi* and the professor.

At first, Sarah was not given *zemi* classes. She was told, 'You are teaching so many other classes anyway. Your time is better used doing that. Besides, who would want to come to your class anyway?' Several years later, the school asked her to teach a *zemi* course, but it was soon discontinued because of a lack of student enrolment.

She was recently asked to teach a *zemi* again, namely because a hiring freeze meant there were fewer tenured professors than before who could conduct them. Unlike her previous experience with *zemi* classes, this time she was better prepared and more confident. She warned prospective students that she would be unable to help them in the same way that their Japanese professors could, such as correcting Japanese essays and providing introductions to companies for jobs. She told them, 'You're on your own here. You'll have to do a lot of things on your own.'

Students still registered for her *zemi*, and now she has two groups: one with foreign students that focuses on reading about social issues in English and the other with less ambitious students who want to focus on the history of cartoons in various countries. Sarah says that the students in the latter group are 'not terribly career-oriented', and so they hope to find an 'easy job in an old people's home and be useful'. They are not keen to study for the welfare exams, so they are content in researching in areas related to their hobbies. Nonetheless, she still watches over them and checks if they have been to job interviews. She enjoys developing close relationships with her students and watching them progress over time.

Graduate degree

When Sarah was hired with tenure in 1990, the only academic qualifications she had were a British teaching license, a BA and university teaching experience. In Japan at that time, few Japanese had PhDs, although many did have MAs. The only requirement for teaching at university was holding a BA (Nagasawa, 2004), but in fact, Sarah reported that some of her colleagues had never even attended university. Instead, they were 'some sort of specialists in welfare who worked for years and years'. This illustrates that in that university during those years, academic requirements were not as important as practical work experience. But most universities in Japan went through significant academic overhauls in the 1990s, and hiring practices became stringent all around (Eades *et al.*, 2005). This might also be true at Sarah's school, because over time, all incoming tenured teachers held at minimum MAs, and some even had PhDs.

Sarah began feeling 'embarrassed', almost like the 'the poor relation' when 'everyone was talking about what they did for their doctorate'. She decided to enroll in a distance MA program from a British university. Because her tenured position at the university was secure and because she was confident with her EFL pedagogical knowledge, she studied *Japanese* instead of TESOL and focused not only on linguistic and literary issues but on social issues as well. These topics fit her undergraduate background in social science and they fit her workplace context as well. Obtaining the MA gave Sarah educational capital (Bourdieu, 1991) that resulted in greater confidence and feelings of ease among her colleagues.

Promotion

In 2009, Sarah was promoted to full professor. She had fulfilled the requirements of the school by having the appropriate number of publications and the minimum number of years as associate professor. The publication requirements, however, are not so rigid, because publishing in the university's own *kiyo* (a Japanese university's in-house journal, which may or may not be peer refereed) was sufficient. This reflects a common philosophy in many universities in which greater importance is accorded to internal affairs than to research and other outside activities (see Poole, 2010).

On being marginalized

Despite being a tenured full professor, Sarah says that she occasionally feels marginalized at the university. One reason for this is that the subject that she is hired to teach and her area of research is peripheral to the main function and goals of the university. This is true not only for Sarah but also for other general-education teachers as well. Not surprisingly, Sarah is also marginalized because of her lack of Japanese skills. Although she is fluent in Japanese, she cannot manage committee work in the same way as her Japanese colleagues. In the beginning, she was assigned to more committees, but

> Somebody realized although I did everything I was supposed to do, there would be a lot of, 'oh, I see you can't write, ok I'll write that for you. You just read it and I'll write that.' Or whatever. And I think people sort of noticed that it was difficult. Certain things were difficult for me to do. So the last maybe seven or eight years I haven't been put on important committees.

Sarah decided not to be offended by this exclusion because, after consideration, she admitted to herself, 'No, actually I can't do the job, and I'm better off.' Instead, she concentrates on doing the jobs that she *can* do, like accompanying the students abroad.

She says has never particularly felt marginalized as a *woman*, although there were several colleagues who used to say 'sexist things' to her in pathetic attempts to be funny. Neither does she feel marginalized because she is a foreigner (except for language difficulties). However, some of her colleagues are 'a bit dim about the foreigner aspect.... They just say silly things.' She described a recent conversation with a professor of nursery-school education where they were discussing the tendency that Japanese children have to draw the sun red, whereas English children draw the sun yellow. Sarah was astonished when the woman commented, 'It must be amazing that you are looking at something through blue eyes and it's a different color (laughs).'

Sarah's future

With the retirement age at Sarah's university set at 70, she has five more years of work ahead of her. Although she is unsure of whether she will continue that long, she knows the longer she works the greater her pension benefits will be. This is important because she started paying into the pension system late. Nevertheless, Sarah looks forward to a leisurely and pleasant retired life. She hopes to spend time playing the ukulele, making handicrafts, growing vegetables in her garden and spending time with her three sons.

Among all of my participants, Sarah is not only the oldest but she is also the most successful. However, her success came after she suffered from many hardships. She also acknowledges that to some extent she has been 'lucky'. Her luck, however, came from making the right choices when the right opportunities came along. She also admits that being a white woman in Japan in the 1970s and 1980s, when she was developing her career, also helped:

> Now I think yeah I have been very lucky. I don't know what is, but if you are offered an opportunity and you have got the common sense to take the good one or not. Maybe there is an element of that choice. I think that I have done well. Some people just haven't had the same opportunities, and have not been offered such good jobs or just haven't been there at the right time or place for this that and the other. And I think a lot of is luck. And the timing and taking up the opportunity when it was offered was also important. Because I've seen a lot of people working harder than me for less, you know. But they just didn't have the opportunity. At one point there, I think it was easier for me to get a job because I was a woman. In the same way because I have blue eyes and fair hair. It was easier for me to get a job than it would have been for some Asian person. And in that respect it was easier for me in the beginning.

Sarah's placement in her CoP

With tenure, Sarah's future is secure as a member of her university's CoP. Her story shows how people can be full participating members of their communities and yet not be insiders. Although this does not cause many limitations in Sarah's professional life, it certainly shapes it. As an English teacher, in fact as the *only* English teacher in the university, she naturally operates on a peripheral trajectory in a social welfare world. Sarah and the other liberal arts teachers do important work, and they teach important courses for the university. Ultimately, though, decision-making power lies with those social welfare academics who occupy the insider trajectory and with the university's administrators.

Nevertheless, English is accorded importance because of its placement in Japanese society as a desired language, and because of its role in the students' exchange programs. Sarah's identity as a university English professor in this particular university may be quite different to her identity if she were teaching English majors in a university that places greater emphasis on language learning and language teaching.

Summary of Chapter 9

This chapter provided rather lengthy descriptions of the working lives of the three women in this study who teach or who have taught English in various full-time positions in Japanese institutions. As full-time workers, they have invested themselves heavily into their workplaces, but the degrees to which they belong to their communities differ; they are shaped by the local and by the broader sociopolitical contexts.

Sara, for example, has tenure, and her position is financially secure. As a university professor, she has reached the pinnacle of the EFL hierarchy and she has no worries. And yet, she is not an insider member of her workplace either. One reason for this is her teaching area: English is accorded less importance in the school than other academic topics. Another reason is her Japanese ability, which is not quite sufficient to take part in day-to-day committee work. But instead of accepting these limitations as hindrances, she focuses on the things that she can do that are directly related to the teaching of English (such as managing the part-time teachers and taking students abroad). In addition, when considering the struggles that she had when she was a juggler like the women described in Chapter 9, she is entirely grateful and satisfied with her work.

Andrea has held two types of full-time position. She worked for 11 years in a high school where she felt increasingly marginalized and was disappointed to lose her insider status, and her attempts to regain it through obtaining educational credentials were unsuccessful. Now, she is working in a contracted position where there is no permanent security; she will need to find another position by the time her contract expires. Nonetheless, she feels more satisfied now because the rules are clearer this time. From the beginning, she has understood her placement on the school's trajectory as a peripheral member, and she is learning how to manage her career from this standpoint. At the very least, she feels more appreciated and more respected for the work that she is doing now.

Annie may be the only teacher in this study who experienced feelings of full participation in her workplace. From the beginning, she was on an inbound trajectory, which she later understood to be contingent upon her obtaining the necessary academic qualifications to secure a full-time appointment. Once she became full time, she worked diligently with her colleagues, and during the 18 years she worked full time, she could initiate and implement programs, and her ideas and suggestions were considered and adopted. Although the work became tiresome for Annie as she got older, as a retired teacher now operating on the periphery, she feels somewhat nostalgic for the days when she was in the midst of everything.

In the next chapter, the conclusion of this book, I will tie together some of the major themes that emerged from the narrative data provided by the ten women in this study.

Note

(1) Mary, who had completed her MA in a different graduate program earlier that year, had also found university work and resigned from CCHS at the same time.

10 Concluding Comments

Introduction

In this book, I have attempted to illustrate how ten foreign women have created and sustained their personal and professional identities as foreign women teaching English in various locations and in various contexts in Japan. Unlike those teachers of English as a foreign language (EFL) who move from country to country or those who exit EFL teaching entirely for more lucrative careers, these women have established roots in Japan through marriage to Japanese nationals, and they intend to reside in Japan permanently. Although there are many common issues influencing the lives of *all* non-Japanese English teachers in Japan, for this study I chose to only examine foreign *women* married to Japan men. These women's personal and professional lives are likely to be significantly different from their male counterparts with Japanese spouses, as well as being different from those living in Japan as single women or with non-Japanese spouses.

As women with Japanese husbands, they are expected to conform, to a certain extent, to the same societal norms that shape Japanese women's lives, and yet all the women in my study have constructed solid and fairly lucrative careers as English language teachers and have maintained their own personal sense of self.

These women are not Japanese, and yet they are not entirely outsiders to Japan either. They have become accustomed to living in Japan and strongly identify as members of their local communities. They have established roots and have a solid network of friends that are Japanese and non-Japanese. Most of them are proficient in Japanese – some to the extent that they can read and write it as well. Those with children have navigated the ins and outs of complicated educational waters and have still managed to raise them to be bilingual and bicultural people.

My intent in embarking upon this study was to examine English language teaching in Japan through the eyes of one specific group of teachers. To do that, I first situated my study within the broader sociopolitical context described in Chapters 1–4, because English-language education that occurs in Japan today remains closely tied to those issues. Chapter 2, for example, described the progression of foreign-language education from the time Japan first encountered Westerners until after

World War II. Language learning was connected mainly with information gathering. The first wave of language learners in the Meiji era *needed* language as a tool in order to acquire necessary information to modernize the country. Barely one generation later, that information came to be available through the new Japanese experts *in Japanese*. Thus, English was no longer necessary for practical purposes, and it became used as a gate-keeping tool to select university applicants. The chapter closed with a discussion of issues that hindered English-language education and English-language learning in the 1970s.

In Chapter 3, I described the type of English-language teaching carried out by foreigners in both formal and informal educational contexts. Although there had been foreign English teachers in Japan prior to the 1980s, they were rare and usually located in urban areas like Tokyo. During the 1980s and 1990s, many foreign teachers came to Japan, both in government-sponsored programs such as the Japanese Exchange Teaching (JET) program and as independent teachers for the *eikaiwa* industry. Although most returned home after their contracts were completed, some, like my participants, chose to stay. One reason why many remained in Japan was their marriage to a Japanese national.

Chapter 4 focused on gendered issues that underlie the experiences of foreign male and female teachers in Japan. First it described interracial relationships from a historical perspective and discussed issues that have shaped attitudes toward such relationships. Then it covered gendered attitudes toward English language study itself and how these attitudes influence the teaching experiences of male and female teachers. The chapter closed with an overall discussion of gendered expectations of women in Japan.

Chapter 5 briefly introduced the participants of my study, how the data was collected and analyzed and the theoretical frameworks (Gee, 2000 and Wenger, 1998) that were used for analysis. In that chapter, I also established my position as an insider researcher to this study.

Chapter 6 described my participants in greater detail by providing brief biographical backgrounds and introducing their initial motivations for coming to Japan, their early teaching experiences, how they met their husbands and how well they were accepted into their husbands' families as foreign brides. In this chapter, I also detailed three of the participants' current teaching experiences, as they do not appear in the subsequent chapters.

Chapter 7 was the first of the three analytical chapters. It focused on those who operate their own *eikaiwa* schools as cottage-industry businesses. Chapter 8 described the processes and difficulties of those piecing together a living through teaching multiple types of classes in multiple locations. Chapter 9, the final discussion chapter in this book, covered three teachers who are employed as full-time workers in one institution.

Summing It All Up

This section summarizes some of the themes that emerged from my participants' narrative data. I hesitate to use the word 'findings' in my summation because, as Wolcott (2001: 120–121) cautions, qualitative research is not 'decision-oriented or conclusion-oriented' and as such, does not need a 'dramatic climax' to close with. He writes,

> I do not work toward a grand flourish that might tempt me beyond the boundaries of the material I have been presenting, or might detract from the power (and exceed the limitations) of the observations themselves or what I have been able to make of them.

I have no 'dramatic climax' to attach to my ten participant's stories other than several general themes that have been previously discussed throughout Chapters 6–9, particularly concerning the four perspectives of identity (N-Identity, I-Identity, D-Identity and A-Identity) as classified by Gee (2000). Therefore, I will avoid making broad claims but instead will close this book with a brief discussion of those themes. It is also important to reiterate that the themes that emerged from the data are not only directly related to the particular women that took part in my study but also to what they chose to tell me during the exact times of our interviews. Had I interviewed ten different women, it is likely I would have heard ten different stories. Had I interviewed these same ten women on different days, it is also possible they would have told me ten different stories.

My analysis and interpretation of these women cannot apply to all female EFL teachers in Japan with Japanese spouses, but I do believe the stories my participants told might resonate with other foreign teachers in Japan as well, whether or not they are male or female and whether or not they are married to Japanese.

Next, let us return to the research questions that guided this study. The first one was:

RQ 1: How do foreign women, with Japanese spouses, develop and sustain careers in Japan as English language teachers?

In answering this first research question, I found that the participants' careers were developed and sustained mainly on the basis of the following three points: (1) the time they first arrived in Japan, (2) where they reside in Japan and (3) their resourcefulness.

Time of arrival

All of the participants arrived in Japan with the intention of teaching English (or at least, as assistant language teachers [ALTs]), including Andrea, who had returned to Japan as a wife. However, the time of their arrival in Japan may be an important factor contributing to how their language-teaching careers were first developed. It seems that there might have been more opportunities available in earlier years when there were fewer foreign teachers. Annie and Sarah, for example, both arrived in Japan during the 1970s, when foreigners were relatively few and teaching opportunities were bountiful. Both taught in various contexts for more than ten years, but they obtained full-time permanent employment in 1990 when the schools they were working for needed foreign teachers to help expand their English education programs. Essentially, they were in the right place at the right time. Nowadays, the more prestigious the job, the more stringent the requirements. For example, tenured teachers nowadays are selected from a wider pool of applicants and are hired after their educational backgrounds and research publications have been carefully scrutinized. This is why Theresa is engaged in doctoral studies and professional development; she knows that competition for tenured positions is fierce.

Location

Another factor that has shaped these women's teaching experiences is the locations in which they live. Clearly, not all places in Japan provide equal teaching opportunities. One locale is not necessarily better than another, but different areas provide different sorts of benefits and challenges for the foreigners living in them. In a way, there are more career opportunities in urban areas because there are more schools and more universities, but at the same time, there could be more competition to gain entry to them. Both Andrea and Theresa are on limited-term contracts in the Tokyo area, but because there are many universities in this area, they are likely to receive another appointment if they so desire *and* as long as they are willing to commute. Louisa, who now works part time in three universities and conducts oral examinations in Tokyo, is situated in an ideal location. She can be in central Tokyo within an hour (a reasonable commute) and she can reach universities on the outskirts of her prefecture or in neighboring prefectures in about the same amount of time. Occasionally, universities in such areas have difficulty filling spots because the commute is too far for teachers living in Tokyo, and this might also partially explain why she now has a full university teaching schedule with only a BA.

There can be good opportunities for foreigners in country areas – as long as the areas are not *too countrified*. Pat in Iwate and Lisa in Fukushima, for example, have always had good part-time jobs – especially good ones that had been passed on to them by other foreigners who were leaving the area. They have built their reputations as teachers, and their schools depend upon them. If, however, they were employed on limited-term contracts like Theresa and Andrea, they might experience difficulty in finding subsequent employment, because there simply not enough schools to move around to every three to five years. As part-time teachers, however, their jobs are quite secure – that is, as long as the schools' budgets allow.

On the other hand, for Victoria in Kyushu and for Margaret in Hokkaido, there are few good local jobs. With 20 years of teaching experience, for example, Victoria is still an ALT – an *assistant* teacher – and is unlikely to obtain full-time employment elsewhere because she must have a flexible schedule because of her temple work. Nonetheless, being an ALT provides a steady income that supplements her private teaching, and as one of two foreign women in her town who both work as ALTs, she believes she can keep the job indefinitely. Margaret's work is essentially limited to her home-based *eikaiwa* school. With decreasing enrolment, Margaret is not averse to taking on other work if her financial situation deteriorates and if the opportunity arises. While there may not be that many schools in her area, as the only foreigner in town, she may find work, although that would be quite an adjustment after having been in charge of her own business for so long.

Resourcefulness

The most important factor that has enabled these women to develop and sustain their careers as English teachers in Japan is their resourcefulness. As Neilsen (2009: 49) said, successful long-term ELT teachers must be 'flexible and have a high tolerance for change in life circumstances', and this statement certainly applies to my participants. As the stories throughout this book have indicated, the participants have adjusted and adapted well to living and teaching in Japan. Perhaps my most resourceful participant is Victoria, who resisted being pigeonholed as a financially dependent and powerless temple wife. Through obtaining the highest-level priest qualifications *and* through establishing a successful teaching career in her town, she was able to construct an independent life for herself. She sees opportunities and acts upon them. For example, when she realized her son's martial-art team had a bus but no driver, she went to driving school and obtained a bus-driving license. She became the team driver and as such removed herself from the petty parental hierarchy she had been subject to as a parent of an underclassman.

The women in this study have successfully structured their working lives around their families. This is especially important for those who are married to Japanese corporate employees – whose work takes them out of the house for 12 or more hours each day – because the bulk of family matters are left to them. Those participants with full-time jobs, like Theresa or Andrea, qualified to send their very young children to public daycare centers, and they could focus on their careers without much worry. But for the part-time workers, securing spots in daycare centers is not easy. Some, such as Louisa and Margaret, taught from home with their own children in attendance, earning under-the-table money to maintain their spousal dependency status. Both women had been experienced teachers, and after their children no longer needed constant attention, they opened up language schools. Nonetheless, they did so in such a way that they were still always available for their families. Pat has also restructured her teaching activities so that they better fit around the needs of her family by consolidating much of her teaching at the same school her daughters attend.

Two participants, Sarah and Lisa, devised ways to support themselves as single divorced parents. Sarah did this by moving her family into a tiny apartment above a shop she had rented to use as a language school, since the income she had at that time from university teaching was insufficient to live on. Since it was still the peak of the *eikaiwa* boom of the 1980s, she quickly acquired more students than she could handle. After she earned enough money from university teaching to support her family, she closed the school. Shortly after that, she obtained tenure. At first not having a graduate degree was not a disadvantage, because many teachers at her university did not. Lisa and her husband also opened a language school in Fukushima, but later in 2003, because of increasing marital difficulties and the difficulties of operating a business with her husband, she jumped at the offer of English classes in a local technical college and shortly after that at a high school, even though she hated having to leave her infant son with a babysitter. That work provided a stable income, and she could proceed with her divorce.

Another means of resourcefulness found among the participants is how they increased their educational capital to enhance their career opportunities. Theresa, for example, returned to Japan with a graduate degree, which enabled her to step directly into university teaching. Andrea had believed an MA would enhance her standing at the high school where she worked, but when she found that it did not, she used it to obtain a university position instead. Louisa, in wanting to quit her home *eikaiwa* business, looked into graduate degrees and into the Certificate in English Language Teaching to Adults (CELTA). At her age, she decided that it might not be worth the time and expense a graduate degree would entail, so she took the short-term CELTA course instead. That investment paid off, and she was able to convert that educational capital directly into university work. Sarah, on the other hand, did not need an MA to enhance her career prospects, but she decided to obtain one in order to feel more at home within her university with the incoming professors who were becoming increasingly more and more educated.

Finally, Carrie, the youngest and most inexperienced teacher in this study, has used her brief time in Japan to transform herself from a shy girl afraid of trying new things to a self-confidant woman ready to take on new challenges as she moves to a different prefecture with her husband. In other words, Carrie was resourceful at developing skills to become the kind of person that she wants to be.

Now, let us turn to the second research question:

RQ 1: What factors shape the personal and professional identity development of these women?

In answering the second research question, I found that, regardless of the teaching contexts, the strongest factors shaping the participants' identity were mostly their non-Japaneseness, their native-speakerness and their female gender. These three factors, which fall under Gee's N-Identity perspective, strongly influence the other three identity perspectives (I-Identity, D-Identity and A-Identity).

Being a non-Japanese native English speaking teacher

The participants' non-Japaneseness and their native-speakerness form, without a doubt, a double-edged identity sword. These two identity traits are what brought them to Japan in the first place as teachers and/or as assistants, and they enabled these women to develop I-Identities as teachers. In some instances, opportunities were made available to the participants *because of this*. Louisa, for example, obtained her first university position despite not having a graduate degree, because the school specifically wanted someone (a foreigner) to teach 'fun' English to their nursing students, because they were unhappy with the previous Japanese English teacher whose class had been too difficult. Regardless of the school's initial motivations for hiring her, Louisa is a conscientious and dedicated teacher, and once she got her foot through the university teaching door, other part-time positions followed, enabling her to embark upon a new career. Sarah's case also shows some similarities. She was offered tenure because the university felt that, as a British woman, she would be the ideal teacher to help them with their expanding international program in the United Kingdom. Furthermore, they believed she would be able to take charge of students on overseas trips.

Whereas Louisa and Sarah's native-speakerness worked to their advantage, we also saw how hindrances can be attached to this N-Identity. Foreign teachers, as native English speakers, are often ascribed with characteristics that make them seem like ideal English teachers. However, this is true only *to a certain extent.* Native-speaker teachers are considered ideal for exposing students to the fun and games of English, but the real meat and potatoes of English-language teaching clearly lies in the hands of the Japanese teachers. Their achieved I-Identities as teachers were formed from having studied English under the Japanese system and from having various degrees and licenses that denote their qualifications. As discussed throughout this book, this attitude creates the image that one person is a real teacher with the attending benefits and responsibilities, but the other is not. This issue is particularly noticeable in the public-school system that employs ALTs like Victoria and Carrie. There are also restrictions for those in charge of their own classrooms. Andrea, for example, had the authority to teach alone, but her extracurricular activities with students were curtailed when the school reinforced school-board regulations prohibiting foreign teachers from traveling across the city limits with students, even though she had been taking such trips with students for years.

Related to this are assumptions that foreign teachers do not 'teach'; they just do what comes naturally as native English speakers. In Chapter 7, we saw how surprised one of Margaret's student's mothers was when she came across Margaret's teaching plan. Apparently she had assumed that the English lessons taught by Margaret consisted mainly of songs and games. The mother had held on to that belief even though she had attended regular parent–teacher meetings in which Margaret had outlined her school's curriculum. We also saw how Margaret's rival school attempted to lure her students away through negative advertising stating that native

English-speaking teachers are incapable of teaching the English that is appropriate for Japanese students. In fact, as a result of such advertising, Margaret did lose several students.

While it is true that nearly all of my participants first began teaching English with little prior experience, this is certainly no longer the case. They have developed teaching expertise through on-the-job experience, through membership in professional organizations such as the Japan Association of Language Teachers (JALT) and/or by keeping abreast of the language-teaching field through teachers' books and manuals. In addition, as mentioned earlier, they have increased their educational capital as well: Out of the ten women in this study, one has nearly completed her PhD, three have MAs, three have certifications related to teaching English as a second language (TESOL) and one is currently pondering graduate school. Three also have teaching licenses from their own countries. Furthermore, these women are no longer fresh-off-the-boat *gaijin* with no knowledge of Japanese language or culture. Now, they are not only proficient in Japanese and knowledgeable about Japanese culture but are also extremely knowledgeable about their own local contexts. However, as illustrated by Victoria's experiences with some of the teachers she team-teaches with, there may be hesitation to acknowledge foreigners' status as knowledgeable cultural insiders to Japan. What is important to question is whether or not the strengths of teachers like these women are being sufficiently recognized and utilized. If not, an opportunity for real language learning and real cultural exchange might be being missed.

Gender issues

The third factor that shapes these women's professional identity is gender. We have already discussed how these women have organized their teaching around the needs of their families, whether they work to supplement their family's income or whether they solely support their family. Many of their initial decisions concerning work were shaped by the gender roles of men and women in Japan. Had Sarah been a man, for example, it is unlikely that she would have left a tenured track position upon marriage in order to be at home for children that had yet to be born. Louisa and Margaret moved with their husbands during their job transfers during the early years of their marriages, preventing them from establishing lucrative career-building connections. Margaret, for example, had just begun teaching part-time at a local university in Nagano in the 1990s when her husband was transferred to Hokkaido, and she had to quit. Had this transfer not occurred, would her professional life have been different? Later, Margaret's decision to *only teach women and children* because she wished to avoid gossip if men were 'going in and out of the house at all hours' was certainly motivated by gendered concerns.

Interestingly, being a wife and mother is given a high priority in Japan, but the two divorced women felt respected by their workplace colleagues and administrators for their struggles as single mothers. Lisa's school, for example, maintained the number of her classes during recent cutbacks because, as she believes, they know she needs the money. Sarah, after some negotiation with her university, was allowed to bring her young sons with her on a school trip abroad, with the university covering the expenses for one of them. Although Annie was not a single mother, her school understood that she was unwilling to leave her daughter in Japan to go abroad with students, so they also allowed her to bring her daughter along.

At the same time, there is an overall attitude in Japan that children with working mothers somehow suffer because of a lack of attention. Annie spoke about this Chapter 9 when she described her relationship with the nonworking mothers in her daughter's elementary school, who seemed to look down working mothers *and* their children. This leads to a slight sense of guilt that perhaps working mothers *aren't* doing the best by their children by Japanese standards. Margaret and Louisa said they were somewhat regretful that their children could not attend after-school enrichment classes because their mothers were too busy conducting their own classes for other children. Andrea was made to feel guilty by her mother-in-law for being too busy to take her kindergarten-aged daughter to extra lessons. Now, having more time as a university teacher, she has enrolled her daughter (who is now in elementary school) in dance classes.

During the interviews, I did not ask the participants to discuss their relationships with their Japanese husbands in detail, but of course some participants did. As with every marriage, regardless of nationality, some marriages are better than others, and some survive and some do not. None of the women spoke about their husbands in cultural terms; in other words, no one spoke about their husbands *as Japanese men*. They were just men that they were married to who happen to be Japanese.

However, those women that seemed the happiest with their marriages were those whose husbands did not expect them to conform entirely to Japanese ways, but who accepted them for who they are – foreign women living in Japan. Some of the husbands were too busy to offer much practical help during weekdays due to their work schedules, but many did help out on the weekends. Andrea's husband, for example, babysat or took the children to his parents' house on the weekends while she was studying for her MA or when she needed to mark essays. Annie's husband also took charge of their daughter when she was writing the final papers for her Royal Society of Arts (RSA) Diploma. Victoria's husband, even though he had cancer at the time, helped watch the children while she studied for the priest's exam.

The only participant who reported having recent work-related problems that seemed rooted in gender harassment was Andrea. As we saw in Chapter 9, she was squeezed out of a job that she had loved and ultimately moved on to university teaching. Andrea's 'fall', so to speak, began after she returned from her second maternity leave to find that work that had been previously been hers was increasingly being allotted to a foreign male teacher, 'Mike', who had befriended a powerful Japanese male teacher. After entering graduate school, she was warned by an ally that she was under close scrutiny for any infraction. It was not until she relinquished some of her prime classes that would have involved collaboration with 'Mike' and moved to a different teacher's room that she felt the harassment lessened. By the time she resigned, she was more than ready to leave. According to Creaser (2015), people who are victims of this type of treatment, known as mobbing or workplace bullying, often leave their jobs willingly. However, if they had not been emotionally abused in the first place, they would not be forced to tender their resignations. Luckily, Andrea was resourceful enough that when she realized that she could not stay longer at the school, she completed her graduate degree first so she was able to make an upward career change.

Other women did not speak of instances of gender discrimination and/or harassment, although several (such as Margaret and Victoria) complained that they did experience this when they first came to Japan. The others did not, which suggests that, for the most part, their professional lives have been quite comfortable. Most of the women (with the exception of Theresa, who has many foreign male and female colleagues) work where there are few, if any, other foreigners. Such an atmosphere is less likely to bring about problems that can arise due to homosocial relationships among colleagues in the workplace, which can cause exclusionary feelings for members of the opposite sex (Hicks, 2013).

Closing Thoughts

Although my original plan for this study had been to examine 15 women in three educational contexts – private, secondary and tertiary – I found that there was a substantial amount of border crossing across these educational contexts. Some of the women work in all three contexts, deftly juggling a variety of lessons with a variety of students – teaching kindergarteners in one hour and university students in the next. Others, like Andrea and Louisa, moved from one context to another during the course of our interviews. All had changed jobs numerous times during their teaching careers in Japan. No-one's careers remained static; they fluidly moved from one context to another as necessary, and in general, the participants have moved up the EFL teaching hierarchy in Japan – from JET teacher or *eikaiwa* school employee to self-employed business owner, high-school teacher or university professor. To be able to do this, the women proved to be very resourceful in recognizing and seizing opportunities as they occurred. Margaret and her husband, for example, purchased their home because of its potential as a school. Victoria utilizes rooms in her family mausoleum to hold group lessons when it is not being used for funerals. Theresa, still in her thirties, realizes that to gain security in tertiary education she will need a doctorate, and thus she works full time, raises small children and writes her dissertation. Carrie, the youngest person in the study, may exit EFL teaching entirely (for now) and return to school to study an entirely different subject.

The women in this study have also displayed much resilience. Personal difficulties such as family illnesses, divorces or natural disasters have brought great struggles to some of the participants, and yet these difficulties were overcome in original and practical ways. What is certain is that these women have made successful lives for themselves in Japan, and they resisted being pigeonholed into stereotypical categories that are often imposed on women in Japan, particularly *foreign* women in Japan and especially foreign women *married to Japanese men*. They are survivors, and they are making their mark on Japan.

References

Abe, Y. and Oishi, A.S. (2009) The 1.03 million yen ceiling and earnings inequality among married women in Japan. *Economics Bulletin* 29 (2), 1510–1519.
Aoki, M. (2014) Schools fret about assistant teachers ahead of proposed 2020 reforms. *The Japan Times*. http://www.japantimes.co.jp/news/2014/01/02/national/schools-fret-about-assistant-teachers-ahead-of-proposed-2020-reforms/#.U26z68dtoUA (accessed 11 May 2014).
Appleby, R. (2012) Desire in translation: White masculinity and TESOL. *TESOL Quarterly*, doi:10.1002/tesq.51.
Appleby, R. (2013) Singleness, marriage, and the construction of heterosexual masculinities: Australian men teaching English in Japan. *Journal of Multidisciplinary International Studies* 10 (1), 1–21.
Appleby, R. (2014) *Men and Masculinities in Global English Language Teaching*. Bristol: Palgrave Macmillan.
Aspinal, R. (2005) University entrance in Japan. In J.S. Eades, R. Goodman and Y. Hada (eds) *The 'Big Bang' in Japanese Higher Education: The 2004 Reforms and the Dynamics of Change* (pp. 199–218). Victoria: Trans Pacific Press.
Bailey, K. (2006) Marketing the *eikaiwa* wonderland: Ideology, *akogare,* and gender alterity in English conversation school advertising in Japan. *Environment and Planning D: Society and Space* 24, 105–130.
Bailey, K. (2007) Akogare, ideology, and 'Charisma Man' mythology: Reflections on ethnographic research in English language schools in Japan. *Gender Place and Culture: A Journal of Feminist Geography* 14 (5), 585–608.
Bazeley, P. (2007) *Qualitative Data Analysis with NVivo*. London: Sage Publications.
Beauchamp, E.R. (1987) The development of Japanese educational policy, 1945–85. *History of Education Quarterly* 27 (3), 299–324.
Beijaard, D. (1995) Teachers' prior experiences and actual perceptions of professional identity. *Teachers and Teaching: Theory and Practice* 1, 291–294.
Beijaard, D., Meijer, P.C. and Verloop, N. (2004) Reconsidering research on teachers' professional identity. *Teaching and Teacher Education* 20, 107–128.
Bell, J.S. (2002) Narrative inquiry: More than just telling stories. *TESOL Quarterly* 36 (2), 207–213.
Benjamin, G.R. and James, E. (1989) Public and private schools and educational opportunity in Japan. In J.J. Shields (ed.) *Japanese Schooling: Patterns of Socialization, Equality and Political Control* (pp. 152–162). University Park, PA: Pennsylvania State University Press.
Bird, S. (2005) Language learning edutainment: Mixing motives in digital resources. *RELC Journal* 36, 311–339.
Bourdieu, P. (1991) *Language and Symbolic Power*. Malden, MA: Polity Press.
Bourdieu, P. and Wacquant, L. (1992) *An Invitation to Reflexive Sociology*. Chicago: University of Chicago Press.

Braine, G. (1999a) *Non-Native Educators in English Language Teaching*. Mahwah, NJ: Lawrence Erlbaum Associates.

Braine, G. (1999b) Introduction. In G. Braine (ed.) *Non-Native Educators in English Language Teaching* (pp. xiii–xx). Mahwah, NJ: Lawrence Erlbaum Associates.

Briggs, C.L. (2002) Interviewing, power/knowledge, and social inequality. In J.F. Gubium and J.A. Holstein (eds) *Handbook of Interview Research* (pp. 911–922). Thousand Oaks, CA: Sage Publications.

Brooks, D. (2015) University teachers in Japan work under the shadow of a falling axe. *The Japan Times Online*. Retrieved 7 May 2015 from http://www.japantimes.co.jp/community/2015/03/22/issues/university-teachers-in-japan-work-under-the-shadow-of-a-falling-ax-2/#.VUq3mRcYxto

Brotherstone, C. (2015) *Lifer: How to be a bald middle-aged English conversation teacher in Japan* [e-reader version] Varty Books.

Brown, J. (1994) Courtiers and Christians: The first Japanese emissaries to Europe. *Renaissance Quarterly* 47 (4), 872–906.

Browne, C. and Evans, B. (1994) The ALT as cultural informant: A catalyst for developing students' communicative competence. In M. Wada and A. Cominos (eds) *Studies in Team Teaching* (pp. 1728). Tokyo: Kenkyusha.

Bueno, E.P. (2003) A leading language school. In E.P. Bueno and T. Caesar (eds) *I Wouldn't Want Anybody to Know: Native English Teaching in Japan* (pp. 98–114). Tokyo: JPGS Press.

Bueno, E.P. and Caesar, T. (eds) (2003) *I Wouldn't Want Anybody to Know: Native English Teaching in Japan*. Tokyo: JPGS Press.

Burrows, C. (2007) The effect of limited-term contracts on teaching standards at tertiary-level education in Japan. *OnCUE Journal* 1 (1), 64–73.

Burton, S.K. (2004) Interviews with female Japanese study abroad students in England. *NUCB JLCC* 6 (1), 1–11.

Butler Y. and Iino, M. (2005) Current Japanese reforms in English language education: The 2003 "Action Plan". *Language Policy* 4, 25–45.

Caesar, T. and Bueno, E.P. (2003) Introduction. In E.P. Bueno and T. Caesar (eds) *I Wouldn't Want Anybody to Know: Native English Teaching in Japan* (pp. 14–27). Tokyo: JPGS Press.

Canagarajah, A.S. (1999) *Resisting Linguistic Imperialism in English Teaching*. Oxford: Oxford University Press.

Casey, K. (1995–1996) The new narrative research in education. *Review of Research in Education* 21, 221–253.

Charisma Man website. 2013, Online, available: http://www.charismaman.com/ (accessed 20 January 2013).

Chase, S. (2002) Learning to listen: Narrative principles in a qualitative research methods course. In R. Josselson, A. Lieblich and D. McAdams (eds) *Up Close and Personal: The Teaching and Learning of Narrative Research*. Washington D.C.: American Psychological Association.

Chase, S. (2005) Narrative inquiry: Multiple lenses, approaches, voices. In N.K. Denzin and Y.S. Lincoln (eds) *Handbook of Qualitative Research* (3rd ed.) (pp. 651–679). Thousand Oaks: CA: Sage.

Chesney, R. (2008) *Senseitional! Confessions of English Teachers in Japan*. Lulu.com.

Clandinin, D.J. (1985) Personal practical knowledge: A study of teachers' classroom images. *Curriculum Inquiry* 15 (4), 361–385.

Clandinin, D.J. (1986) *Classroom Practice: Teacher Images in Action*. London: The Falmer Press.

Clandinin, D.J. and Connelly, E.M. (1987) Teachers' personal knowledge: What counts as personal in studies of the personal. *Journal of Curriculum Studies* 19, 487–500.
Clandinin, D.J. and Connelly, E.M. (1996) *Teachers' Professional Knowledge Landscapes.* Teachers College Press, New York.
Clandinin, D.J. and Connelly, E.M. (2000) *Narrative Inquiry: Experience and Story in Qualitative Research.* San Francisco: Jossey Bass.
Clarke, M. (2008) *Language Teacher Identities: Co-constructing Discourse and Community.* Clevedon: Multilingual Matters.
Clavell, J. (1975) *Shogun.* U.S.: Delacort Press
Cohen, E. (ed.) (2010) *Planet Eigo* 2nd *Ed.* Yamagata: Association for Japan Exchange and Teaching.
Connelly, E.M. and Clandinin, D.J. (1985) Personal practical knowledge and the modes for knowledge: Relevance for teaching and learning. In E. Eisner (ed.) *Learning and Teaching the Ways of Knowing* (Vol. 84th yearbook of the National Society for the Study of Education, Part II, pp. 174–198). Chicago: University of Chicago Press.
Connelly, E.M. and Clandinin, D.J. (1990) Stories of experience and narrative inquiry. *Educational Researcher* 19 (5), 2–14.
Connelly, E.M. and Clandinin, D.J. (1995) Narrative and education. *Teachers and Teaching: Theory and Practice* 1 (1), 73–85.
Connelly, E.M. and Clandinin, D.J. (1999) *Shaping a Professional Identity: Stories of Educational Practice.* New York: Teachers College Press.
Crawford, M., Hayashi, K. and Suenaga, S. (2010) *Japanese War Brides in America: An Oral History.* Santa Barbara, CA: Praeger.
Creaser, F. (2012) Harassment prevention policies at a Japanese university. *The Journal and Proceedings of the Gender Awareness in Language Education (GALE) Special Interest Group of the Japan Association for Language Teaching* 5, 22–37.
Creaser, F. (2015) Mobbing in the Workplace. Pan Sig. JALT Pan Sig [Conference]. Kobe. 16 May 2013.
Daizen, T. and Yamanoi, A. (2008) The changing academic profession in the era of university reforms in Japan. *The Changing Academic Profession in International Comparative and Quantitative Perspectives: RIHI International Seminar Reports* 12. Hiroshima: Research Institute for Higher Education.
Davies A. (1991) *The Native Speaker in Applied Linguistics.* Edinburgh: Edinburgh University Press.
Davies, B. and Harré, R. (1990) Positioning: The discursive production of selves. *Journal for the Theory of Social Behaviour* 20 (1), 43–63.
Davies, B. and Harré, R. (1999) Positioning and personhood. In R. Harré and L. van Langenhove (eds) *Positioning Theory.* Oxford: Blackwell Publishers Ltd.
De Mente, B. (1969/2001) *Mistress Keeping in Japan: The Pitfalls and the Pleasures* [Google Books Version]. Retrieved from http://books.google.co.jp/books?id=O19aKfoUG9kC&pg=PP1&lpg=PP1&dq=Mistress+Keeping+in+Japan:+The+Pitfalls+and+the+Pleasures&source=bl&ots=xVhKbnD879&sig=B5zaDz8xB6eKYpBaHTwh2zsRpQg&hl=ja&sa=X&ei=fjNMVIODtL38QXUogI&redir_esc=y#v=onepage&q=Mistress%20Keeping%20in%20Japan%3A%20The%20Pitfalls%20and%20the%20Pleasures&f=false
De Mente, B. (1988) *Japan at Night* (1988) [Google Books Version] Retrieved from http://books.google.co.jp/books?id=fQg_AQAAIAAJ&q=de+mente+Japan+at

+Night&dq=de+mente+Japan+at+Night&hl=ja&sa=X&ei=1zNMVLvnNtb5 8AW-n4KAAg&ved=0CB8Q6AEwAA
De Mente, B. (2000) *Bachelor Japan*. Tokyo: Tuttle.
De Mente, B. (2006) *Sex and the Japanese: The Sensual Side of Japan* (2006) [Google Books Version] Retrieved from http://books.google.co.jp/books?id=PSXRAgAAQBAJ&pg=PT142&dq=Sex+and+the+Japanese:+The+Sensual+Side+of+Japan&hl=ja&sa=X&ei=MjRMVKG1DIj88QWDzYD4BQ&ved=0CB4Q6AEwAA#v=onepage&q=Sex%20and%20the%20Japanese%3A%20The%20Sensual%20Side%20of%20Japan&f=false
Derivry-Plard, M. (2013) The native speaker language teacher: Through time and space. In S. Houghton and D. Rivers (eds) *Native-speakerism in Japan: Intergroup Dynamics in Foreign Language Education* (pp. 243–255). Bristol: Multilingual Matters.
Diggs, N.B. (2001) *Looking Beyond the Mask: When American Women Marry Japanese Men*. New York: State University of New York Press.
Dower, J. (1999) *Embracing Defeat: Japan in the Wake of World War II*. New York: W.W. Nortan & Company.
Duff, P.A. and Uchida, Y. (1997) The negotiation of teachers' sociocultural identities and practices in postsecondary EFL classrooms. *TESOL Quarterly* 31 (3), 451–486.
Eades, J.S., Goodman, R. and Hada, Y. (eds) (2005) *The "Big Bang" in Japanese Higher Education: The 2004 Reforms and the Dynamics of Change*. Melbourne: Trans Pacific Press.
Earns, L.R. (1997) A Miner in the deep and dark places: Guido Verbeck in Nagasaki, 1859–1869. *Crossroads* 5 http://www.uwosh.edu/home_pages/faculty_staff/earns/verbeck.html (accessed 23 November 2013).
Edge, J. (1996) Cross-cultural paradoxes in a profession of values. *TESOL Quarterly* 30 (1), 9–28.
EIKEN, Test in Practical English Proficiency (2015), retrieved 28 March 2015 http://stepeiken.org/
Ekiken, K. (1905) *Women and the Wisdom of Japan*. London: John (reprinted by Kessinger Publishing 10 September 2010)
Elbaz, F. (1983) The teacher's "practical knowledge": Report of a case study. *Curriculum Inquiry* 11 (1), 43–71.
Erikson, E.H. (1968) *Identity, Youth and Crisis*. New York: W.W. Norton & Company.
Evanoff, R. (1993) Making a career of university teaching in Japan. In P. Wadden (ed.) *A Handbook for Teaching English at Japanese Colleges and Universities* (pp. 15–26). New York: Oxford University Press.
Fang, Z. (1996) A review of research on teacher beliefs and practices. *Educational Research* 38 (1), 47–65.
Fichtner, F. and Chapman, K. (2011) The cultural identities of foreign language teachers. *L2 Journal* 3 (1), 116–140.
Flynn C. (2009) ALT furniture: A look at dispatch ALT contracts. *The Language Teacher* 33 (5), 39–40.
Fraser, M. (2011) Exploring the nature and process of professional identity of teachers of English in Japanese higher education. Doctor of Education thesis, Faculty of Education, University of Woolongong. http://ro.uow.edu.au/theses/3431
Freeman, D. and Richards, J. (1996) *Teacher Learning in Language Teaching*. New York: Cambridge University Press.
Fujimura-Fanselow, K. (1989) Women's participation in higher education in Japan. In J.J. Shields (ed.) *Japanese Schooling: Patterns of Socialization, Equality, and Political Control*. University Park, PA: Pennsylvania State University Press.

Fujimura-Fanselow, K. (1995) College women today: Options and dilemmas. In K. Fujimura-Fanselow and A. Kameda (eds) *Japanese Women: New Feminist Perspectives on the Past, Present and Future* (pp. 125–154). New York: The Feminist Press.
Fukase, H. (2015) Conversation between Random Foreign Male (RFM) and Heather. *AFWJ Journal April 29.*
Fukuzawa, R. (1994) The path to adulthood according to Japanese middle schools. *Journal of Japanese Studies* 20 (1), 61–86.
Fukuzawa, R. (2001) *Intense Years: How Japanese Adolescents Balance School, Family and Friends*. New York, Routledge.
Gatbonton, E. (1999) Investigating experienced ESL teachers' pedagogical knowledge. *The Modern Language Journal* 83 (1), 33–50.
Gee, J.P. (1996) *Social Linguistics and Literacies: Ideology in Discourses* (2nd ed.). London: Taylor & Frances.
Gee, J.P. (2000) Identity as an analytic lens for research in education. In W.G. Secada (ed.) *Review of Research in Education* (Vol. 25). Washington, DC: American Educational Research Association.
Geertz, C. (1988) *Works and Lives: The Anthropologist as Author.* Retrieved from http://books.google.co.uk/books?id=_EMEZKVE8UcC&pg=PR7&source=gbs_selected_pages&cad=2#v=onepage&q&f=false
Geluso, J. (2013) Negotiating a professional identity: Non-Japanese teachers of English in pre-tertiary education in Japan. In S. Houghton and D. Rivers (eds) *Native-speakerism in Japan: Intergroup Dynamics in Foreign Language Education* (pp. 92–104). Bristol: Multilingual Matters.
General Union (2007) blog posting General Union anti-dispatching campaign makes the news http://www.generalunion.org/alt/news/77?lang=jp retrieved 10 May 2014.
General Union (2013) blog posting University & School teachers won't be victims of new Labour Contract Law http://www.generalunion.org/News/1008 retrieved 7 May 2015.
Gibbs, G.H. (2002) *Qualitative Data Analysis: Explorations with NVivo.* Maidenhead, UK: Open University Press.
Glaser, B.G. and Strauss, A.L. (1967) *The Discovery of Grounded Theory: Strategies for Qualitative Research.* Chicago: Aldine.
Goffman, E. (1959) *The Presentation of Self in Everyday Life.* London: Penguin.
Golembek, P.R. (1998) A study of language teachers' personal practical knowledge. *TESOL Quarterly* 23 (3): 447–464.
Goodman, R. (2007) The concept of Kokusaika and Japanese educational reform. *Globalisation, Societies and Education* 5 (1), 71–87.
Gordon, B. (1997) *The Only Woman in the Room.* Chicago: University of Chicago Press.
Gorsuch, G. (1999) Mombusho approved textbooks in Japanese high school EFL classes: An aid or hindrance to educational policy innovations? *The Language Teacher* 23 (10), 5–15.
Gorsuch, G. (2000) EFL educational policies and educational cultures: Influences on teachers' approval of communicative activities. *TESOL Quarterly* 34 (4), 675–709.
Gorsuch, G. (2001) Japanese EFL teachers: Perceptions of communicative, audiolingual and yakudoku activities: The plan versus the reality. *Education Policy Analysis Archives* 9 (10). http://epaa.asu.edu/epaa/v9n10.html (accessed 20 May 2007).

Griffis, W.E. (1900) *Guido Verbeck of Japan: A Citizen of No Country; A Life Story of Foundation Work Inaugurated by Guido Fridolin Verbeck*. Chicago: Fleming H. Revell. [reprinted by Oliphant, Anderson and Ferrire, London, 1901.]

Griffis, W.E. (1902) *A Maker of The New Orient: Samuel Robbins Brown, Pioneer Educator in China, America and Japan*. Forgotten Books: www.ForgottonBooks.org

Guest, M. (2000) 'But I have to teach grammar!': An analysis of the role 'grammar' plays in Japanese university English entrance examinations. *The Language Teacher* 24 (11), 23–29.

Guest, M. (2011) How to talk to Japanese women—EFL style. *ELTNews.com*. Retrieved 12 December 2013 from http://www.eltnews.com/columns/uni_files/2011/07/how_to_talk_to_japanese_women.html.

Habu, T. (2000) The irony of globalization: The experience of Japanese women in British higher education. *Higher Education* 39 (1), 43–66.

Hadley, G. and Yoshioka Hadley, H. (1996) The culture of learning and the good teacher in Japan: An analysis of student views. *The Language Teacher* 20 (9), 53–55.

Hall, H.T. (1998) *Cartels of the Mind: Japan's Intellectual Closed Shop*. New York: W.W. Norton & Company.

Hanna, P. (2012) Using Internet technologies (such as Skype) as a research medium: A research note. *Qualitative Research* 12 (2), 239–242.

Hara, Y. (1977) From Westernization to Japanization: The replacement of foreign teachers by Japanese who studied abroad. *The Developing Economies* 15(4) 440–461.

Harasawa, M. (1974) A critical survey of English language teaching in Japan. *ELT* 29 (1), 71–79.

Harasawa, M. (1978) Japanese culture: The ultimate destiny of English language teaching in Japan. In I. Koike, M. Matsuyama, Y. Igarashi and K. Suzuki (eds) *The Teaching of English in Japan* (pp. 547–557). Tokyo: Eichosha Publishing Co., Ltd.

Harré, R. and van Langenhove, L. (1999) *Positioning Theory*. Oxford: Blackwell Publishers, Ltd.

Harshbarger, B. (2012) A faulty ivory tower: Reflections on directing the ELP from 2006–2012. *Language Research Bulletin* 27. ICU: Tokyo.

Hashimoto, K. (2013) The construction of the 'native speaker' in Japan's educational policies for TEFL. In S. Houghton and D. Rivers (eds) *Native-speakerism in Japan: Intergroup Dynamics in Foreign Language Education* (pp. 159–169). Bristol: Multilingual Matters.

Hayes, B.E. (2012) Institutional change in gendered recruitment patterns in Japanese academia: Tempered radical or subversive? *The Journal and Proceedings of the Gender Awareness in Language Education (GALE) Special Interest Group of the Japan Association for Language Teaching*, 5–21.

Hayes, B.E. (2013) Hiring criteria for Japanese university English-teaching faculty. In S. Houghton and D. Rivers (eds) *Native-speakerism in Japan: Intergroup Dynamics in Foreign Language Education* (pp. 132–146). Bristol: Multilingual Matters.

Heimlich, E. (2013) The meaning of Japan's role of professional foreigner. In S. Houghton and D. Rivers (eds) *Native-speakerism in Japan: Intergroup Dynamics in Foreign Language Education* (pp. 169–182). Bristol: Multilingual Matters.

Henrichson, L. (1987) Diffusions of innovations in English language teaching: The English language exploratory committee's promotion of C. C. Fries' oral approach in Japan, 1956–1968. Doctoral Dissertation, University of Hawaii.

Henrichson, L. (1989) *Diffusion of Innovations in English Language Teaching: The ELEC Effort in Japan, 1956–1968*. Westport, CN: Greenwood Press.

Herbison, C. and Schultz, J. (1990) *Quiet Passage: The Japanese-American War Bride Experience*. Lawrence, KS: The University of Kansas, 1990.
Hinchman, L. and Hinchman, S. (eds) (2001) *Memory, Identity, Community. The Idea of Narrativity in the Human Sciences*. New York: New York University Press.
Hino, N. (1988) Yakudoku: Japan's dominant tradition in foreign language learning. *JALT Journal* 10 (1), 4–5.
Hogg, M.A. and Abrams, D. (1988) *Social Identifications: A Social Psychology of Intergroup Relations and Group Processes*. New York: Routledge.
Holliday, A. (1994) *Appropriate Methodology and Social Context*. Cambridge: Cambridge University Press.
Honda, Y. (2004) The formation and transformation of the Japanese system of transition from school to work. *Social Science Japan Journal* 7 (1), 103–115.
Houghton, S. (2013) The overthrow of the foreign lecture position and its aftermath. In S. Houghton and D. Rivers (eds) *Native-speakerism in Japan: Intergroup Dynamics in Foreign Language Education* (pp. 60–74). Bristol: Multilingual Matters.
Houghton, S. and Rivers, D. (eds) (2013) *Native-speakerism in Japan: Intergroup Dynamics in Foreign Language Education*. Bristol: Multilingual Matters.
Ike, M. (1995) A historical review of English in Japan (1600–1880). *World Englishes* 14 (1), 3–11.
Imamura, M. (1978) Junior high school: English teaching policies for lower secondary schools. In I. Koike, M. Matsuyama, Y. Igarashi and K. Suzuki (eds) *The Teaching of English in Japan* (pp. 134–140). Tokyo: Eichosha Publishing Co., Ltd.
Imura, S. (1978) Critical views on TEFL: Criticism on TEFL in Japan. In I. Koike, M. Matsuyama, Y. Igarashi and K. Suzuki (eds) *The Teaching of English in Japan* (pp. 15–22). Tokyo: Eichosha Publishing Co., Ltd.
Ion, H. (2009) *American Missionaries and Christian Oyatoi and Japan 1859–73*. Vancouver: UBC Press.
Ishida, G. (1973) A shallow view of mixed marriage. *Asahi Evening News*, 28 May 1973.
Ishida, H. (1993) *Social Mobility in Contemporary Japan: Educational Credentials, Class and the Labour Market in a Cross National*. Stanford, CA, Stanford University Press.
Ishigaki, A. (1940/2004) *Restless Wave: My Life in Two Worlds*. NY: Feminist Press.
Ishikida, M.Y. (2005a) *Japanese Education in the 21st Century*. Lincoln, NE: Universe.
Ishikida, M.Y. (2005b) *Higher Education and Lifelong Learning. Japanese Education in the 21st Century*. Lincoln, NE, Center for US–Japan Comparative Social Studies.
Ito, K. (1978) Traditional methods and new methods: A study on the methods suited for the Japanese. In I. Koike, M. Matsuyama, Y. Igarashi and K. Suzuki (eds) *The Teaching of English in Japan* (pp. 204–219). Tokyo: Eichosha Publishing Co., Ltd.
Jansen, M.B. (2000) *The Making of Modern Japan*. USA: First Harvard University Press.
Japan Society for the Promotion of Science (2006) JSPS's new restart postdoctoral fellowship. *JSPS Quarterly* 18, 2. www.jsps.go.jp/english/e-quart/19/jsps19.pdf (accessed 24 June 2011).
JET Programme (n.d.) History of the JET program. Retrieved from http://www.jetprogramme.org/e/introduction/history.html 13 May 2015.
Johnston, B. (1997) Do EFL teachers have careers? *TESOL Quarterly* 31 (4), 681–712.
Johnston, B. (1999) The expatriate teacher as postmodern paladin. *Research in the Teaching of English* 34 (2), 255–280.
Josselson, R. (ed.) (1996) *Ethics and Process in the Narrative Study of Lives*. Newbury Park, CA: Sage Publications.

Kachru, B.B. (1985) Standards, codification and sociolinguistic realism: The English language in the outer circle. In R. Quirk and H.G. Widdowson (eds) *English in the World: Teaching and Learning the Language and Literatures* (pp. 11–30). Cambridge: Cambridge University Press.

Kachru, B.B. (ed.) (1992) *The Other Tongue: English Across Cultures.* Urbana, IL: University of Illinois Press.

Kamhi-Stein, L.D. (ed.) (2004) *Learning and Teaching from Experience: Perspectives on Nonnative English-speaking Professionals.* Ann Arbor, MI: The University of Michigan Press.

Kan, S. English offers mothers control over careers. *The Daily Yomiuri*, 28 April 2009.

Kariya, T. and Rosenbaum, J. (1987) Self-selection in Japanese junior high schools: A longitudinal study of students' educational plans. *Sociology of Education* 60 (3), 168–180.

Kashper, E. (2003) Cometh the man, cometh the charisma. *The Japan Times Online*, 19 August. http://www.japantimes.co.jp/community/2003/08/19/issues/cometh-the-man-cometh-the-charisma/#.U6d176hhvTo (accessed 23 June 2014).

Kawagoe, A. (2010) ED *Education in Japan community Blog* educationinjapan.wordpress.com/about (accessed 15 April 2014).

Kawasaki, I. (1973) *Alien Rice.* Tokyo: Tuttle Publishing.

Keene, D. (1969) *The Japanese Discovery of Europe, 1720–1830.* Stanford, CA: Stanford University Press.

Kelly, W. (2014) Applying a critical metatheoretical approach to intercultural relations: The case of U.S.–Japanese Communication. In M. Asante, Y. Miiki and J. Yin (eds), *The Global Intercultural Communication Reader* (pp. 357–373). New York: Routledge.

Kelsky, K. (2001) *Women on the Verge: Japanese Women, Western Dreams.* Durham, NC: Duke University Press.

Kemper, K. and Makino, M. (1993) Cultural influences on the construction of knowledge in Japanese higher education. *Comparative Education* 29 (2), 185–199. https://books.google.co.jp/books/about/The_Social_Role_of_Higher_Education.html?id=CwPgqhHjZXIC&hl=ja (p. 27–55)

Kennett, B. and Jackson, L.R. (2014) 'What if [your] boyfriend was a foreigner?' Romance, gender, and second language learning in an edutainment context. *Asian Englishes* 16 (2), 157–172.

Kiernan, P. (2010) *Deconstructing Narrative Identity in English Language Teaching: Exploring Teacher Interviews in Japanese and English.* Basingstoke: Palgrave MacMillan.

Kinmouth, E. (2005) From selection to seduction: The impact of demographic change on private higher education in Japan. In J.S. Eades, R. Goodman and Y. Hada (eds) *The 'Big Bang' in Japanese Higher Education: The 2004 Reforms and the Dynamics of Change* (pp. 106–135). Melbourne: Trans Pacific Press.

Kitao, K. and Kitao, S.K. (1995) *English Teaching: Theory, Research and Practice.* Tokyo: Eichosha.

Kobayashi, Y. (2002) The role of gender in foreign language learning attitudes: Japanese female students' attitudes toward English learning. *Gender and Education* 14 (2), 181–197.

Kobayashi, Y. (2007a) Japanese working women and English study abroad. *World Englishes* 26 (1), 62–71.

Kobayashi, Y. (2007b) TEFL policy as a part of stratified Japan and beyond. *TESOL Quarterly* 41 (3), 566–571.

Kobayashi, Y. (2011) Global Englishes and the discourse on Japaneseness. *Journal of Intercultural Studies* 32 (1), 1–14.
Kobayashi, Y. (2014) Gender gap in the EFL classroom in East Asia. *Applied Linguistics* 35(2), 219–223.
Koike, I. and Tanaka, H. (1995) English in foreign language education policy in Japan: Toward the twenty-first century. *World Englishes* 14 (1), 13–25.
Koike, I., Matsuyama, M., Igarashi, Y. and Suzuki K. (eds) (1978) *The Teaching of English in Japan* (pp. 15–22). Tokyo: Eichosha Publishing Co., Ltd.
Koike, M. (2000) American studies and the liberation of a Japanese woman: A personal narrative. *American Studies Journal* 38 (3), 72–78.
Koyama, N. (1995) *Noboru Kokusai Kekkon Daiichigo: Meiji Hitotachi no Zakkon Kotohajime* [*The First International Marriage: The Beginnings of Mixed Marriages of Meiji People*] Tokyo: Kodansha, 1995 p. 263–271. As republished on Yoshi Research (www.weatherall.org)   http://members.jcom.home.ne.jp/yosha/yr/nationality/Naturalization_1873.html (accessed 25 June 2014).
Koyama, N. (2002) Three Meiji marriages between Japanese men and English women. In H. Cortazzi (ed.) *Biographical Portraits: Britain and Japan, Volume IV* (pp. 383–396). London: Japan Library, 2002 London: Routledge.
Kubo, M. (2006) Support for female researchers in Japan: Current actions of Japanese funding agencies to assist female researchers. *JSPS Quarterly* (from Japan Society of the Promotion of Science) 18 Winter. http://www.jsps.go.jp/english/e-quart/18/index_01.html (accessed 1 June 2011).
Kubota, R. (1998) Ideologies of English in Japan. *World Englishes* 17 (3), 295–306.
Kubota, R. (2011) Learning a foreign language as leisure and consumption: Enjoyment, desire, and the business of *eikaiwa*. *International Journal of Bilingual Education and Bilingualism* 14 (4), 473–488.
Kubota, R. and Fujimoto, D. (2013) Racialized native speakers: Voices of Japanese American English language professionals. In S. Houghton and D. Rivers (eds) *Native-speakerism in Japan: Intergroup Dynamics in Foreign Language Education* (pp. 196–206). Bristol: Multilingual Matters.
Kubota, R. and McKay, S. (2009) Globalization and language learning in rural Japan: The role of English in the local linguistic ecology. *TESOL Quarterly* 43, 593–619.
Kvale, S. (2006) Dominance through interviews and dialogues. *Qualitative Inquiry* 12 (3), 480–500.
Lah, K. (2010) Comic spoofs Western nerds' dating success in Japan. *CNN Connect the World*   http://edition.cnn.com/2010/WORLD/asiapcf/03/02/japan.charisma.man.comic/ (accessed 23 June 2014).
Lave, J. and Wenger, E. (1991) *Situated Learning: Legitimate Peripheral Participation*. Cambridge: Press Syndicate of the University of Cambridge.
Law, G. (1995) Ideologies of English language education in Japan. *JALT Journal* 17 (2), 213–224.
Leupp, G. (2003) *Interracial Intimacy in Japan: Western Men and Japanese Women 1543–1900*. New York: Continuum.
Lewis, C. (2010) One more time – with Charisma, *The Japan Times Online*, 13 July. Online, available: http://search.japantimes.co.jp/cgi-bin/fl20100713zg.html (accessed 23 June 2014).
Liddle, J. and Nakajima, S. (2000) *Rising Suns, Rising Daughters: Gender, Class and Power in Japan*. New York: Zed Books Ltd.

Lincoln, Y.S. and Denzin, N. (1994) *Handbook of Qualitative Research*. Thousand Oaks, CA: Sage Publications.
Liu, D. (1998) Ethnocentrism in TESOL: Teacher education and the neglected needs of international TESOL students. *ELT Journal* 52 (1), 3–9.
Liu, J. (1999) Nonnative-English speaking professionals in TESOL. *TESOL Quarterly* 33 (1), 85–102.
LoCastro, V. (1996) English language education in Japan. In H. Coleman (ed.) *Society and the Language Classroom* (pp. 40–59). Cambridge: Cambridge University Press.
Loti, P. (1887; 2010) *Madame Chrysanthème*: A public domain book: Kindle version
Lummis, D. (1976) *English Conversation as Ideology*. Tokyo: Kirihara Shoten.
Lyons, N. and LaBoskey, V.K. (2002) Why narrative inquiry or exemplars for scholarship of teaching? In N. Lyons and V.K. LaBoskey (eds) *Narrative Inquiry in Practice: Advancing the Knowledge of Teaching* (pp. 11–30). New York: Teachers College Press.
Ma, K. (1996) *Modern Madam Butterfly*. Tokyo: Charles E. Tuttle Company.
MacNaughton, A. (2008) Company and personal character in the eikaiwa industry: An ethnography of a private language school in Japan. Unpublished doctoral dissertation, the University of Hong Kong.
Marx, E. (2013) *When East Weds West*. Lexington KY: Botchan Books.
Masden, K. (2013) Kumamoto General Union vs. the Prefectural University of Kumamoto: Reviewing the decision rendered by the Kumamoto Court. In S. Houghton and D. Rivers (eds) *Native-speakerism in Japan: Intergroup Dynamics in Foreign Language Education* (pp. 42–59). Bristol: Multilingual Matters.
Matsui, M. (1995) Gender role perceptions of Japanese and Chinese female students in American universities. *Comparative Education Review* 39 (3), 356–378.
Matsuyama, M. (1978) Entrance examinations: College entrance examinations and English education in Japan. In I. Koike, M. Matsuyama, Y. Igarashi and K. Suzuki (eds) *The Teaching of English in Japan* (pp. 35–46). Tokyo: Eichosha Publishing Co., Ltd.
McConnell, D. (2000) *Importing Diversity: Inside Japan's JET program*. Berkeley, CA: University of California Press.
McCormick, K. (1988) Vocationalism and the Japanese Education System. *Comparative Education* 24 (1), 37–51.
McCrostie, J. (2010) The right stuff: Hiring trends for tenured university positions in Japan. *The Language Teacher* 34 (5), 31–35.
McCrostie, J. (2014) Harassers exploit Gaba's 'man-to-man' lesson format: Teachers cite unique classroom method and management behind prevalence of abuse by students. *The Japan Times* http://www.japantimes.co.jp/community/2014/06/16/issues/harassers-exploit-gabas-man-man-lesson-format/#.VEwjauegbw0 (accessed 26 October 2014).
McNeill, D. (2007) Few women reach the top in Japanese universities [electronic version]. *The Chronicle of Higher Education* 54, NA. http://find.galegroup.com/itx/start.do?prodId=EAIM (accessed 22 April 2009).
McVeigh, B.J. (2001) Higher Education, apathy and post-meritocracy. *The Language Teacher* 25 (10), 29–32.
McVeigh, B.J. (2002) *Japanese Higher Education as Myth*. Armonk, NY: M.E. Sharp, Inc.
Mead, G.J. (1934) *Mind, Self and Society*. Chicago: University of Chicago Press.
MEXT (2006) OECD Thematic review of tertiary education – Country background report of Japan. http://www.oecd.org/document/16/0,3746,en_2649_33723_35580240_1_1_1_1,00.html (accessed 15 October 2007).

MEXT (N.D.) Statistics (accessed 17 June 2015). http://www.mext.go.jp/english/statistics/index.htm.

Minakawa, S. (1955) *Christian Education and English Teaching in Early Japan*. Tokyo: Gakuseisha.

Ministry of Economy, Trade and Industry (2005) 2005 Survey on Selected Service Industries. Retrieved from <www.meti.go.jp/english/statistics/tyo/tokusabizi/index.html> (accessed 15 June 2013).

Ministry of Economy, Trade and Industry (2015) Monthly report on the current survey of selected services industries, February 2015. Retrieved from http://www.meti.go.jp/statistics/tyo/tokusabido/result/pdf/hv201502kj.pdf (accessed 31 August 2015).

Mizuta, A. (2009) The unchanged images of English in changing Japan: From modernization to globalization. *Intercultural Communication Studies* XVIII (2), 38–53.

Morita, N. (2004) Negotiating participation and identity in second language academic communities. *TESOL Quarterly* 38 (4), 573–603.

Mulvey, S. (2012) Becoming part-time (and grasping at straws) [Blog post, 29 July]. http://thebasementblogbyme.wordpress.com/ (accessed 1 June 2013).

Mulvey, S. (2012a, June 16) A reexamination of gender in the classroom. JALT Pan Sig [Conference]. Hiroshima. 18 May 2012.

Murray, A. (2013) Teacher burnout in Japanese higher education. *The Language Teacher* 37 (4), 51–55.

Nagai, M. (1971) *Higher Education in Japan: Its Take-off and Crash*. Tokyo: University of Tokyo Press.

Nagasawa, K. (2004) Teacher training and development. In V. Makarova and T. Rodgers (eds) *English Language Teaching: The Case of Japan* (pp. 280–295). Minchen: Lincom Europa.

Nagatomo, D.H. (2011) A case study of how beliefs toward language learning and language teaching influence the teaching practices of a teacher of English in Japanese higher education. *The Language Teacher* 35 (6), 25–29.

Nagatomo, D.H. (2012a) *Exploring Japanese University English Teachers' Professional Identity*. Bristol: Multilingual Matters.

Nagatomo, D.H. (2012b) Gender counts: Women in Japanese higher education. *The Language Teacher* 36 (4), 29–32.

Nagatomo, D.H. (2013) The advantages and disadvantages faced by housewife English teachers in the cottage industry *eikaiwa* business. *The Language Teacher* 37 (1), 3–7.

Nagatomo, D.H. (2014a, May) Language learning in the 21st Century: Approaches, needs and contexts: Merging the competing ideologies of *eigo* and *eikaiwa*. Plenary address at the NEAR Conference at University of Niigata Prefecture, Niigata, Japan.

Nagatomo, D.H. (2014b) In the ivory tower and out of the loop: Racialized and gendered identities of university EFL teachers in Japan. In Y.L. Cheung, S.B. Said and K. Park (eds) *Advances and Current Trends in Language Teacher Identity Research* (pp. 102–115). Abingdon: Routledge.

Nagatomo, D.H. (2015) How being an "insider" or an "outsider" shapes EFL teachers' professional identity: One teacher's story from Japan. *Asian EFL Journal* 17 (3) 111–130.

Nakao, K. (1978) The oral method: With particular reference to the work of Harold Palmer. In I. Koike, M. Matsuyama, Y. Igarashi and K. Suzuki (eds) *The Teaching of English in Japan* (pp. 228–241). Tokyo: Eichosha Publishing Co., Ltd.

Nakata, Y.F. and C Mosk (1987) The demand for college education in postwar Japan. *The Journal of Human Resources* 22 (3), 377–404.
Neilsen, R. (2009) *Travellers' Tales: The Expatriate English Teacher in the New Global Culture*. Newcastle upon Tyne: Cambridge Scholars Publishing.
Neilsen, R. (2011) 'Moments of disruption' and the development of expatriate TESOL teachers. *English Australia Journal* 27 (1), 18–32.
Neilsen, R., Gitsaki, C. and Honan, E. (2007) Traveller's tales. ELT teachers in a globalising world. In C. Gitsaki (ed.) *Language and Languages: Global and Local Tensions* (pp. 1–14). Newcastle upon Tyne: Cambridge Scholars Publishing.
Newby H., Weko, T., Breneman, D., Johanneson, T. and Maassen, P. (2009) OECD reviews of tertiary education: Japan. http://www.google.co.jp/url?sa=t&rct=j&q=&esrc=s&source=web&cd=1&ved=0CCIQFjAAahUKEwiZ17LJkZDGAhVjKqYKHR44AJo&url=http%3A%2F%2Fwww.oecd.org%2Fjapan%2F42280329.pdf&ei=Q_N9VdmpLuPUmAWe8IDQCQ&usg=AFQjCNHdOg6lNcGZY3ivjTxpAmlWqA24w&sig2=42j8EMjpzYSywigdQWH8cQ&bvm=bv.95515949,d.dGY (accessed 15 June 2015).
Nishino, T. (2011) Japanese high school teachers' beliefs and practices regarding Communicative Language Teaching. *JALT Journal* 33 (2), 131–155.
Nishino, T. and Watanabe, M. (2008) Communication-oriented policies versus classroom realities in Japan. *TESOL Quarterly* 42 (1), 133–138.
Nitta, F. (1988) *Kokusai Kekkon:* Trends in intercultural marriage in Japan. *International Journal of Intercultural Relations* 12, 205–232.
Normile, D. (2001) Women faculty battle Japan's *Koza* system [electronic version]. *Science* 291.5505, 817. http://find.galegroup.com/itx/start.do?prodId=EAIM (accessed 22 April 2009).
Nunan, D. (1988) *The Learner-Centered Curriculum: A Study in Second Language Teaching*. Cambridge: Cambridge University Press.
NVivo (2002) QSR International Pty. Melbourne, Australia.
Oguri, S. (2002) *Daarin wa gaikokujin [My Darling is a Foreigner]*. Tokyo: Media Factory.
Okano, K. (2000) Social justice and job distribution in Japan: Class, minority and gender. *International Review of Education/Internationale Zeitschrift für Erziehungswissenschaft/Revue Internationale de l'Education* 46 (6), 545–563.
Okano, K. and Tsuchiya, M. (1999) *Education in Contemporary Japan: Inequality and Diversity*. Cambridge: Cambridge University Press.
O'Leary, V.E. and Mitchel, J.M. (1990) Women connecting with women: Networks and mentors in the United States. In S. Stiver Lie and V.E. O'Leary (eds) *Storming the Tower: Women in the Academic World*. New York: Nichols/GP Publishing.
Omura, K. (1978) Prewar (before 1945): From the Phaeton Incident up to the Pacific War. In I. Koike, M. Matsuyama, Y. Igarashi and K. Suzuki (eds) *The Teaching of English in Japan* (pp. 91–103). Tokyo: Eichosha Publishing Co., Ltd.
Ono, H. (2001) Who goes to college? Features of institutional tracking in Japanese higher education. *American Journal of Education* 109 (2), 161–195.
Ono, H. (2003) Pursuing quality: Migration among college students in Japan. *Research in Sociology of Education* 14, 103–123.
Ono, H. (2004) College quality and earnings in the Japanese labor market. *Industrial Relations* 43 (3), 595–617.
Ono, H. and Piper, N. (2004) Japanese women studying abroad, the case of the United States. *Women's Studies International Forum* 27 (2), 101–118.

Ota, Y. (1994) The 'decline' of English language competence in modern Japan. *Journal of Asian Pacific Communication* 5 (4), 201–206.
Pavlenko, A. (2002) Bilingualism, gender and ideology. *International Journal of Bilingualism* 5 (2), 117–151
Pennycook, A. (1994) *The Cultural Politics of English as an International Language*. New York: Longman.
Phan Le Ha (2008) *Teaching English as an International Language: Identity, Resistance and Negotiation*. Clevedon: Multilingual Matters.
Phillipson, R. (1992) *Linguistic Imperialism*. Oxford: Oxford University Press.
Piller, I. (2002) *Bilingual Couples Talk: The Discursive Construction of Hybridity*. Amsterdam: Benjamins.
Piller, I. and Takahashi, K. (2006) A passion for English: Desire and the language market. In A. Pavlenko (ed.) *Bilingual Minds: Emotional Experience Expression and Representation* (pp. 59–83). Clevedon: Multilingual Matters.
Pomatti, D. (2007) Westernization and English education in the Meiji public schools. *Foreign Languages and Literature* 32 (1), 116–145.
Poole, G. (2010) *The Japanese Professor*. Rotterdam: Sense Publishers.
Rampton, M.B.H. (1990) Displacing the 'native speaker': Expertise, affiliation, and inheritance. *English Language Teaching Journal* 44 (2), 97–101.
Raymo, J. (2003) Educational attainment and the transition to first marriage among Japanese women. *Demography* 40 (1), 83–103.
Riessman, C.K. (1993) *Narrative Analysis* (Vol. 30). Newbury Park, CA: Sage Publications.
Riessman, C.K. (2002) Analysis of personal narrative. In J.F. Gubrium (ed.) *Handbook of Interview Research*. Thousand Oaks, CA: Sage Publications.
Riessman, C.K. (2008) *Narrative Methods for the Human Sciences*. Thousand Oaks, CA: Sage Publications.
Rivers, D. (2010) Ideologies of internationalisation and the treatment of diversity within Japanese higher education. *Journal of Higher Education Policy and Management* 32 (5), 441–454.
Rivers, D. (2011) Japanese national identification and English language learning processes. *International Journal of Intercultural Relations* 35, 111–123.
Rivers, D. (2013) Institutionalized native-speakerism: Voices of dissent and acts of resistance. In S. Houghton and D. Rivers (eds) *Native-speakerism in Japan: Intergroup Dynamics in Foreign Language Education* (pp. 75–91). Bristol: Multilingual Matters.
Rivers, D. and Ross, A. (2013) Idealized English teachers: The implicit influence of race in Japan. *Journal of Language, Identity, and Education* 5 (12), 321–339.
Ruxton, I. (1998) Britain 17 August–16 December 1872: The Mission's aims, objectives, and results. In I. Nish (ed.) *The Iwakura Mission in America and Europe: A New Assessment* (pp. 35–44). Surrey, U.K.: Japan Library Curzon Press Ltd.
Said, E. (1978) *Orientalism*. London: Penguin.
Sakata, K. and McKenzie, C.R. (2005) The impact of tax reform in 2004 on the female labour supply in Japan. *MODSIM05 – International Congress on Modeling and Simulation: Advances and Applications for Management and Decision Making*, Proceedings, 1084–1090.
Sato, K. (2002) Practical understandings of CLT and teacher development. In S.J. Savignon (ed.) *Interpreting Communicative Language Teaching: Contexts and Concerns in Teacher Education* (pp. 41–81). New Haven: Yale University Press.
Schodt, F. (2003) *Native American in the Land of the Shogun: Ranald MacDonald and the Opening of Japan*. Berkeley, CA: Stone Bridge Press.

Seargeant, P. (2009) *The Idea of English in Japan: Ideology and the Evolution of a Global Language*. Bristol: Multilingual Matters.

Seargeant, P. (2013) Ideologies of nativism and linguistic globalization. In S. Houghton and D. Rivers (eds) *Native-speakerism in Japan: Intergroup Dynamics in Foreign Language Education* (pp. 231–242). Bristol: Multilingual Matters.

Seidman, I. (2006) *Interviewing as Qualitative Research: A Guide for Researchers in Education and the Social Sciences* (3rd edn). New York: Teachers College Press.

Shibusawa, N. (2006) *America's Geisha Ally: Reimagining the Japanese Enemy*. USA: Harvard University Press.

Shimbori, M. (1981) The Japanese academic profession. *Higher Education* 10 (1), 75–87.

Shimizu, K. (1995) Japanese college student attitudes towards English teachers: A survey. *The Language Teacher* 19 (10), 5–8.

Shulman, L.S. (1987) Knowledge and teaching: Foundations of the new reform. *Harvard Educational Review* 57 (2), 1–22.

Silverman, D. (1993) *Interpreting Qualitative Data: Methods for Analyzing Talk, Text and Interaction*. London: Sage Publications.

Simon-Maeda, A. (2004) The complex construction of professional identities: Female EFL educators in Japan speak out. *TESOL Quarterly* 38 (3), 405–436.

Simon-Maeda, A., Churchill, E. and Cornwell, S. (2006) Negotiating academic practices, identities and relationships in a doctoral program: A case from an overseas institution in Japan. *TESL-EJ* 10 (2), 1–25.

Smith, R.C. (2007) Harold E. Palmer's life and career. Retrieved from http://www2.warwick.ac.uk/fac/soc/al/research/collect/elt_archive/halloffame/palmer/life (accessed 1 December 2013).

Smith, R.C. and Imura, M. (2004) Lessons from the past: Traditions and reform. In V. Makarova and T. Rodgers (eds) *English Language Teaching: The Case of Japan* (pp. 29–48). Munich: Lincom-Europa.

Sodei, T. (2005) A comparative study of the research conditions of women scientists and the present states of women's/gender studies in Asian countries toward the sustainable development. Paper presented at the Fifth Conference of the Science Council of Asia (SCA).

Stanley, P. (2012) Superheroes in Shanghai: Constructing transnational Western men's identities. *Gender Place and Culture: A Journal of Feminist Geography* 19 (2), 213–231.

Stanley, P. (2013) *A Critical Ethnography of "Westerners" Teaching English in China: Shanghaied in Shanghai*. Oxon, Canada: Routledge.

Stewart, A. (2005) Teaching Positions: A Study of Identity in English Language Teachers in Japanese Higher Education. PhD thesis, the University of London.

Stewart, A. (2006) An inquiry into the social aspects of language teacher expertise. In A. Yoshitomi, T. Umino and M. Negishi (eds) *Readings in Second Language Pedagogy and Second Language Acquisition: In Japanese Context* (pp. 101–118). Amsterdam: John Benjamins Publishing Co.

Strauss, A.L. and Corbin, J. (1990) *Basics of Qualitative Research. Grounded Theory Procedures and Techniques*. London: Sage Publications.

Suemori, S (2014) A preliminary exploration of one group of pre-service EFL Teachers' beliefs concerning NESTs and JTEs. *Eigokenkenkyu* 10 (44), 29–46.

Sugiyama, M. (2010) The politics of learning foreign languages – learning language in an imaginary reality in Japan. *Osaka Furitsu Daigaku Kiyo* 59, 39–50.

Suzuki, W. (1969) *Nurtured by Love*. Hicksville, N.Y.: Exposition Press, Inc.

Suzuki, W. (1987) *My Life with Suzuki*. USA: Summy-Brichard, Inc.

Tajfel, H. (ed.) (1978) *Differentiation Between Social Groups. Studies in Social Psychology.* London: Academic Press.
Tajima, K. (1978) The grammar-translation method: Its historical and social background. In I. Koike, M. Matsuyama, Y. Igarashi and K. Suzuki (eds) *The Teaching of English in Japan* (pp. 220–227). Tokyo: Eichosha Publishing Co., Ltd.
Takahara, K. (2008) Assistant language teachers in trying times. info.japantimes.co.jp/rss/nn20080105f1.html (accessed 10 May 2014).
Takahashi, K. (2013) *Language Learning, Gender and Desire: Japanese Women on the Move.* Bristol: Multilingual Matters.
Tanabe, Y. (1978) English as an international language: qualifications, adaptation and perspective. In I. Koike, M. Matsuyama, Y. Igarashi and K. Suzuki (eds) *The Teaching of English in Japan.* Tokyo: Eichosha Publishing Co., Ltd. 47–57.
Tang, C. (1997) On the power and status of nonnative ESL teachers. *TESOL Quarterly* 31 (3), 577–580.
Terasaki, G. (1985) *Bridge to the Sun.* Newport, Tennessee: University of North Carolina.
Thornbury, S. (2002) Unbearable lightness. *ELT Journal* 55 (4), 397–402.
Toh, G. (2013) Scrutinizing the native speaker as referent, entity, and project. In S. Houghton and D. Rivers (eds) *Native-speakerism in Japan: Intergroup Dynamics in Foreign Language Education* (pp. 183–195). Bristol: Multilingual Matters.
Tokiwamatsu Gakuen English Department (1998) *Go Global: A Global Education Resource Book for Language Teachers.* Tokyo: Kagensha.
Tope, A. (2003) Japan rethinks goodwill assistance. *The Guardian.* http://www.theguardian.com/education/2003/oct/23/tefl (accessed 11 May 2014).
Torii, T. (1978) Teacher training: English teacher training in postwar Japan. In I. Koike, M. Matsuyama, Y. Igarashi and K. Suzuki (eds) *The Teaching of English in Japan* (pp. 58–70). Tokyo: Eichosha Publishing Co., Ltd.
Torikai, K. (2009) *Voices of the Invisible Presence: Diplomatic Interpreters in Post-World War II Japan.* Philadelphia, PA: John Benjamins, B.V.
Tsang, W.K. (2004) Teachers' personal practical knowledge and interactive decision. *Language Teaching Research* 8 (2), 163–198.
Tsuneyoshi, R. (2013) Communicative English in Japan and "native speakers" of English. In S. Houghton and D. Rivers (eds) *Native-speakerism in Japan: Intergroup Dynamics in Foreign Language Education* (pp. 119–131). Bristol: Multilingual Matters.
University of Tokyo (n.d.) Gender-equal participation basic plan for the University of Tokyo. http://www.google.co.jp/url?sa=t&rct=j&q=&esrc=s&source=web&cd=2&ved=0CCYQFjABahUKEwiC_bjKI5DGAhXRM7wKHaN0AJw&url=http%3A%2F%2Fkyodo-sankaku.utokyo.ac.jp%2Fen%2Fabout%2Fhistory%2Fdocuments%2FBasicPlanEN.pdf&ei=kPl9VYL1ItHn8AWj6YHgCQ&usg=AFQjCNFHgkkOpYE1U9dKnxeBe0mtpI__9g&sig2=ouJhuE8RFm6i8V7q7vYu3g&bvm=bv.95515949,d.dGc (accessed 15 June 2015).
Uzama, A. (2012) Yokoso Japan: Classifying foreign tourists to Japan for market segmentation. *Journal of Hospitality and Management* 21, 132–154.
Webster, L. and Mertova, P. (2007) *Using Narrative Inquiry as a Research Method: An Introduction to Using Critical Event Analysis in Research on Learning and Teaching.* Oxford: Routledge.
Wenger, E. (1998) *Communities of Practice: Learning, Meaning and Identity.* Cambridge: Cambridge University Press.

Wetherall, W. (2008) Becoming Japanese in the Meiji Period: Adopted sons, income husbands, and naturalization. http://Members.jcom.home.ne.jp/yosha/yr/nationality/Naturalization_Meiji.html (accessed 10 May 2014).

Whitsed, C. (2011) Standing in the genkan: Adjunct foreign English language teachers in the Japanese higher education internationalization context (unpublished doctoral thesis). Perth, Australia: Murdoch University.

Whitsed, C. and Volet, S. (2011) Fostering the intercultural dimensions of internationalisation in higher education: Metaphors and challenges in the Japanese context. *Journal of Studies in International Education* 15 (2), 146–170.

Whitsed, C. and Wright, P. (2011) Perspectives from within: Adjunct, foreign, English-language teachers in the internationalization of Japanese universities. *Journal of Research in International Education* 10 (1), 28–45.

Widdowson, H.G. (1994) The ownership of English. *TESOL Quarterly* 28 (2), 377–381.

Wolcott, H. (2000) *Writing Up Qualitative Research* 2nd *Edition*. Thousand Oaks, CA: Sage Publications.

Woods, D. (1996) *Teacher Cognition in Language Teaching: Beliefs, Decision-Making and Classroom Practice*. Cambridge: Cambridge University Press.

Wordell, C. (1992) Politics and human relations in the Japanese university. In P. Wadden (ed.) *A Handbook for Teaching English at Japanese Colleges and Universities* (pp. 145–155). New York: Oxford University Press.

World Economic Forum (2014) The Global Gender Gap Report 2014. Retrieved 25 May 2015 from http://reports.weforum.org/global-gender-gap-report-2014/.

Worthington, C. (1999) Combating discrimination at a Japanese university. *JPRI Working Paper* 58. http://www.jpri.org/publications/workingpapers/wp58.html. Retrieved 7 May 2015.

Yamamoto, B.A. (2010) International marriage in Japan: An exploration of intimacy, family and parenthood. 18th Biennial Conference of the Asian Studies Association, http://asaa.asn.au/ASAA2010/reviewed_papers/Yamamoto-_Beverley.pdf (accessed 6 August 2012).

Yamamoto, N.Y. (1978) The oral method: Harold E. Palmer and the reformation of the teaching of the English language in Japan. *ELT Journal* 32 (2), 151–158.

Yoshida, A. (2002) The curriculum reforms of the 1990s: What has changed? *Higher Education* 43, 43–63.

Yoshino, K. (2002) English and nationalism in Japan: The role of the intercultural-communication industry. In S. Wilson (ed.) *Nation and Nationalism in Japan* (pp. 135–145). New York, NY: Routledge Curzon.

Yphantides, J. (2013) Native-speakerism though English-only policies: Teachers, students and the changing face of Japan. In S. Houghton and D. Rivers (eds) *Native-speakerism in Japan: Intergroup Dynamics in Foreign Language Education* (pp. 207–216). Bristol: Multilingual Matters.

Author Index

Abe, Y. 138, 213
Abrams, D. 100, 218
AJET 118, 213
Aoki, M. 46–47, 213
Appleby, R. 5, 7, 78, 79, 80–87, 124, 213
Aspinal, R. 35, 213

Bailey, K. 2, 40, 76, 77, 78, 136, 213
Bazeley, P. 98, 213
Beauchamp, E.R. 42, 213
Beijaard, D. 91, 213
Bell, J.S. 92, 93, 104, 213
Benjamin, G.R. 49, 213
Bird, S. 77, 213
Bourdieu, P. 42, 100, 197, 213
Braine, G. 4, 101, 214
Briggs, C.L. 96, 214
Brooks, D. 54, 214
Brotherstone, C. 40, 214
Brown, J. 13, 214
Browne, C. 152, 214
Bueno, E.P. 37, 40, 51, 214
Burrows, C. 56, 214
Burton, S.K. 76, 214
Butler, Y. 1, 12, 35, 214

Caesar, T. 3, 37, 40, 51, 214
Canagarajah, A.S. 3, 101, 214
Casey, K. 92, 214
Charisma Man 78, 214
Chase, S. 92, 214
Chesney, R. 40, 215
Clandinin, D.J. 3, 91, 92, 214, 215
Clarke, M. 3, 215
Clavell, J. 13, 61, 215
Cohen, E. 118, 215
Connelly, E.M. 92, 214, 215
Corbin J. 98, 227
Crawford, M. 66, 215
Creaser, F. 83, 211, 215,

Daizen, T. 49, 215
Davies, A. 9, 100, 215
De Mente 70, 215, 216
Denzin, N. 98, 215, 222
Derivry-Plard, M. 38, 216
Diggs, N.B. 73, 74, 216
Dower, J. 65, 216
Duff, P.A. 40, 92, 101, 136, 216

Eades, J.S. 49, 196, 213, 216, 220, 225
Earns, L.R. 18, 216
Edge, J. 9, 216
EIKEN 145, 216
Ekiken, K. 61, 62, 82, 216
Elbaz, F. 2, 91, 92, 216
Erikson, E.H. 99, 216
Evanoff, R. 54, 216
Evans, B. 152, 216

Fang, Z. 91, 216
Fichtner, F. 2, 216
Flynn, C. 45, 46, 216
Fraser, M. 2, 50, 54, 56, 182, 217
Fujimoto, D. 39, 221
Fujimura-Fanslow, K. 75, 216
Fukase, H. xiv, 216
Fukuzawa, R. 41, 217

Gatbonton, E. 2, 91, 217
Gee, J.P. vii, ix, 7, 8, 99, 100, 101, 102, 103, 130, 143, 144, 146, 148, 173, 190, 202, 203, 207, 217
Geertz, C. 105, 217
Geluso, J. 2, 47, 217
General Union 80, 217
Gibbs, G.H. 98, 217
Gitsaki, C. 4, 224
Glaser, B.G. 98, 217
Goodman, R. 196, 213, 216,
Gordon, B. 68, 218

Gorsuch, G. 1, 12, 217
Griffis, W.E. 17, 18, 19, 218
Guest, M. 12, 80, 81, 82, 218

Habu, T. 76, 218
Hada, Y. 196, 213, 216,
Hadley, G. 57, 218
Hadley, Y. 57, 218
Hall, H.T. 51, 218
Hanna, P. 76, 218
Harasawa, M. 3, 12, 31, 32, 218
Harré 100, 215
Harshbarger, B. 87, 88, 218
Hashimoto, K. 41, 44, 46, 47, 218
Hayashi, K. 14, 66, 215
Hayes, B.E. 51, 52, 58, 218
Heimlich, E. 39, 218
Henrichson, L. 11, 14, 15, 16, 17, 18, 26, 27, 28, 30, 218, 219
Herbison, L. 66, 219
Hinchman, L. 92, 218
Hinchman, S. 92, 218
Hino, N. 11, 12, 33, 219
Hogg, M.A. 100, 218
Holliday, A. 3, 219
Honan, E. 4, 224
Honda, Y. 1, 219
Houghton, S. 39, 54, 55, 180, 216, 217, 218,

Iino, M. 1, 12, 35, 214
Ike, M. 14, 16, 23, 26, 27, 28, 30, 31, 33, 219
Imamura, S. 3, 29, 32, 219
Imura, M. 27, 28, 226
Ion, H. 17, 219
Ishida, G. xv, 72, 219
Ishida, H. 1, 42, 219
Ishigaki, A. 66, 219
Ishikida, M.Y. 42, 50, 75, 219
Ito, K. 14, 219

Jackson, L. 77, 220
James, E. 49, 213
Jansen, M.B. 14, 16, 17, 18, 19, 219
Japan Society for the Promotion of Science 83, 219
JET 43, 219
Johnston, B. 3, 4, 219

Josselson, R. 104, 215, 220

Kachru, B.B. 3, 101, 220
Kamhi-Stein, L.D. 4, 101, 220
Kan, S. 76, 220
Kariya, T. 1, 42, 220
Kashper, E. 78, 220
Kawagoe, A. 46, 220
Kelly, W. 69, 220
Kelskey, K. 66, 76, 77, 78, 220
Kemper, K. 49, 220
Kennett, B. 77, 220
Kiernan, P. 92, 220
Kinmouth, E. 26, 50, 52, 220
Kitao, K. 26, 220
Kitao, S.K. 26, 220
Kobyashi, Y. 5, 57, 75, 76, 77, 76, 86, 220, 221
Koike, I. 17, 28, 30, 31, 76, 77, 218, 219,
Koyama, N. 63, 64, 220
Kubo, M. 83, 221
Kubota, R. 2, 9, 38, 39, 40, 76, 101, 129, 132, 136, 221
Kvale, S. 96, 221

LaBoskey, V.K. 92, 222
Lah, K. 78, 221
Lave, J. 100, 102, 221
Law, G. 2, 3, 41, 221
Leupp, G. 61, 62, 221
Liddle, J. 5, 82, 101, 162, 187, 221
Lincoln, Y.S. 92, 214, 219, 222
Liu, D. 9, 222
Liu, J. 9, 222
Lo Castro, V. 60, 75, 222
Loti, P. 63, 222
Lummis, D. 38, 39, 101, 106, 129, 222
Lyons, N. 92, 222

Ma, K. 73, 74, 222
MacNaughton, A. 40, 222
Makino, M. 49, 220
Marx, E. 64, 222
Masden, K. 54, 55, 223
Matsui, M. 76, 222
Matsuyama, M. 31, 32, 218, 219, 222
McConnell, D. 43–45, 110, 117, 222
McCormick, K. 1, 222
McCrostie, J. 57, 80, 222

McKay, S. 101, 221
McKenzie, C.R. 138, 226
McKnight, A. 68, 223
McNeill, D. 83, 223
McVeigh, B.J. 51, 223
Mead, G.J. 99, 223
Mertova, P. 92, 228
MEXT 41, 52, 83, 84, 223
Minakawa, S. 12, 13, 33, 222
Ministry of Economy, Trade and Industry 37, 38, 223
Mitchel, J.M. 90, 224
Mizuta, A. 2, 3, 37, 38, 77, 129, 144, 222
Morita, N. 102, 223
Mosk, C. 35, 224
Mulvey, S. 80, 82, 87, 223

Nagai, M. 90, 223
Nagasawa, K. 51, 196, 223
Nagatomo, D.H. 2, 5, 7, 38, 40, 41, 49, 57, 76, 86, 92, 96, 102, 134, 182, 221, 222
Nakajima, S. 5, 82, 101, 162, 187, 221
Nakao, K. 27, 224
Nakata, Y.F. 35, 224
Neilsen, R. 3–5, 205, 224
Newby, H. 90, 224
Nishino, T. 1, 12, 224
Nitta, F. 70, 71, 224
Normile, D. 83, 224
Nunan, D. 2, 224
NVivo 98, 213, 217, 224

O'Leary, V.E. 90, 224
Oguri, S. 74, 124, 224
Oishi, A.S. 138, 213
Okano, K. 42, 224
Omura, K. 15, 16, 25, 224
Ono, H. 1, 42, 75, 77, 224, 225
Ota, Y. 17, 21–26, 33, 225

Pavlenko, A. 7, 92, 93, 225
Pennycook, A. 9, 225
Phan Le Ha 2, 3, 9, 225
Phillipson, R. 9, 225
Piller, I. 69, 76, 78, 225
Pomatti, D. 14, 16, 17, 19, 21, 225
Poole, G. 17, 52, 56, 87, 225

Rampton, M.B.H. 4, 101, 225
Raymo, J. 76, 225
Richards, J. 2, 91, 216
Riessman, C.K. 92, 225
Rivers, D. 38, 39, 51, 55, 58, 78, 180, 216, 217, 218, 219
Rosenbaum 1, 42, 220
Ross, A. 38, 51, 225
Ruxton, I. 18, 226

Said, E. 62, 216
Sakata, K. 138, 226
Sato, K. 1, 2, 226
Schodt, F. 15, 226
Schultz, J. 66, 219
Seargeant, P. 38, 39, 226
Seidman, I. 95, 98, 226
Shibusawa, N. 65–68, 124, 226
Shimbori, M. 51, 52, 226
Shimizu, K. 58, 226
Shulman, L.S. 2, 92, 226
Silverman, D. 98, 226
Smith, R.C. 26, 226
Sodei, T. 83, 226
Stanley, P. 82, 226
Stewart, A. 56, 92, 226
Strauss A.L. 98, 217, 227
Suemori, S. 48, 227
Suenaga, S. 66, 215
Sugiyama, M. 37, 38, 39, 227
Suzuki, W. 64, 227

Tajfel, H. 100, 227
Tajima, K. 11, 227
Takahara, K. 45, 47, 227
Takahashi, K. 2, 37, 38, 39, 60, 70, 76, 77, 78, 80, 90, 124, 136, 225, 227
Tanabe, Y. 14, 25, 227
Tang, C. 4, 101, 227
Terasaki, G. 64, 227
Thornbury, S. 107, 227
Toh, G. 38, 227
Tokiwamatsu Gakuen English Department 185, 227
Tope, A. 46, 227
Torii, T. 29, 227
Torikai, K. 14, 227
Tsang, W.K. 2, 227
Tsuneyoshi, R. 38, 227

Uchida, Y. 40, 92, 101, 135, 216
University of Tokyo 83, 227
Uzama A. 70, 228

Volet, S. 52, 56, 228

Watanabe, M. 1, 224
Webster, L. 92, 248
Wenger, E. vii, 7, 8, 57, 99, 100, 102, 103, 167, 171, 173, 180, 181, 202, 221, 228
Wetherall, W. 63, 64, 248
Whitsed, C. 2, 50 52, 56, 85, 87, 228

Wolcott, H. 105, 203, 228
Woods, D. 2, 91, 228
Wordell, C. 57, 228
World Economic Forum 82, 228
Worthington, C. 55, 228
Wright, P. 2, 50

Yamamoto, B.A. 6, 27, 70, 124, 228
Yamanoi, A. 50, 215
Yoshida, A. 30, 36, 52, 228
Yoshino, K. 38, 39, 228
Yphantides, J. 58, 228

Subject Index

A-Identity (affinity-identity) 100, 102, 155, 161, 171, 173, 191, 203, 207
Adams, William 13, 14
adventure 8, 40, 106, 107, 108, 110
akogare 69, 76, 77, 80, 82, 213
Alien Rice 72
Assistant Language Teachers (ALT) vi, ix, xiii, xvii, xx, 1, 44–47, 113–116, 118, 146, 147, 151, 155, 159, 205, 214, 217
assistants xiv, xvii, 1, 24, 36, 43, 47, 84, 109, 131, 141, 146, 153, 174, 183, 184, 204, 205, 207, 213, 227
Association of Foreign Wives of Japanese (AFWJ) xvi, x, 71, 72, 95, 162, 217

bicultural children x, 103, 186, 188, 201
bilingual/ bilingualism 103, 135, 153, 201, 221, 225
Blomhoff, Jan Cook 15
Board of Educations (BOE) 46, 47
brides vi, 65, 66, 146, 202, 215
British English Teaching (BET) 43
Brown, Samuel Rollins 18
Business Language Testing Servicd 164

Certificate in English Language Teaching to Adults (CELTA) 94, 112, 164, 165, 170, 207
Charisma Man vii, 77–79, 193, 213
Christianity/ Christians 13, 14, 16, 17, 19, 21, 33, 34, 61, 214, 219
Clark, William Smith 21
classroom vii, 2, 3, 16, 32, 36, 40, 41, 43, 44, 46, 47, 48, 80, 82, 111, 112, 117, 119, 129, 130, 131, 151, 153, 154, 170, 171, 180, 183, 184, 185, 198, 192, 193, 208
clown 110, 114
collaboration 178, 179

colleagues 6, 38, 56, 78, 82, 83, 86, 114, 118, 121, 128, 151, 159, 162, 173–181, 186, 189, 190, 197, 198, 200, 210, 211
colonialism 16, 23, 27
Community of Practice (CoP) vii, x, xi, 100, 102, 103, 173, 180, 199
connections 52, 103, 119, 132, 163, 169, 181
contracts 4, 45, 48, 51, 53, 54, 55, 106, 130, 193, 202, 204, 205, 214, 217
Coordinator of International Relations (CIR) 45
Council of Local Authorities for International Relations 44, 114
Course of Study 28, 35, 41, 47
cultural capital 62
culture xiv, 2, 3, 20, 31, 33, 37, 38, 61, 62, 72, 74, 75, 77, 85, 87, 98, 106, 107, 123, 169, 184, 187, 189, 209

D-Identity (discourse-identity) 100, 102, 143, 146, 151, 171, 173, 203, 207
Daring wa gaikokujin 74
data collection 95–96
degrees (bachelors) xiii, 40, 51, 94, 196, 205
degrees (masters) 7, 51, 52, 55
degrees (PhD/doctorate) 7, 94, 116, 117, 118, 122, 209
direct hire teachers xiii, 45, 150
discrimination 44, 86, 88, 187, 188, 211
dispatch companies/ dispatched teachers 36, 45, 46, 48, 52, 192, 194, 201
divorce 64, 122, 124, 157, 162, 163, 206, 210, 212

earthquake, 2011 Great Tohoku Earthquake 122, 157, 158, 159
economy vi, 35, 36, 37, 69, 70, 109, 133, 142, 146, 163, 223

Subject Index

educational capital 75, 181, 197, 209
Ei-Bei Taiwa Shokei 16
eigo xiii, xvii, 10, 12, 25, 27, 30, 35, 26, 38, 41, 89, 108, 134, 137, 152, 170, 215, 334
Eigo Dai Ronso 30
eikaiwa vi, ix, xiii, xvii, 1–3, 6, 9, 10, 35–41, 45, 50, 53, 58, 75–80, 88, 89, 93, 94, 99, 103, 108, 111, 115, 116, 138–145, 150, 152, 155, 156, 163, 164, 166, 169, 170, 171, 174, 182, 184, 193, 202, 205–207, 212, 213, 221, 222, 223, 224
eikaiwa industry 35–37, 202, 222
eikaiwa school, operating own 122, 123 129–145
eikaiwa schools 2, 9, 37–40, 45, 78, 79, 80, 128, 129–145
ekiben daigaku 49
elite universities 42
employment requirements 39, 40, 48, 51, 52, 57, 164, 196, 204
English Language Exploratory Committee (ELEC) 29
English language Teaching (ELT) 1, 3, 4, 27, 86, 120, 183, 205, 218, 222, 224, 227
entrance exams 1, 2, 10, 12, 26, 27, 30, 31, 32, 34, 37, 41, 42, 48, 49, 60, 75, 131, 213, 218, 222
exclusion 87, 197, 211

F-ranking schools 50
family 5, 6, 34, 49, 55, 56, 63, 66, 68, 74, 83, 84, 87, 98, 99, 104, 108, 113, 115, 116, 118, 119, 120, 123, 125, 126, 127, 129, 130, 131, 138, 142, 143, 144, 145, 146, 147, 148, 149, 150, 154, 156, 157, 158, 161, 170, 172, 178, 187, 206, 210, 212
financial independence ix, 124, 138, 140, 141, 199
financial struggle 20, 50, 55, 124, 132, 138, 139, 154, 159, 161, 163
foreign experts 20–24
Freame, William Henry 63
Fries, Charles C. 29
Fukuzawa Yukichi 25
full-time vi, 7, 36, 38, 42, 46, 48, 51, 52, 53, 54, 55, 84, 103, 105, 120, 122, 139, 141, 146, 155, 167, 168, 173, 174, 177, 182, 184, 189, 191, 194, 199, 200, 203, 204, 205, 206, 212

gaijin xvii, 77, 82, 112, 121, 134, 151, 209
gaijin on parade 112
gaikokujin kyoushi 54
gender discrimination 64, 88, 211
General Union 80
Gentaku Otsuki 11
Gentaku Otsuki 11
Gilmour, Leonie 64
GIs 65–66
Global Gender Report 82
global issues 185
graduate school 175, 196

harassment, academic 83
harassment, power 83
harassment, sexual 79, 83
hardships 64, 68, 198
Harris, Townsend 11
Hensoku 25
Hepburn, James Curtis 18
high schools/secondary schools vi, xiii, 27, 28, 29, 31, 35–37, 41, 42, 43, 48–50, 79, 89, 93, 95, 110, 115, 132, 149, 154, 179, 182, 184, 190, 219, 220
hijokin koshi 52
Hiraizumi Wataru 30
hiring practices 41, 189, 196
HMS *Phaeton* 14
Hollywood vi, 62, 67, 90
hostile environment 83, 86, 87, 88, 141
housewife/housewives 73, 132
husband viii, xiv, xvi, 6, 8, 61, 62, 63, 64, 68 70, 71, 72, 73, 74, 84, 86, 90, 106, 108, 110, 112, 113, 114, 119, 120, 122, 124, 125, 127, 129, 131, 132, 138, 139, 141, 142, 148, 149, 150, 156, 157, 162, 172, 186, 201, 202, 206, 207, 210, 211, 212

I-Identity (institutional-identity 100, 101, 150, 153, 159, 170, 173, 190, 203, 207
in-laws 104, 126, 146
inappropriate behavior 80, 82, 83, 87

Subject Index 235

income/salary ix, 6, 9, 23, 38, 40, 42, 48, 53, 54, 55, 70, 75, 76, 86, xi, 111, 112, 122, 123, 124, 129–133, 138, 139, 141, 142, 146, 147, 150, 156, 189,
Institute for Research in English Teaching (IRET) 27
Institute for the Investigation of Barbarian Writings 16
insurance 138
International English Language Testing System (IELTS) 163
interracial vi, xix, 8, 60, 61, 66, 67, 70, 72, 74, 75, 95, 89, 106, 124, 202, 221
Iwakura Mission 18,

Japan Exchange Teaching (JET) Program vi, xvii, 36, 41, 42, 43, 44, 45, 47, 55, 94, 107, 108, 109, 110, 112, 113, 114, 115, 117, 118, 119, 127, 130, 147, 150, 183, 202, 212, 219, 222
Japanese culture 31, 33, 61, 62, 69, 72, 77, 85, 107, 123, 184, 189, 209, 218
Japanese language proficiency 52, 122, 153, 169, 186, 196
Japanese proficiency exam 122, 186
Japanese teachers 2, 3, 10, 21, 25, 36, 41, 43, 44, 46, 47, 48, 50, 56, 57, 58, 97, 118, 120, 151, 152, 153, 170, 176, 177, 178, 181, 183, 185, 189, 191, 192, 194, 208
Jessie Roberta Cowan 64
Joan Burk 71
juken eigo xvii, 1, 38
juku 123, 133, 155

Katakana 16
kindergarden, daycare centers, *yochien* ix, xiii, 6, 94, 130, 132, 147, 149, 151, 155, 158, 160, 161, 187, 206, 210, 211
Kitagawa Sei 63
kokusai kekkon 66
kokusaijin 144
kyoiku inkai 150, 153
Kyoiku Jimusho 114

Labor Contract Law 53
labor laws 46
language school 18, 39, 107, 112, 114, 122, 123, 206, 214, 222

love, students/job 160, 165, 189, 221,
love, with Japan 107, 108

MacDonald, Ranald 15, 16
Madam Butterfly 62
Madame Chrysantheme 62
Marden, Orison Swett 26
marginalization x, 87 102, 180, 182, 197–199
marriage, opposition to 125–127
Meiji era 16–25
Mickey Mouse University 49
Minami Teisuke 63
Ministry of Education 28
Ministry of Education, Culture, Sports, Science and Technology (MEXT) xvii, 41, 43, 63, 152, 223
Ministry of Foreign Affairs 43, 63
Ministry of Health, Labor, and Welfare (MHLW) 46
Missionaries 17–19
Mombusho English Fellow 43, 111, 171
money 5, 6, 30, 42–44, 49, 58, 75, 98, 111, 112, 119, 123, 130, 132, 134–138, 140–142, 145, 147, 154, 159, 161, 165, 171, 182, 183, 206, 210
Mori Arinori 22
Moriyama Einosuke 15
Moriyama Einosuke 15
Morse, Edward S. 21
mother-in-law 126, 147, 150, 210
Murray, David 22
Murry, Lindley 15
Murry's English Grammar 15

N-Identity (nature-identity) 100, 101, 143, 148, 161, 203, 207, 208
nagai kekkon 63
Nagasaki Tsuji 14
Nakahama Manjiro 16
narrative inquiry 92–93
narrative research 92–93
narrative study 92–93
nationality 63, 57, 64, 90, 210
Nihon Jin 23
Niijima Jo 16
ninkisei 54
Nitobe Inazo 21
Noguchi Isamu 64

non-Japanese xi, xx, 2, 3, 9, 27, 39, 51, 52, 53, 56–58, 70, 90, 101, 129, 143, 144, 146, 148, 161, 185, 186, 190, 201, 207, 217
non-Japanese xi, xx, 2, 3, 9, 27, 39, 51, 52, 53, 56, 58, 64, 70, 90, 101, 129, 143, 144, 146, 148, 161, 180, 185, 186, 190, 191, 201, 207, 217
nonstandard employment 51

Office for the Translation or Examination of Barbarian Books 16
Okakura, Yoshizaburo 12
Okuma Shigenobu 18
Onna Daigaku 61, 62
opportunities 2, 4, 32, 43, 52, 53, 70, 76, 87, 89, 90, 107, 116, 172, 198, 204, 205, 206, 207 212,
oral approach 29
Oranda-tsuji 14
outsourcing teachers vi, 45, 46, 47, 192

Palmer, Harold 26–27
parents 1, 2, 43, 75, 76, 113, 119, 125, 126, 127, 130, 132, 133, 135, 140, 141, 150, 154, 155, 158, 161, 186, 187, 188, 206, 210
part-time vi, 9, 36, 37, 38, 51, 52, 53, 54, 58, 83, 87, 103, 112, 113, 116, 123, 124, 159, 164, 166, 167, 171, 188, 189, 191, 192, 194, 199, 205, 206, 208, 223
Participant Andrea viii, x, xv, 94, 95, 106, 107, 108, 120, 121, 173, 174, 175–183, 189–191, 200, 204–212
Participant Annie viii, x, xv, 94, 95, 106, 107, 119, 120, 125, 173, 183–191, 200, 204, 210
Participant Carrie xiii, x, xv, 94, 95, 107, 108, 117–120, 127, 128, 207, 208, 212
participant confirmations 99
Participant Lisa viii, ix, xv, 94, 95, 107, 109, 110, 121, 122, 146, 156–163, 171, 172, 205, 206
Participant Louisa viii, ix, xv, 94, 95, 107, 108, 110, 111, 112, 115, 129–144, 163–170, 204, 206, 207, 208, 210, 212

Participant Margaret viii, ix, xv, 94, 95, 107, 108, 109, 112, 113, 114, 115, 124, 125, 126, 127, 129, 130, 131, 132, 133, 134, 135, 136, 137, 138, 140, 141, 142, 143, 144, 145, 154, 205, 206, 208, 209, 210, 211, 212
Participant Pat viii, xv, 94, 95, 107, 108, 115, 116, 127, 128, 205, 206
Participant Sarah vii, x, xi, xv, 94, 95, 106, 107, 122, 123, 124, 129, 142, 163, 173, 191–198, 204, 206–210
Participant Theresa viii, xv, 94, 96, 107, 109, 116–117, 127–128, 204–207, 211–212
Participant Victoria xiii, ix, xv, 59, 94–96, 107–109, 114, 115, 125–127, 146–156, 171, 172, 205, 208, 209, 211, 212
pension 138, 163, 198
permanent residency 57, 124, 191
Pittman, Eliza 63
pregnant, pregnancy 66, 83, 112, 113, 116, 174
private schools 36, 41, 42, 44, 48, 94, 118
process of analysis 98–99
professional development 55, 168, 204
prostitutes 9, 62, 66, 142
public schools 28, 41, 42, 48, 94, 116, 118, 147, 183, 184, 225

race 9, 38, 57, 60, 63, 66, 67, 71, 90, 100, 225,
racial bias 66
renewable contracts 53, 54
resourcefulness xi, 146, 155, 171, 172, 204, 205, 207, 211, 212
retirement x, 27, 42, 48, 57, 120, 132, 139, 142, 183, 188, 191, 198, 200
Rockefeller Foundation 29
Rollins, Samuel 18
romance/love/dating vi, 60, 65, 66, 67, 70, 78, 84, 85, 89, 90, 115, 117, 126, 127, 220, 221
Royal Society of Arts (RSA) Diploma 183, 184

Sawayanagi, Masataro 26
Sayonara 67
Seisoku 25
seniority 53, 55, 120, 177

Subject Index 237

sexist 69, 85, 87, 89, 113, 197
shijuku 16, 17
single mother 156, 159, 161, 194, 210
Sorai Ogyu 11
sotomuki 56
spousal benefits 138
standard employment 42, 51
stereotypes 6, 67, 72
Suzuki, Shinichi 64
Suzuki, Waltred 64

Taisho era 64
taxes ix, 38, 130, 131, 139, 140, 144, 168 169 226
teacher beliefs 1, 91, 92, 93
teacher identity xix, xx, , 91–92, 102, 182, 224
teaching adults viii, xiii, 112, 123, 132, 136, 137, 140, 164, 184
teaching children xiv, 119, 136 165, 168, 170
teaching group lessons 131, 132, 136, 137, 148, 151, 154, 170, 212
teaching private lessons ix, 94, 103, 123, 140, 151, 156, 161
teaching university students x, 117, 167, 179, 193, 212
tenure 4, 7, 26, 51–58, 83, 88, 103, 116, 117, 123, 124, 191, 195–197, 204, 205, 209, 209, 222
terakoya 17
Terasaki, Gwen 64
The Teaching of English in Japan 31
Tokugawa Ieyasu 13, 14
Toyotomi Hideyoshi 13

trajectories 57, 86, 103, 173
transcription method 96–97
traveling abroad with students 194, 195
Tsuda Juku 30
Tsuda, Ume 18, 30

uchimuki 56
University of Tokyo 18, 21, 22, 23, 24, 83

Valignano Allesandro 13
Verbek, Guido Fridolen 17–18
visas 400, 45, 66, 80, 106, 107, 113, 116, 120

Watanabe Shoiji 30
Watanabe Shoiji 30
Westerners vi, xix, 8, 9, 16, 60, 61, 70, 74, 75, 124, 124, 201, 226
Westernization 22, 23, 218, 225
wife/wives xv, xvi, 5, 6, 61, 62, 64, 70, 71, 72, 73, 82, 84, 86, 90, 101, 115, 123, 126, 127, 132, 138, 139, 143, 146, 148, 155, 162, 204, 206, 210
working mothers 186–187
World Economic Forum 82
WWII xix, 28, 29, 34, 35, 37, 41, 64, 65, 66, 69, 124, 202, 216

Xavier, Francis 13

Yakudoku 10, 11, 25, 33, 37
yellow cabs 70
Yoshizaburo Okakura 12

zakkon 63

For Product Safety Concerns and Information please contact our EU Authorised Representative:

Easy Access System Europe

Mustamäe tee 50

10621 Tallinn

Estonia

gpsr.requests@easproject.com

www.ingramcontent.com/pod-product-compliance
Lightning Source LLC
Chambersburg PA
CBHW070559300426
44113CB00010B/1319